CLARENDON STUDIES IN THE HISTORY OF ART

General Editor: Dennis Farr

JOHN WEBB

Architectural Theory and Practice in the Seventeenth Century

JOHN BOLD

CLARENDON PRESS · OXFORD
1989

Oxford University Press, Walton Street, Oxford OX2 6DP
Oxford New York Toronto
Delhi Bombay Calcutta Madras Karachi
Petaling Jaya Singapore Hong Kong Tokyo
Nairobi Dar es Salaam Cape Town
Melbourne Auckland
and associated companies in
Berlin Ibadan

Oxford is a trade mark of Oxford University Press

Published in the United States
by Oxford University Press, New York

British Library Cataloguing in Publication Data
Bold, John
John Webb: architectural theory and practice
in the seventeenth century.—(Clarendon
studies in the history of art.)
1. Architectural design. Webb, John,
1611–1672
I. Title
720'.92'4
ISBN 0–19–817503–5

Library of Congress Cataloging in Publication Data
Bold, John.
John Webb: architectural theory and practice in the seventeenth century/John Bold.
(Clarendon studies in the history of art)
Bibliography. Includes index.
1. Webb, John, 1611–1672—Criticism and interpretation. 2. Webb, John, 1611–1672—Catalogs. 3. Architecture, Modern—17th and 18th centuries—England—Catalogs. 4. Architecture—Philosophy. 5. Chinese language—History and criticism. I. Title. II. Series.
NA997.W38B6 1989 720'.92'4—dc19 88–28995
ISBN 0–19–817503–5

Typeset, printed and bound in Great Britain by
Butler & Tanner Ltd, Frome and London

GENERAL EDITOR'S FOREWORD

THIS is the second volume to appear in the Clarendon Studies in the History of Art, and the first in the series to be devoted to architecture. The seventeenth-century architect and theorist, John Webb, was a pupil of Inigo Jones and the first professionally trained British architect. He almost certainly would have succeeded Jones as Surveyor of the Works if it had not been for the upheavals caused by the Civil War and its aftermath, but he was twice passed over; after his death his reputation was virtually eclipsed and some of his work was wrongly attributed to Inigo Jones in the eighteenth century.

Dr John Bold, in this first full-length study of John Webb, reveals to us a man of great ability who enjoyed a good measure of material success in his profession, as testified by the Catalogue of Architectural Works published here, even though the highest office eluded him. He also discusses Webb's preoccupation with architectural theory, his speculations on the Chinese language and the history of Stonehenge, and sets these scholarly forays in the wider context of seventeenth-century intellectual enquiry. Webb emerges as an engaging, dedicated man, who was perhaps too self-effacing a professional to earn immediate posthumous fame. Dr Bold now brings us closer to understanding the full range of his achievements and of his importance for the neo-Palladians of the eighteenth century.

Dennis Farr

PREFACE

In writing this book, my intention has been to demonstrate the range and the importance of the work of England's first trained, professional architect, John Webb, and to distinguish his individual achievement from that of his master, Inigo Jones.

My interest in the subject was stimulated by the teaching of Professor Kerry Downes at the University of Reading, and my growing awareness of the extent to which Webb had been undervalued in histories of architecture led to the completion of a Ph.D. thesis in 1979. More recently, work for the Royal Commission on the Historical Monuments of England on *Wilton House and English Palladianism* has prompted me to look again at his work and to reconsider many of my original conclusions. Throughout these periods of research and consideration, Kerry Downes has been unfailingly helpful and encouraging and I am greatly indebted to him for his support and counsel.

My debts to other scholars are numerous. I wish to thank particularly John Harris for his generosity in making material available to me, and Esther Caplin (Eisenthal), Dr Robin Evans, Professor Jim Hankinson, Richard Hewlings, Dr Gordon Higgott, Professor George Knox, John Newman, Charles Newton, and Peter Reid for information and for many illuminating discussions. Amongst my colleagues at the RCHME, my thanks go individually to Stephen Croad, Diana Hale, and Tony Rumsey; to the staff of the photographic department, and to the organization as a whole for providing a period of study leave to enable me to complete the book.

Little of Webb's built work survives, but I am none the less grateful to all those owners who allowed me access to their houses and to their private archives, and to the Commander of the Royal Naval College, Greenwich, for permitting access to the King Charles Building. I am grateful also to the many archivists, curators, and librarians who enabled research to take place, particularly Mrs Lesley Le Claire at Worcester College, Oxford, Mr Peter Day at Chatsworth, Canon Martin at Wells Cathedral, and the staff of the following: the RIBA Library and Drawings Collection, the Bodleian and British Libraries, the Conway Library, the Public Record Office, and the County Record Offices of Hampshire, Kent, Leicestershire, Northamptonshire, Somerset, and Wiltshire.

My final debt, personal rather than professional, is to Sarah Bold, for her encouragement, support, and advice over many years.

J.B.

London
January 1988

ILLUSTRATION ACKNOWLEDGEMENTS

ALL of the text figures were drawn by Robin Evans, with the exception of figs. 6 and 7 which were drawn by Nancy Sutcliffe.

I am indebted to the following for kind permission to reproduce original material:

The British Architectural Library, RIBA: pls. 19, 49, 66, 69, 89, 92–7, 100, 105.
The British Library: pls. 21, 23, 24, 107.
Devonshire Collection, Chatsworth; by permission of the Chatsworth Settlement Trustees: pls. 5, 67, 75, 80–6, 108, 111, 116–18, 120.
Olive, Countess Fitzwilliam's Wentworth Settlement Trustees and the Director of Libraries, Sheffield: pl. 112.
Gunnersbury Park Museum, London Boroughs of Ealing and Hounslow: pls. 60, 61.
The Lamport Hall Trust: pls. 51, 52, 55–9.
The Duke of Northumberland: pl. 113.
The Earl of Pembroke and the Wilton House Trustees: pls. 30, 37.
The Dean and Chapter of St Paul's Cathedral: pl. 14.
Society of Antiquaries of London: pls. 25, 26, 32.
The Victoria and Albert Museum; by courtesy of the Board of Trustees: pl. 72.
The Provost and Fellows of Worcester College, Oxford: pls. 3, 7–10, 12, 15–17, 31, 35, 36, 46, 70, 74, 76–9, 88, 102, 109, 110, 119.

The photographs are reproduced by kind permission of the following: Conway Library, Courtauld Institute of Art: pls. 3, 4, 6–10, 12, 15–17, 19, 22, 31, 35, 36, 46, 49, 69, 70, 74, 76–9, 88, 89, 92–7, 102, 105, 109, 110, 119.
Country Life: pl. 99.
Courtauld Institute of Art (Photographic Survey): pls. 5, 67, 75, 80–6, 108, 111, 116–18, 120.
A. F. Kersting: pl. 1.
The Royal Commission on the Historical Monuments of England: pls. 2, 11, 13, 14, 18, 20, 25–30, 32–4, 37–45, 47, 48, 50–9, 62–5, 68, 71, 73, 87, 91, 98, 101, 103, 104, 106, 113–15.

CONTENTS

LIST OF PLATES

Details of author, location of original material, and publication are given in parentheses. Original drawings by John Webb are identified by 'JW'. Engravings after Webb are from originals in the RIBA.

LIST OF FIGURES

The plans are redrawings of plans drawn by John Webb; the perspectives are reconstructions of schemes, based on Webb's drawings. The location of these originals is given in parentheses.

ABBREVIATIONS

Bk. of Caps.	John Webb, 'Book of Capitols', MS in Devonshire collection, Chatsworth
BL	British Library
Bod.	Bodleian Library
Campbell	C. Campbell, *Vitruvius Britannicus,* i (1715), ii (1717); iii (1725)
CRO	County Record Office
CSPD	*Calendar of State Papers, Domestic* (several volumes)
HMC	Royal Commission on Historical Manuscripts
Kent	W. Kent, *Designs of Inigo Jones* (1727)
King's Works	H. M. Colvin (gen. ed.), *The History of the King's Works,* iii. *1485–1660 (pt. I)* (1975); iv. *1485–1660 (pt. II)* (1982); v. *1660–1782* (1976)
Palladio	A. Palladio, *I quattro libri dell'architettura* (1570; repr. 1980); published in English by Isaac Ware as *The Four Books of Andrea Palladio's Architecture* (1738; repr. 1965); references are to the original Italian edition unless specified otherwise
PRO	Public Record Office
C 7	Chancery Papers
C 8	Chancery Papers
E 351	Exchequer, Pipe Office, Declared Accounts
SP	State Papers
PCC	Probate Registers of the Prerogative Court of Canterbury
PROB	Probate Registers (PRO numeration)
Works 5	Office of Works Accounts
RCHME	Royal Commission on the Historical Monuments of England
RIBA	Royal Institute of British Architects
RIBA Cat.	J. Harris, *Catalogue of the Drawings Collection of the RIBA: Inigo Jones and John Webb* (1972); references are to the catalogue number unless specified otherwise
Vertue	G. Vertue, *Notebooks,* I–VI; published by Walpole Society as follows—I: 18 (1930); II: 20 (1932); III: 22 (1934); IV: 24 (1936); V: 26 (1938); VI: 30 (1950)
Worcs. Coll. Cat.	J. Harris and A. A. Tait, *Catalogue of the Drawings by Inigo Jones, John Webb and Isaac de Caus at Worcester College, Oxford* (1979); references are to the catalogue number unless specified otherwise

CHRONOLOGY

Entries in small capitals refer to Webb's architectural works and projects.

1611	John Webb born in Little Britain, Smithfield, London.
1615	Inigo Jones succeeds Simon Basil as Surveyor of Works.
1625	Death of James I; accession of Charles I.
1625–8	Education at Merchant Taylors' School.
1628	Goes to live with Inigo Jones and begin training.
*c.*1628–*c.*1634	Assisting Jones at SOMERSET HOUSE.
1630s	Assisting Jones on masque designs.
1632–3	Designing auditorium, Paved Court Theatre, SOMERSET HOUSE.
1633–41	Jones's clerk engrosser at ST PAUL'S CATHEDRAL.
1635	Designing auditorium, Great Hall, WHITEHALL PALACE.
*c.*1635–*c.*1650	Work on theoretical architectural treatise.
1636	First finished drawings of Jones's buildings—Temple Bar and Barber Surgeons' Anatomy Theatre.
1637	Redrawing of design for fountain, GREENWICH.
*c.*1637–9	Assisting Jones with designs for WHITEHALL PALACE—P & K schemes.
1638	Work with Jones at SOMERSET HOUSE. First independent designs—HALE LODGE and HASSENBROOK HALL.
*c.*1638/9(?)–1640s	WILTON HOUSE
1639	Receives Office of Works payment for Survey of King's Stables, etc. Transcribes Jones's instructions for ceiling paintings at Queen's House.
*c.*1641(?)–*c.*1650	DURHAM HOUSE
1642	Outbreak of Civil War. Charles I and Jones both leave London. To the King at Beverley; brief imprisonment.
1642–3	Acting Surveyor of Works in Jones's absence.
1643	Sends plans of fortifications about London to the King at Oxford. Thrust out of office by a Committee of the Revenue; replaced by Edward Carter.
*c.*1644–50	MAIDEN BRADLEY
*c.*1645	WHITEHALL PALACE—E scheme
*c.*1647	COLESHILL HOUSE

*c.*1647–8	Attends the King at Hampton Court and Carisbrooke Castle. WHITEHALL PALACE—T scheme
1648	COBHAM HALL
1648–*c.*1651	WILTON HOUSE
1649	Execution of the King; institution of the Commonwealth.
*c.*1650	NUN APPLETON HOUSE WREXHAM
1651–3	PHYSICIANS' COLLEGE
1652	Death of Inigo Jones; acts as Jones's executor.
1653	Purchase of manor of Butleigh, Somerset. Edward Carter replaced in office by John Embree. DRAYTON HOUSE
1654–7	LAMPORT HALL THE VYNE
1654–68	BELVOIR CASTLE
1655	Advising Sir Justinian Isham on pictures. Publication of *The Most Notable Antiquity of Great Britain Vulgarly called Stone-Heng.* CHEVENING LUDLOW.
*c.*1655–60	NORTHUMBERLAND HOUSE
1656	SYON HOUSE Designs for *Siege of Rhodes.*
1657	Design for frontispiece of Walton's *Biblia polyglotta.* Name put forward for nomination as a Commissioner for the regulating of building in London.
*c.*1658–63	GUNNERSBURY HOUSE
*c.*1659–64	AMESBURY ABBEY
1660	Preparing Whitehall for the King's return and acting to gather together Charles I's dispersed collections. Restoration of King Charles II. Petition for Surveyorship of the Works; granted the Reversion of the post. Surveyorship granted to Sir John Denham.
1660–2	Improvements to COCKPIT THEATRE, WHITEHALL.
1661	WHITEHALL PALACE—D scheme
1661–5	SOMERSET HOUSE
*c.*1662–5	ASHBURNHAM HOUSE
1663	Investigation of fabric of ST PAUL'S CATHEDRAL—minor repairs. Publication of Dr Walter Charleton's *Chorea gigantum,* which attacked the Jones–Webb interpretation of Stonehenge. Recalled by Charles II to work at GREENWICH.
*c.*1663–4	WHITEHALL—S scheme

1663–72	GREENWICH PALACE
1664	Referred to as Denham's deputy.
1665	Designing auditorium of HALL THEATRE, WHITEHALL. Publication of *A Vindication of Stone-Heng Restored.*
1666	Indisposition of Denham; Hugh May deputizes as Surveyor. Put in charge of the works at GREENWICH PALACE. Designs for *Tragedy of Mustapha.*
1667(?)	WOOLWICH DOCKYARD
1669	Death of Denham; appointment of Christopher Wren as Surveyor. Second petition to the King. Publication of *An Historical Essay Endeavouring a Probability that the Language of the Empire of China is the Primitive Language.*
*c.*1670(?)	BUTLEIGH COURT
1672	Will dated 24 Oct. Died 30 Oct. Buried 4 Nov., Butleigh Parish Church.

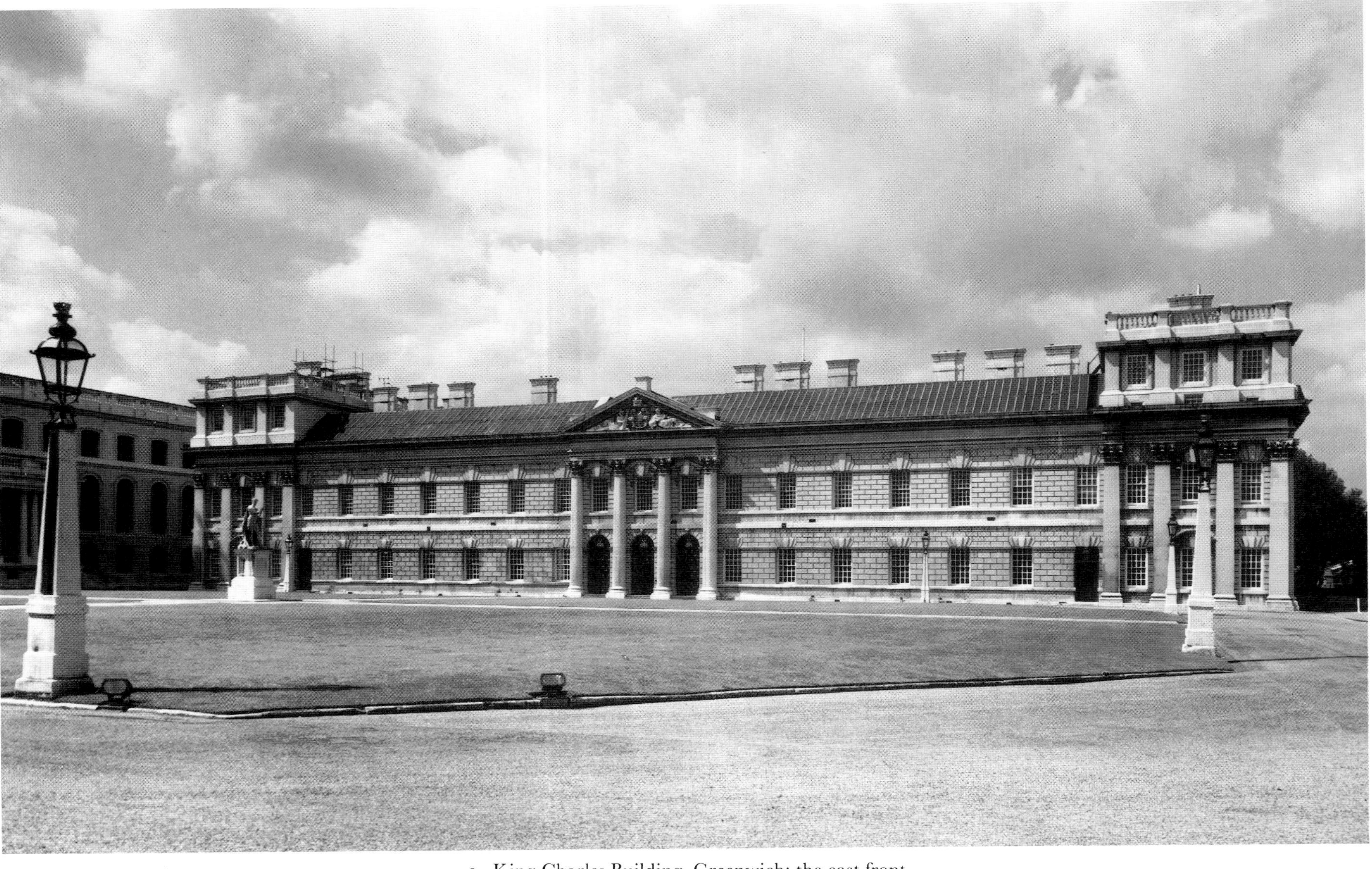

1. King Charles Building, Greenwich: the east front

1

LIFE AND BACKGROUND

> ... few ages can bragg of a good surveyor of building, or such as wee call architects. Inigo Jones was one, who did all things well and great. But since there has bin Pratt for Clarendon hous, Webb for Greenwich gallery, and Gonnersbury, and at present Sir Christopher Wren; dexterous men ...
>
> (Roger North, *c.*1695–6)[1]

IN 1671, one year before his death, John Webb, Surveyor *manqué* of the King's Works, was putting the finishing touches to an expanded version of his *Historical Essay* on the origins of the Chinese language. He found himself, he observed with Ciceronian detachment in his 'Address to the Reader', 'very fairely at leasure, until his Majesty shall bee gratiously pleased to proceed towards the perfecting of his new Royall Palace at Greenwich; the designing and ordering whereof comanded formerly my cheifest time'.

Unfortunately, King Charles II was not pleased to do as Webb hoped and in October 1672 England's first trained professional architect died, a somewhat disappointed man, although 'rich and wealthy' in 'real and personal estate'.[2] He had been, for a period of over fifteen years from *c.*1650 until *c.*1665, the best qualified and the most successful architect in the country. He was survived by his wife Anne, a close relative of his former master Inigo Jones, eight children, and a sister, Bridgett. His legacy included, in addition to houses and lands in Butleigh, Somerset, a large collection of drawings by himself, Jones, and Palladio, a substantial library of books, and three masterpieces: Gunnersbury House, Amesbury Abbey, and the King Charles Building at Greenwich. Of these, only the last survives. It is one of the most important classical buildings in England, the first which properly can be called Baroque, and the basis of one of the most exciting architectural ensembles in Europe.

The King Charles Building represents the King's side of an incomplete royal palace fronting the Thames (pl. 1). Financial and political constraints prevented the execution of its pendant across the court and the linking range whose dome would have provided the appropriate Baroque climax to the whole. The buildings which we see now at Greenwich take their mood from Webb's block, but they did not begin to go up until after the granting of the site to the Royal Naval Hospital a quarter of a century after the King Charles Building had been boarded up, its interior unfinished and its architect dead.

[1] H. M. Colvin and J. Newman, *Of Building: Roger North's Writings on Architecture* (1981), 23.

[2] PRO C7/386/66.

Notwithstanding its incomplete state, the King Charles Building revealed Webb to be a truly original architect in a way in which his other masterpieces did not. Gunnersbury and Amesbury certainly were influential, particularly in the eighteenth century, but as triumphs of synthesis and summation they did not extend the possibilities of architectural expression.[3] The King Charles Building broke new ground. It was distinguished not only by a consummate command of detail and mass, but also by that rhetorical largeness of scale, characteristic of Baroque art, which confers a grandeur which has nothing to do with the bathos of mere size. For Webb, the building represented the distillation of over thirty years of training and practice. For the next generation, the builders of Chatsworth, Castle Howard, and Blenheim, as well as of the Naval Hospital itself, it provided a precedent of inestimable importance. For the historian, it remains a piece of undeniably great architecture, which provides the best single reason for embarking on a study of its architect.

The circumstances of Webb's birth and early life are vague. Born in 1611 in Little Britain, Smithfield, he was the son of a gentleman of a Somersetshire family who had, according to Webb's own son James, 'had some crosses in the World'.[4] The relative lateness and limited nature of his formal education certainly suggest that the family fortunes could not have been great. He entered Merchant Taylors' School in 1625[5] and, after attaining a 'competent perfection in all schole learning', went in 1628 to live with Inigo Jones, the Surveyor of the King's Works, who, acting upon the 'speciall command' of King Charles I, educated him in the study of Architecture, 'with an intention that hee should have succeeded him in his place'.[6] The question which arises here is whether Webb was chosen by the King himself, after a recommendation at Court, or whether Jones knew him already and brought his name forward. It could be that Webb's late education was the direct result of Jones's intervention. Jones himself had been christened at the church of St Bartholomew the Less, Smithfield: he might have been a local friend of the family.

Webb did not have any official Office of Works position under Jones, but, in accordance with the 'Orders to be Observed by the Officers', drawn up in 1609, was employed by him directly.[7] He succeeded Francis Carter as Jones's deputy and worked for him as 'Clerk engrosser' from 1633 until 1641 on the rebuilding of old St Paul's Cathedral. This was not, strictly speaking, within the province of the Royal Works, although the initiative behind the rebuilding was the King's. Webb's tasks there included the drawing out of Jones's ideas for the workmen, which would have provided an invaluable training for him as well as removing a considerable burden from Jones, who, as Dr Margaret Whinney has suggested, probably did not care greatly for this aspect of the building process.[8] Webb

[3] Cf. A. Gomme and D. Walker, *Architecture of Glasgow* (1987), 123, from whom I have borrowed this definition of originality.

[4] A. Pritchard, 'A Source for the Lives of Inigo Jones and John Webb', *Architectural History*, 23 (1980), 138–40.

[5] Revd C. J. Robinson (ed.), *Register of Merchant Taylors' School* (1882).

[6] Pritchard, 'Source', p. 139.

[7] *King's Works*, iii. 112: 'Where an officer employs a deputy, the deputy's wage is not to be charged to the King.' The only official payment which Webb received from the Crown, prior to the Restoration, was for 'engrossing and makeinge two copies of a year Booke of Survey of his Mats Stables Barnes and Coach Houses' (PRO E 351/3272; Account of Henry Wicks, *c.*1639).

[8] M. Whinney and O. Millar, *English Art 1625–1714* (1957), 33.

also was employed during the early 1630s on work at Somerset House, and he was certainly drawing out the Surveyor's ideas for new palaces there and at Whitehall towards the end of the decade. By 1636 his association with Jones was such that they were being mentioned in the same breath,[9] and two years later he was branching out into domestic practice, assisting Jones in making designs for ceilings at Wilton and making his first independent designs at Hale and Hassenbrook.

All, therefore, seemed set fair for Webb to take over the Surveyorship from Jones, but any hopes which he might have entertained for the future were to prove misplaced, for in 1642, at the beginning of the Civil War, the King, after governing in a manner ironically akin to the hermetic allegories which were enacted before him in the Banqueting House, left London, shortly to be followed by Jones, who, as he was entitled to do, left Webb to discharge his official duties.[10] In July of the same year, Webb took £500 to the King at Beverley, lent to him by the Surveyor, 'sewed up in his waistcoate', carrying it 'through all ye enemys quarters'. This was discovered afterwards and Webb was imprisoned for a period, 'being close prisoner for a month'.[11] The following year he was thrust out of office by a Committee of the Revenue and replaced by Edward Carter, Jones's executive officer at St Paul's and the son of Francis, whom Webb had succeeded as Jones's deputy. Carter's 'false suggestion' that the Surveyor was at Oxford with the King created a climate in which Webb clearly could not be allowed to continue in office.[12] His punishment certainly would have been the greater if it had been known that he had sent to the King at Oxford 'designs of all the fortifications about London'.

To a Royalist, Jones, during the Interregnum, was still 'Mr Surveyor', and Webb still regarded himself as his deputy when he attended the King at Hampton Court and Carisbrooke in 1647–8 and received his command to design a palace for Whitehall. But over the next decade, in the absence of Royal Works, Webb turned increasingly to domestic architecture and his undoubted success in this area of practice perhaps was the root cause of his undoing at the Restoration, since he did not confine his attentions to houses owned by Royalists. Indeed, in working for two of the leading Parliamentarian Lords, Pembroke and Fairfax, he would have appeared to have been, politically, a trimmer at best, and he appears to have compounded his sin by entertaining the idea of official employment during the Interregnum (see p. 52). Even so, with the return of King Charles II in 1660, Webb, although having no official post to reclaim, could with justice, as the most experienced architect in the country, have expected to be granted the Surveyorship of the Works.

He pointed out in his petition that King Charles I had intended that he should succeed Jones and that, having 'consumed thirty years study', there were 'scarce any of the greate Nobility or eminent gentry of England but he hath done service for'. Furthermore, he continued, at the request of the Council of State he had prepared Whitehall against the

[9] By Samuel Hartlib; see G.H. Turnbull, 'Samuel Hartlib's Connection with Sir Francis Kynaston's Musaeum Minervae', *Notes & Queries* (19 Jan. 1952), 34. A further minor reference to Webb occurs in 1634, when he witnessed a contract between Lord Cottington and Hubert le Sueur, the sculptor, for work on a tomb at Westminster Abbey (*CSPD 1634–5*, p. 158, 18 July 1634).

[10] *King's Works*, iii. 156.

[11] PRO SP 29/5, 74.1 (see App. II).

[12] *Wren Society*, 18 (1941), 155.

King's return, spending over £8,000, of which only £500 had been repaid.[13] He was too late. Charles II had granted the post to Sir John Denham at Breda before he had even set sail. Denham, who, as the diarist John Evelyn observed, was 'a better poet than architect',[14] had also been promised the reversion of the post by the late King[15] and, with more foresight than Webb, made sure that he was in the right place at the right time to underline his claims to reward for loyal service to the royal cause. Webb, undaunted, continued to petition before the empty stable: 'Mr Denham may possibly as most gentry in England at this day have some knowledge in the Theory of Architecture but nothing of ye practique ... whereas Mr Webb himselfe designes, orders and directs ... without any other mans assistance.'[16] In a separate petition made to the Council of State before he became aware of Denham's appointment, Webb noted the circumstances of his dismissal in 1643 and 'hee doubteth not wth yor favourable assistance to discharge the said trust to yor Honors good satisfaction and the best advantage of the State'.[17] He supported this petition with certain proposals for the running of the Office of Works 'whereby the State may be eas'd in ye payments of mony (in future)'.[18] His diligence was rewarded only by the granting of the reversion of the Surveyorship, dated 3 July 1660, but even this was to prove an empty promise because Denham, according to Webb's later petition of 1669, 'under pretence ... that if I had his reversion hee could not sell it', prevented its passing the Great Seal.[19]

Following his disappointment, Webb claimed that he withdrew to his house at Butleigh, purchased in 1653, not returning to London until 1663, when he was recalled to 'react for your Majestie at Greenwich'. The evidence here is ambiguous, because one of the Whitehall drawings is dated 1661, and he also appears to have been responsible for work at Somerset House, the Cockpit Theatre, and possibly Ashburnham House at this time. He was referred to as Denham's deputy in May 1664 and was put formally in charge of the Greenwich works in 1666 at a salary of £200 per year, which rapidly fell into arrears, so he found himself again in a position where the granting of the Surveyorship would have been no more than just. However, in April 1666, during the period of Denham's mental indisposition, it was the Paymaster of the Works, Hugh May, who received the warrant to act as substitute. May must have been as disappointed as Webb when Denham eventually was succeeded by the new man, Christopher Wren, although he was better treated than his rival for the post, being granted a pension to add to the Comptrollership to which he had been promoted in 1668. Wren's appointment in March 1669 was the result of the personal favour of King Charles II and here the King, although dealing shabbily with Webb, was exhibiting his customary prescience as well as his practical management abilities. He recognized Wren as a man of genius whose scientific and mathematical abilities could be well utilized in the royal service, but he gave him time to find his feet: May was in charge at Windsor and Webb was still at Greenwich.

[13] PRO SP 29/5 74.1 (see App. II).

[14] J. Evelyn, *The Diary of John Evelyn*, ed. E. S. de Beer (1959), 430, 19 Oct. 1661.

[15] Vertue, II. 53.

[16] PRO SP 29/5 74.1 (see App. II).

[17] *Wren Society*. 18 (1941), 155.

[18] Ibid.

[19] PRO SP 29/251 120, pub. in *Wren Society*, 18 (1941), 156 (see App. II). The Grant of the Reversion, dated 3 July 1660, lacking the Great Seal, is at Somerset CRO DD/S/BTO.

Webb's petition of 1669, written when it had become clear that he had again been passed over, states that 'he conceives it much beneath him ... [to serve] ... under one ... who ... is his inferior by farr' and rather poignantly continues:

> May yor Majestie please if not to confirm yor Petitioner's Grant as in the honor of a King you appear to bee obliged, then to Joyne him in Patent with Mr Wren and hee shalbee ready to instruct him in the course of the office of yor works, whereof he professeth to bee wholy ignorant, and yor Petitioner, if you vouchsafe, may take care of your Majesties works at Greenwich, or elsewhere as hitherto hee hath done.

The plea was disregarded; the work at Greenwich was progressing slowly, and Webb, with only three more years to live, spent most of them at Butleigh, possibly engaging in building works on his own house but also, for much of the time, endeavouring to forward his literary reputation. His books on Stonehenge had appeared in 1655 and 1665, his work on China in 1669, and the manuscript of the expanded version of it was completed in 1671.

Inigo Jones's training of Webb, bringing him up 'in the study of Architecture, as well that wch relates to building as for masques Tryumphs and the like', made him England's first professional architect at a time when there was still no architectural profession as such. Jones himself was an artist and myth-maker who provided, in his masque designs, settings for the celebration of the Solomonic Stuart kingship. He came relatively late to architecture and stands in the same relation to Webb as Wren was to do to Hawksmoor: the polymathic teacher of a dedicated professional. In both cases, the pupil was to achieve a greatness in the command of architecture comparable with that of the master, yet in the end to find that the due reward of the Surveyorship had eluded him and that he had been superseded by the members of a new generation. It must be acknowledged, however, that, although Webb was unfortunate in his King, the times were such that, even if he had received the expected accolade in 1660 or 1669, his opportunities probably would not have been much greater. The missed opportunities for Webb in the Royal Works occurred in the years before the Restoration when the Court was in flight and exile.

The importance of the Office of Works in the seventeenth century cannot be overstressed, since it provided the most coherent available structure for the training of the prospective architect, in both theory and practice. This theoretical requirement was in itself new, a consequence of the introduction into England of a new, formal system of design based upon Italian exemplars. Jones usually is credited with this innovation, but it must be remembered that there had been stirrings long before he attained his pre-eminent position as the arbiter of the Court's taste. The mid-sixteenth century saw the 'false dawn' of Renaissance architecture in England, during which time a small group of patrons attempted to apply correctly the language of classicism.[20] The mood produced some important results, at, for example, Somerset House, Longleat, and Hill Hall, but it was short lived. In the later Elizabethan period, architecture, in classical terms, 'made

[20] M. Girouard, *Robert Smythson and the Elizabethan Country House* (1983), 30.

no growth, but rather went backwards',[21] succumbing to the influence of Flemish Mannerism, a taste fostered by immigrant craftsmen and readily available pattern books.

The change which Inigo Jones set in train after his Italian journey of 1613–14 was to take up the threads spun during the 'false dawn' and to attempt to apply the principles of classicism as a thoroughgoing system of design, permeating all aspects of the building, a considerable way beyond the merely decorative. This is why his Banqueting House would have impressed the viewer upon its completion in 1622; indeed, this is why it continues to exercise its sway today (pl. 2). Roger North recognized the achievement; in the epigraph quoted at the head of this chapter, he singled out Jones as one who 'did all things well and great', and he went on to praise his 'grand maniere' and 'plaineness', which 'hath more majesty then any thing done since'.

But the Banqueting House did not come into the world Minerva-like.[22] It should be seen, not as a beginning from scratch, but as a turning-point, providing both a consummately masterful conclusion to the period during which classicism in art was being introduced to England, and an inspiration for the future. As a deeply considered, cool, Italianate masterpiece, it must have seemed surprising in the London of the early seventeenth century, but perhaps not quite so great a surprise as some historians would have us believe, for history is not merely a roll-call of the achievements of great individuals. The Banqueting House is rooted by both style and purpose in its time: a halcyon period of unlimited possibilities. It was a place for fantasy, a marvellously wrought casket for the enactment of obscurely symbolic demonstrations; an inspiration rather than a model, and very definitely representative of a Court art.

With a building of the Banqueting House's sophistication facing Whitehall, with the haphazardly arranged buildings of the Tudor palace stretching behind it, down to the river, it is small wonder that both Charles I and Inigo Jones, with their dreams of European architectural grandeur, should have recognized the need for the training of a successor in the Royal Works. Webb, the man chosen, was an apt pupil. He grounded himself in all aspects of the Surveyor's business, receiving a training from Jones which was both theoretical and practical. The training in theory would have culminated in the treatise upon which Webb was working during the Interregnum: this would have set the academic seal on Jonesian classicism. The training in practice involved him, from the start, in working closely with Jones on designs and upon their implementation, and he continued to be, throughout his career, in the words of John Harris, 'a witness to his master's genius'.[23] In his finished drawings of buildings by Jones (pl. 3);[24] in his published accounts of Jones's life in the books on Stonehenge; and in the monument, subsequently destroyed in the Great Fire, which he erected at St Benet's, Paul's Wharf, he saw himself

[21] In the opinion of John Aubrey; see H. M. Colvin, 'Aubrey's *Chronologia Architectonica*', in J. Summerson (ed.), *Concerning Architecture* (1968), 4.

[22] See E. Mercer, *English Art 1553–1625* (1962), 98.

[23] J. Harris, in Macmillan (US) *Encyclopaedia of Architects*, ii, (1982), 512, s.v. Inigo Jones.

[24] Webb produced highly finished, idealized drawings of certain of Jones's designs: Temple Bar (*RIBA Cat.* 53) and the Barber Surgeons' Anatomy Theatre (*Worcs. Coll. Cat.* 1), both dated 1636; Star Chamber (*Worcs. Coll. Cat.* 22–4), *c.*1640; York Water Gate (*RIBA Cat.* 170), dated 1641. These probably were prepared with publication in mind, perhaps as part of the proposed theoretical treatise. The York Water Gate has, in recent years, been attributed to Balthazar Gerbier, but this is by no means certain: Webb is unlikely to have produced a measured drawing of a building which was not by either himself or Jones.

2 (*above*). The Banqueting House, Whitehall: a late-seventeenth-century engraving of Inigo Jones's building of 1619–22

3 (*right*). The Barber Surgeons' Anatomy Theatre: an idealized drawing by Webb of the building designed and built by Inigo Jones in 1636–7

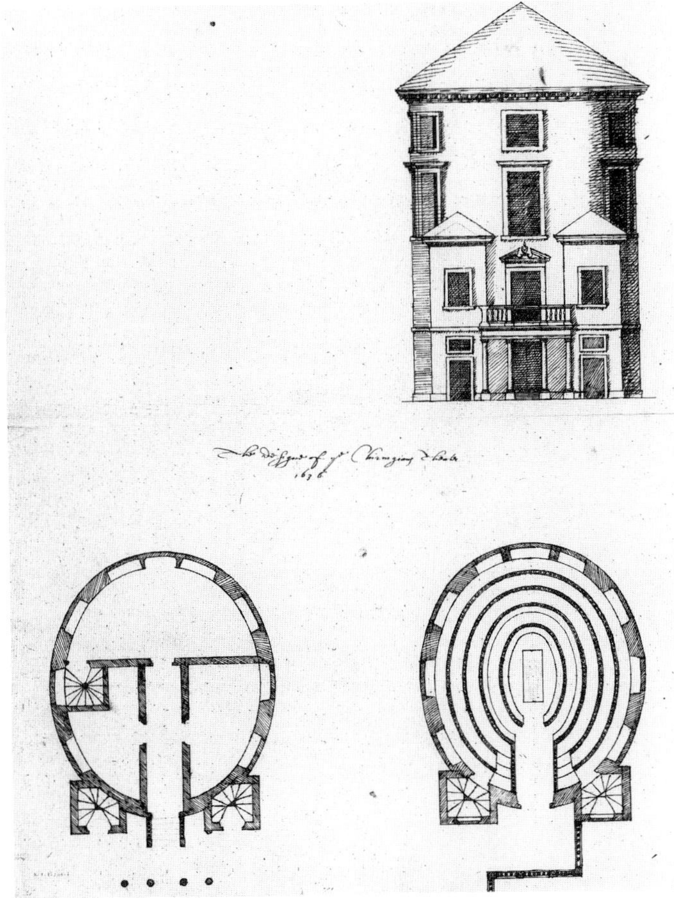

not merely as Jones's executor, but also as the chronicler of his career and the keeper of his reputation—this to the extent that he was referred to still, in 1661, nine years after the master's death, as 'Inigo Jone's man'.[25] The situation in reverse would have been unimaginable. Webb certainly owed a great deal to Jones, both professionally and personally, but the extent to which he allowed himself to remain overshadowed by his master suggests a sense of filial obligation which few sons would feel.

Aside from Roger North's brief acknowledgement, which remained unpublished until recent years, Webb himself had no contemporary apologists. The only direct comments which have been passed down to us about his life come from his own petitions of 1660 and 1669, a letter written by his son-in-law, Dr John Westley, in 1662,[26] two letters from his eldest son James, written in 1681–2 for the benefit of Anthony Wood in his compilation of *Athenae oxonienses*,[27] and a rather tart reference to his collection of drawings 'to ye value of some thousands Stirling' which 'he reserves for additions to his daughters' portions'[28] (which is not surprising, since he had five—see Appendix III).

Bereft of contemporary descriptions,[29] we must turn to his works, but here we find that, although it ought to be the case that by them he can be known, prior to the present century they tended to be attributed to Jones. Jones himself, in comparison with such other acknowledged architectural masters as Wren or Chambers, built little. It was the quality rather than the quantity of his work which gave it the totemic force which caused the English neo-Palladians of the early eighteenth century to see him, in Webb's phrase, as the 'Vitruvius of his Age'.[30] But even they believed that his *œuvre* was rather greater than it was. Colen Campbell, in his monumental celebration of the work of recent British architects, *Vitruvius Britannicus*, published in three lavish folios between 1715 and 1725, laid particular stress upon the work of Jones, seeing him as the fount of all beauty and majesty in English architecture.[31] But, of the fifteen designs which he illustrated and attributed to the master, only three definitely and two possibly were by him. Of this same fifteen, five were by Webb, but Campbell attributed the design of three of them to Jones and only their execution to Webb after Jones's death. The only house which he believed unequivocally to be by Webb himself, Horseheath Hall, was by Sir Roger Pratt.[32] Similar mistaken attributions occurred in the eighteenth century with Webb's drawings.

When Jones died in 1652, Webb inherited his books and his collection of drawings, which included a large group by Palladio. He fully realized the importance of the collection and, when he in turn bequeathed them to his son William, along with his own drawings and library, he enjoined him to 'keepe them intire together without selling or

[25] By John Evelyn (*Diary*, p. 430).

[26] Bod. Carte MS 31, fos. 440–1.

[27] Pritchard, 'Source', pp. 138–40.

[28] Corpus Christi MS *c*.332, fo. 26; quoted by T. Connor, 'The Earliest English Books on Architecture', in *Inigo Jones and the Spread of Classicism* (1987), 62 (papers given at the Georgian Group Symposium, 1986).

[29] G. Vertue mentions a 'picture of Ini. Jones & Webb. Architects' (1.24). There is no further information on this piece. The only existing claimed depiction of Webb is an eighteenth-century profile plaster bas-relief in the coving of the High Room at Lamport Hall.

[30] J. Webb, *A Vindication of Stone-Heng Restored* (1665), 8.

[31] It has been demonstrated recently that Colen Campbell was called in at a late stage in the compilation of *Vitruvius Britannicus*, and that he rearranged the material and added several of his own designs to alter the thrust of a book which had been intended as a national survey of architecture, making it into one with a Palladian and Jonesian message; see E. Harris, '"Vitruvius Britannicus" before Colen Campbell', *Burlington Magazine*, 128 (1986), 340–6.

[32] The Webb buildings which Campbell illustrated and attributed to Jones were Somerset House Gallery, Gunnersbury, Greenwich, Amesbury, and the Jones–Webb–de Caus Wilton.

imbezzling any of them'.[33] But some of the books were already on sale in 1675,[34] before William's death, and by the 1680s, with the Webb family fortunes declining, further dispersal was under way, John Aubrey noting that 'John Oliver, the City Surveyor, hath all [Jones's] papers and designs, not only of St. Paul's Cathedral, etc. and the Banqueting House, but his designe of all Whitehall'.[35] This collection passed to William Talman and then to his son John, from whom it passed in the 1720s to Lord Burlington, who appears to have added to his collection in 1740 by acquiring Webb's Greenwich drawings from Hawksmoor's executors' sale. These probably had been left by Webb in the Office of Works and were used subsequently by Hawksmoor in the preparation of designs for the Royal Naval Hospital.[36]

Burlington's collection is divided now between Chatsworth and the RIBA. The remainder of the Jones–Webb designs, and Jones's library, were acquired by Dr George Clarke of Oxford, who bequeathed them to Worcester College in 1736. He is said in a letter of 1713 to have acquired recently at least some of them, but the precise circumstances of the purchase are not known.[37] The only other large group of Webb drawings outside these major collections is at Northamptonshire County Record Office (for Lamport Hall). There are other drawings at Wiltshire County Record Office (6), the Victoria and Albert Museum (2), Belvoir Castle (1), Alnwick (1), Sheffield Central Library (1), and the British Library (a group of stage designs).

Many of the drawings in Burlington's collection were published by William Kent in his sumptuous folio of 1727 as the *Designs of Inigo Jones*. They became at least as crucial to the promulgation of neo-Palladianism, or, more accurately, the Inigo Jones Revival, as *Vitruvius Britannicus*; possibly more so, since many of the drawings were cast on an ideal plane rather than being illustrations of particular houses. These drawings were by Webb. It was not until J. A. Gotch's examination of the subject in the early part of the present century that Webb began to be seen as a more significant figure than hitherto had been presumed.[38] In fact, his was a very productive career. As the author of roughly five hundred surviving drawings, with almost thirty identifiable architectural commissions to his name, not to mention the theatre designs and three books, we might question why he was overlooked for so long.

The fault does not lie solely with Campbell for his misattribution of Webb's finest buildings; nor does it rest entirely with those accidents of history which caused some projects to be abandoned and some buildings to be demolished. The architect himself must bear some of the blame: his reputation suffered through his own self-effacement and professionalism. Webb's professionalism will be discussed again in the context of his approach to domestic architecture, but it is worth advancing here the view that he was a victim of that peculiarly English tendency to undervalue the achievements of the unflamboyant, dedicated professional and overpraise the often lesser achievements of the

[33] PRO PCC 145 (EURE); dated 24 Oct. 1672.

[34] H. W. Robinson and W. Adams (eds.), *The Diary of Robert Hooke 1672–1680* (1935), 156, 165.

[35] J. Aubrey, *Brief Lives*, ed. Clark, ii (1898), 10.

[36] K. Downes, *Hawksmoor* (Whitechapel Art Galley exhibition catalogue; 1977), cat. no. 36.

[37] H. M. Colvin, *A Biographical Dictionary of British Architects 1600–1840* (1978), 217.

[38] J. A. Gotch, 'The Original Drawings for the Palace at Whitehall attributed to Inigo Jones', *Architectural Review* (June 1912).

gifted amateur. There has been perhaps, in English eyes, something not quite sound in the pursuit of excellence, and Webb pursued it with remarkable dedication. His drawings, in which he worked through various series of possibilities at both the theoretical and the practical levels, demonstrate that he *made* himself into a great architect by hard work. His drawings are always competent and often attractive, but they lack the artistry and flair of those of Jones. This does not mean that they are inferior; rather that, through their drawings, Jones and Webb were expressing different intentions. Those of Webb are generally architectural drawings *per se*; that is, they are essentially purposive rather than ends in themselves. The growing popularity of architectural drawings in recent years as exhibits and as investments has tended to obscure the proper function of architectural draughtsmanship, which is firstly to enable the architect to formulate ideas and then to transmit those ideas or instructions to patrons, other architects, or builders: they are a stage in a process. Aesthetics do enter into the equation but they are secondary, and architectural drawings therefore should not be judged merely in terms of artistic merit.

Webb's finished drawings are carefully drawn, often ruled, with hatching and wash both being employed at different times for shading, without any apparent consistency of purpose. This makes difficult the precise dating of the drawings on stylistic grounds alone, but the overall style of painstaking delineation usually is readily identifiable. It occurs again in the work of Edward Woodroffe, one of Wren's assistants at St Paul's from the later 1660s until his death in 1675.[39] Although little is known about the arrangement of Webb's office, we might infer that at some stage Woodroffe received a training there. The only other draughtsman who can be associated with the office worked in a style which is not paralleled in Webb's own work.[40]

The drawing out and refining of ideas was, for Webb, habitual, not necessarily to be discouraged by the absence of an immediate practical application: even in the most unlikely of his projects, the building of a new Whitehall Palace, he must have entertained hopes that one day the building would progress beyond the drawing board. Through dint of practice, he acquired a degree of expertise in drawing and in design considerably beyond that of all his contemporaries, but being book-learned and home-bred he was open to the partial criticism of gentlemen-architects like Sir Roger Pratt, a later rival in country-house design, who had travelled extensively. Pratt criticized Webb's Gunnersbury for its imitation of foreign models, and advised prospective builders to get advice not only from someone well versed in the literature, but from one who has also 'seen much of that kind abroad', as the result 'will generally fall out better than one which shall be given you by a home bred Architect for want of his better experience, as is daily seen'.[41]

Despite being home-bred, with no evidence of his having travelled abroad,[42] Webb did

[39] K. Downes, *Sir Christopher Wren* (Whitechapel Art Gallery exhibition catalogue; 1982), 73–4.

[40] See Ch. 5, n. 86.

[41] R. T. Gunther, *The Architecture of Sir Roger Pratt* (1928), 60.

[42] A pass was issued to a John Webb on 8 July 1656: 'These are to will and require you to permit and suffer Mr John Webb to transport himselfe to France without any lets hindrance or molestation he carrying nothing with him prejudiciall to this Commonwealth' (PRO SP 25/114, p. 10). There is much in Webb's work to indicate a knowledge of French architecture, but it was all available in pattern books. It would have been quite extraordinary for him to have visited France without mentioning it in his petitions, since it would have represented additional confirmation of his experience and value to the King. It seems likely, therefore, that the pass was written for another Webb. However, there is a gap in the Lamport correspondence (see J. A. Gotch, 'Some Newly found Drawings and Letters of John Webb', *Journal of the RIBA*, 3rd ser. 28 (1921), 574–6), with no letters surviving between May 1655 and June 1657. Although Webb did have some work elsewhere, he might have been away for part of that period.

have a wide knowledge both of European architecture, gleaned from pattern books, treatises, and engravings (in which there was a flourishing market in London), and of painting. John Harris has demonstrated the extent to which Inigo Jones used French engravings as sources for decorative design and Webb followed him, here as elsewhere.[43] Jones's visits to Italy and Charles I's visit to Spain in 1623 (when Prince of Wales) were both formative influences on the taste and aspirations of the English Court—aspirations which had a considerable bearing on Webb's career. The influence of Italian art and architecture upon English practice needs no rehearsal here, and Webb's own particular reliance upon Italian and antique precedent, and his faith in its prescriptions, is apparent in all his work. The influence of Spain is less direct and it has been less explored. The spirit of emulation which fired the impressionable Charles after his stay at the Court of Philip IV was an important factor in the formation of his picture collection as well as in his architectural ambitions, and Charles was not alone in his appreciation: the fascination which Spain holds for the English visitor is one of long standing.

Robert Bargrave's praise of the Escorial is noted below, but this was not the only building to catch his eye during his travels in the 1640s. The Royal Palace in Madrid he considered stately and majestic; the Plaza Mayor, where Charles had watched a bullfight, he found to be 'excelling by joint consent any in the whole world for its largeness together with its uniformity of stately building' (pl. 4); and the Common Prison he thought was 'such a faire fabrick' that it seemed 'fit rather for a Prince's palace than an offenders gaol'.[44] Andrew Marvell, who also travelled in Spain at this time, used his experience in a conceit which gracefully complimented Lord Fairfax on his work at Nun Appleton (where Webb worked in *c.*1650):

> For you, Thessalian Tempe's seat
> Shall now be scorned as obsolete;
> Aranjuez, as less, disdained;
> The Bel-Retiro as constrained; . . .
> ('Upon Appleton House', ll. 753–6)

The Buen Retiro, a pleasure-palace set in elaborate grounds, was newly constructed at the time of Marvell's visit, but information about its progress had been sent to England by Charles's agent in Madrid, Sir Arthur Hopton.[45] News of such a building, the setting for extravagant masques and pageants, could only have encouraged the King's own palatial visions, inchoate in 1623, but steadily gaining strength throughout the 1630s.

This influence notwithstanding, the precise nature of the architectural interchange between England and Spain is not easy to chart, since, apart from the Imperial staircase, there are no obvious borrowings. The influence of Spanish absolutist architecture was rather more inspirational than formal. However, Charles did try to recruit the Surveyor of the Spanish Royal Works to his own service, and the Escorial looms in the background

[43] J. Harris, 'Inigo Jones and his French Sources', *Metropolitan Museum of Art Bulletin*, 19 (1960–1), 253–64.

[44] R. Bargrave, 'A Relation of Sundry Voyages and Journeys', Bod. MS Rawlinson C. 799, fos. 137–8.

[45] J. H. Elliott, 'Philip IV of Spain', in A. G. Dickens (ed.), *The Courts of Europe* (1977), 182.

of the Whitehall Palace Schemes. Further, although the piazza at Leghorn in Tuscany is generally cited, correctly, as the source for Inigo Jones's Covent Garden, the memory of Madrid's Plaza Mayor could not have been far from the King's mind when he approved the scheme.

During their visit to Madrid, Charles and his travelling companion, the Duke of Buckingham, had been greatly impressed by the Spanish royal collection. They procured several paintings and the acquisition of further works from the same source continued after their return. Sir Arthur Hopton was busy throughout the 1630s, attempting to satisfy the requirements of the King and those of his courtiers with an interest in art.[46] Inigo Jones also became involved in the traffic of art objects when in 1638 he sent instructions to Spain for the packing and shipping of plaster moulds taken of three antique marble heads, for casting in England 'for His Majesty's use'.[47]

Jones was an accomplished virtuoso with a considerable knowledge of painting which he put to use in the service of the King: his examination of an important gift of pictures from Cardinal Barberini, which arrived in London in 1636, is graphically recorded.[48] In 1639 he sent instructions to Jacob Jordaens on the ceiling paintings which were required for the Queen's House at Greenwich. In this he was assisted by Webb, who made a transcription of the iconographical and procedural requirements; clearly, Jones was training him in all of the many branches of his work.[49]

The opportunity to study the great collections of the King and of the Earl of Pembroke would have given Webb that intimate knowledge of Italian painting which enabled him to follow Jones along the path of connoisseurship. There was, during the Interregnum, no opportunity for him to exercise his skills on behalf of the Court, but, as he mentioned in his petition in 1660, he could, and did, advise others. During the course of building at Lamport Hall, he undertook to offer advice to Sir Justinian Isham on the purchasing of paintings, advising him always to 'buy principalls' rather than copies, for 'though they are somewhat deerer yet are they of farr more esteeme and hee that buys cann hardly bee a looser'. He commented on copies after Titian (a *Lucretia*, 'tollerable ... but not so pleasing to yor Ladye because of ye naked woman in it') and Guercino ('very hard yett mee thinks might well be placed over ye dore in yor roome ... at wch height much of ye hardness would bee taken off'), and wrote of a version of Van Dyck's late piece, *The Infants Christ and John the Baptist*, that it was 'a pretty thing but hath been much spoiled' and 'indifferently repaired'. This was sold to Isham for £20 as the 'tow boyse' by the dealer and copier, Maurice Wase, to whom he had been introduced by Webb. It remains in the Lamport collection.[50]

As well as acting as an intermediary and as an advisor, it is likely that Webb would himself have dealt in art, although there is only one documented instance of his doing so.

[46] E. du Gué Trapier, 'Sir Arthur Hopton and the Interchange of Paintings between Spain and England in the 17th Century', *Connoisseur* (Apr. 1967), 239–43; (May 1967), 60–3.

[47] E. Harris, 'Velazquez and Charles I'. *Journal of the Warburg and Courtauld Institutes*, 30 (1967), 414–20.

[48] R. Wittkower, 'Inigo Jones—Puritanissimo Fiero', in *Palladio and English Palladianism* (1974), 67–70.

[49] E. Croft Murray, *Decorative Painting in England 1537–1837*, i (1962), 36–7. Webb's transcription is inserted at the back of his copy of Palladio's *Quattro libri* (Worcester College).

[50] Gotch, 'Some Newly Found Drawings and Letters of John Webb', pp. 574–6.

One Henry Carter claimed in 1660 that six years before he had bought from Webb 'a naked Venus, a foot long, for £20'. This, 'being now said to belong to the late King', and therefore to be restored to the royal collections, he promised to keep safe until it was called for and begged that Webb be ordered to repay him.[51] Webb's involvement here is ironic as it was he who had been summoned by the House of Lords to assist in the restoration of 'the late King's goods, jewels and pictures ... to his now Majesty'. In May 1660 the Lords moved the appointment of a committee to receive information about the whereabouts of the goods which had been dispersed after the death of Charles I, and this was afterwards empowered to seize 'all such of the goods as should be discovered to them', the books of inventories being ordered to be delivered to Webb. This ruling clearly was connected with his preparation of Whitehall for the return of Charles II: writing to the Earl of Dorset, he 'requests his Lordship to order that such pictures as the writer may find fitting to be set up in his His Majesty's lodgings at Whitehall may be delivered to him by the committee'.[52]

During their deliberations, the Lords referred to Webb, prematurely, as 'His Majesty's Surveyor'. As we have seen, this was, unfortunately, the closest that he got to being appropriately honoured for all his knowledge and experience, and for his efforts on behalf of the Crown. It is the purpose of this book not only to demonstrate, belatedly, that Charles II made a rare error of judgement in failing to promote Webb, but also to show that 'Inigo Jone's man' is worthy of a position in his own right in the limited ranks of great English architects. To attempt to show why he is worthy of his place is not to detract from the achievements of the men who came before and after, but rather to fill out a figure who succeeded, as Whinney succinctly stated, in bridging the gap 'in style as well as in time between the school of Inigo Jones and that of Wren'.[53]

[51] *CSPD 1660–1*, p. 379, Nov. 1660.

[52] HMC, 7th Report, Pt. I (1879), 88a, 92.

[53] M. Whinney, 'John Webb's Drawings for Whitehall Palace', *Walpole Society*, 31 (1946), 95.

2

THEORY

WHEN Ben Jonson satirized Inigo Jones as Colonel Iniquo Vitruvius, he was fighting a rearguard action. The famous quarrel between the poet and the architect of the Court masques centred upon the role of Invention in their creation. Jonson maintained that this was the preserve of the poet whilst the architect was responsible for providing merely the visual expression of the text. This traditional English view of the architect as craftsman was contested by Jones, who, basing his position on Renaissance and classical theory, propounded his view of Architecture as a liberal rather than a mechanical art, no less dependent than poetry upon Invention.[1]

In the first of the masques to be produced after the break-up of his partnership with Jonson, Jones collaborated with Aurelian Townshend on *Albion's Triumph*. In a design for a scene border the figures of Theory and Practice are depicted, 'shewing that by these two, all works of Architecture, and Ingining have their perfection' (pl. 5). Jones based his figures on those of *Theorica* and *Experientia*, taken from the title-page of Scamozzi's *L'idea della architettura universale*. Scamozzi followed Vitruvius in requiring the architect to be master of all the arts, and Jones too believed that the artist, no less than the poet, needed to draw on all human knowledge for his inventions. But before the invention came the conception, the Idea, which was based on knowledge and reason. The work of building was merely the expression, or realization, of this Platonic Idea; the actual construction of forms immanent in the mind of the creator, the Architect. Although this view was not new in England, it was a comparatively recent one, and Jones was the first architect to promote it.

John Dee, the sage, who had studied both Vitruvius and Alberti, made a plea in 1570 for the inclusion of Architecture among the 'Artes Mathematicall': 'The Architect procureth, enformeth and directeth the Mechanician to handworke and the building actuall . . . and is cheif Iudge of the same. . . . Architecture hath good and due allowance in the honest company of Artes Mathematicall Derivative.'[2] Later, Henry Wotton picturesquely propounded the Renaissance view that the architect should be 'no superficiall, & floating Artificer; but a Diver into Causes'.[3] But, in the creation of the great Elizabethan and Jacobean country houses, if there was one controlling mind at work, it was that of the owner rather than that of an architect:

[1] For a full discussion and analysis of the quarrel, see D.J. Gordon, 'Poet and Architect: The Intellectual Setting of the Quarrel between Ben Jonson and Inigo Jones', *Journal of the Warburg and Courtauld Institutes*, 12 (1949), 152–78.

[2] J. Rykwert, *The First Moderns* (1980) 123.

[3] H. Wotton, *The Elements of Architecture* (1624), 55.

4 (*above*). The Plaza Mayor, Madrid: an arena, forum, and market place laid out by Juan de Herrera for King Philip II and completed in 1617–19 by Juan Gómez de Mora for King Philip III

5 (*left*). Inigo Jones's depictions of *Theorica* and *Practica* on a scene border for the masque *Albion's Triumph*, 1632; by these two, 'all works of Architecture, and Ingining have their perfection'. The young Theory, who looks upwards, is concerned with the light of reason and the sublime, whilst the aged Practice looks down, pointing her compasses and rule towards the ground, thereby demonstrating her concern with earthly matters

The plan might come from one source, the details from a number of others. Designs could be supplied by one or more of the craftsmen actually employed on the building; or by an outside craftsman; or by the employer; or by a friend of the employer; or by a professional with an intellectual rather than a craft background.[4]

This was the prevailing practice, which Jones, in attempting to exalt the role of the architect, was opposing. The idea of the modern architect was a development not from within the ranks of the building trades, with their stress on quotidian practicalities, but from within the realms of theory, supported by artistically enlightened patronage; for Jones, such patronage was provided by the Court.

Coupled with the intellectual position, the idea of the omnicompetent artist carried with it a concern for social position, and it was Jones's social pretensions which Jonson mocked in his lines 'To Inigo Marquess Would be'. Written in 1631, at the height of the quarrel over the masque *Love's Triumph through Callipolis* which ended the long collaboration between poet and architect, Jonson clearly was alluding to the position of Jones's Spanish equivalent, Giovanni Battista Crescenzi. Created Marqués de la Torre in 1626, Crescenzi was made Minister of Public Works and Surveyor of the Royal Works four years later.[5] The impression made upon Charles I when Prince of Wales by his visit to the Spanish Court in 1623 was profound, and, in view of Crescenzi's many skills as architect, painter, and connoisseur, it is not surprising that Charles attempted later to recruit him for the English Royal Works. Although Crescenzi turned down the opportunity to come to England, in 1631, the invitation probably was known well enough in Court circles to give force to Jonson's lines:

> But cause thou hearst ye mighty K. of Spaine
> Hath made his Inigo Marquess, wouldst thou fayne
> Our Charles should make thee such? T'will not become
> All Kings to doe ye self same deeds wth some!
> Besydes, his Man may merit it, & be
> A Noble honest Soule! What's this to thee?
> He may have skill & iudgment to designe
> Cittyes & Temples! thou a Caue for Wyne,
> Or Ale! He build a pallace! Thou a shopp
> Wth slyding windowes, & false Lights a top! . . .[6]

Jonson concluded with the uncharitable suggestion that Inigo might be styled 'ye Marquess of New-Ditch', but Jones stood high in royal favour, not only for his architectural abilities, but also as a great connoisseur of paintings, an invaluable aide to a great collector.[7] It was Charles I's patronage of Jones which paved the way for the acceptance of the architect as a professional man of standing, more than a mere floating artificer.

[4] M. Girouard, *Robert Smythson and the Elizabethan Country House* (1983), 8.

[5] For Crescenzi, see Enriqueta Harris, 'G. B. Crescenzi, Velázquez, and the "Italian" Landscapes for the Buen Retiro', *Burlington Magazine*, 122 (1980), 562–4, and P. Shakeshaft, 'Elsheimer and G. B. Crescenzi', *Burlington Magazine*, 123 (1981), 550–1.

[6] *Ben Jonson*, ed. C. H. Herford and P. Simpson, viii (1947), 406–7; see also J. Brown and J. H. Elliott, *A Palace for a King* (1980), 44–5.

[7] Cf. R. Wittkower, 'Inigo Jones—Puritanissimo Fiero', in *Palladio and English Palladianism* (1974), 67–70.

There was as yet no formal training-ground for the prospective architect, and throughout the seventeenth century, with the exceptions of John Webb and Nicholas Hawksmoor, 'brought up' respectively by Inigo Jones and Sir Christopher Wren, there were therefore no trained, professional architects in the accepted sense of the term. There were men who practised Architecture, but they came to it from other disciplines. Jones himself had not turned seriously to building until early middle age. Wren was a mathematician and Professor of Astronomy. Hugh May, Sir Roger Pratt, Captain Winde, and William Samwell were all gentlemen. Gerbier was a diplomat. Some, Peter Mills and Robert Grumbold for example, like Robert Smythson in the later sixteenth century, developed an ability as 'surveyors' which enabled them to progress beyond their craft origins. Theirs was not an inevitable step, but one which was made possible by changing attitudes towards a developing profession.[8]

Such attitudes also lay behind the increasing desire in the seventeenth century for academic training. Both James I and Charles I displayed an interest in the idea of an 'Academy Royal or College & Senate of Honour', an outline of which was submitted by Edmund Bolton in 1617, and in 1635 Sir Francis Kynaston succeeded in founding the Musaeum Minervae. This was an academy of learning, designed to educate young nobles and gentlemen by means of demonstration and experiment in arts not practised in the universities: Navigation, Riding, Fortification, and Architecture, etc. The last two were to be taught along with Arithmetic, Algebra, and Geometry by the Professor of Geometry, John Spidell. A similar subject range was essayed at Balthasar Gerbier's Academy at Bethnal Green in 1649, Architecture being included, 'as well for building, as for magnificent shewes, and secret motion of Scenes, and the like'.[9] These rather opportunist experiments were short lived and Wren was later to make the point that:

> our English Artists are dull enough at Inventions but when once a foreigne patterne is sett, they imitate soe well that commonly they exceed the originall.... this shows that our Natives want not a Genius, but education in that which is the foundation of all Mechanick Arts, a practice in designing or drawing, to which everybody in Italy, France and the Low Countries pretends to more or less.[10]

The same point was made by John Gwynn in 1749 in his *Essay on Design*, in which he made 'Proposals for Erecting a Public Academy ... for Educating the British Youth in Drawing'. Drawing being the *sine qua non* for designer, painter, or sculptor, Gwynn argued that it could and should be taught. Design, the 'Child of Genius', could not be taught in the same way, but education could call it forth. English artists did not lack capacity,

[8] For the development of the architectural profession and the role of the Office of Works, see H. M. Colvin, *A Biographical Dictionary of British Architects 1600–1840* (1978), 26–41.

[9] C. Rowe, 'The Theoretical Drawings of Inigo Jones: Their Sources and Scope' (University of London MA thesis, 1948); see also G. H. Turnbull, 'Samuel Hartlib's Connection with Sir Francis Kynaston's Musaeum Minervae', *Notes & Queries* (19 Jan, 1952), 33–7. In a letter of Aug. 1650 to Webb's patron at Lamport, Sir Justinian Isham, Bishop Brian Duppa reported on Gerbier's Academy: 'The mushroom Academy which you mention, was onely in request ... when it was new sprung up ... but whether it may not rise again ... I can not tell. For as long as Sir Balthasar is sure, that the major part of men are fooles, he cannot despair of keeping the chair and having disciples' (*The Correspondence of Bishop Brian Duppa and Sir Justinian Isham 1650–60* ed. G. Isham (1955)).

[10] In a letter of Nov. 1694 to Mr Treasurer Hawes of Christ's Hospital, quoted in M. Whinney and O. Millar, *English Art 1625–1714* (1957), 319.

ingenuity, and industry, but they had never been properly initiated. In short, they needed an academy, such as Colbert had founded in France nearly a century before.

In fact, it was the Office of Works during the seventeenth and eighteenth centuries which provided the only English equivalent to an academy for the training of architects, but it could do this only on a limited scale. The standard of instruction received was subject to considerable variation because the Office itself did not run smoothly, its progress being interrupted by the Interregnum and, more consistently, its procedures being hampered by the often overtly political nature of its appointments. In dealing solely with royal buildings, it could hardly be said to be providing a substitute for a general training, but a little was better than nothing at all because until the mid-eighteenth century the opportunities to study and work in the office of a practising architect were few. How, then, were new ideas, as well as basic knowledge, disseminated outside Works' circles?

Professional standing and professional practice alike are dependent upon a body of knowledge and upon theory. England lagged behind both Italy and France in the development of an appropriate, architectural literature. It is a telling comment upon English attitudes that Shakespeare's only reference to a major architect is anachronistic. He refers to a statue [*sic*] by 'that rare Italian master, Julio Romano', who 'would beguile Nature of her custom, so perfectly he is her ape'.[11]

In Italy, the exemplifying remains of the architecture of classical antiquity were given a theoretical context by Vitruvius' account of the practice of classical architecture and the role of the architect. Because of its historical place and the accident of its survival, Vitruvius' manuscript acquired a significance which it did not intrinsically deserve. Here was the architectural language of antiquity as perceived by an Augustan. The manuscript's prolixity and vagueness rendered it capable of considerable variations in interpretation. Several editions of the *De architectura* appeared in Italy and France after the first printed Latin edition had been issued at Rome in *c.*1486,[12] but there was no complete edition published in English until 1791.[13] Robert Pricke published a version taken from Mauclerc's French edition in 1669, which laid stress upon the Orders, and in 1692 an 'Englished' version of Perrault's abridged edition appeared.[14] Christopher Wase's complete edition of *c.*1670 was undersubscribed: it survives in manuscript.[15]

The first of the scholarly treatises of the Italian Renaissance, Alberti's *De re aedificatoria*, was published in Latin (1485), Italian (1546), French (1553), and Spanish (1582), but did not appear in English until Leoni's translation from the Italian was published in 1726.[16] Of far greater significance for England were the books of Serlio, published between 1537 and 1551.[17] The *Regole generali di architettura* broke new ground in being written in the vernacular and in being copiously illustrated. It was as a source book for details that

[11] *The Winter's Tale*, v. ii.

[12] P. Murray, *The Architecture of the Italian Renaissance* (1969), 239. For a general survey of architectural literature, see D. Wiebenson (ed.) *Architectural Theory and Practice from Alberti to Ledoux* (1982).

[13] *The Architecture of M. Vitruvius Pollio*, trans. William Newton (d. 1790) and published in accordance with his will by his brother James.

[14] *A New Treatise of Architecture* (1669), and *De architectura* (1692).

[15] Bod. MS. CCC c. 378.

[16] See J. Rykwert's foreword to the 1965 reprint of Leoni's edition of *Ten Books on Architecture*.

[17] Murray, *Architecture*, pp. 195–6.

it had its greatest influence. The Venetian edition of 1619, *Tutte l'opere d'architettura et prospetiva,* owned by both Inigo Jones and John Webb, included, in Book VII, plans of houses, but the only English version, by Robert Peake (1611),[18] a translation from the Dutch of Books I–V, omitted them. Although covering geometry, perspective, antique buildings, and the Bramante Tempietto, Peake's volume laid most stress upon the Orders and upon details. It is safe to presume that Peake knew his market and that it was the decorative aspects of classicism which appealed to the English audience at this time. In the late sixteenth century the books of Hans Blum, Vredeman de Vries, and Wendel Dietterlin were all in use in England. All dealt with the Orders and with details, Blum's *Quinque columnarum* being considered useful enough to warrant an English translation in 1608.

It was for its clear description and illustration of the Orders that Palladio's *Quattro libri dell'architettura* first appealed to an English audience. This, the most influential treatise in the whole history of architecture, was the first to combine readily reproducible designs with a learned and informative text. It was first published in Venice in 1570, with four reprints being made from the original blocks in 1581, 1601, 1616, and 1642. Both Jones and Webb owned and annotated copies of the 1601 edition.[19] Webb's had been rebound with an interleaved manuscript translation into English, but no published edition was available until that of Leoni a century later. Instead of a complete edition, it was Book I, on the Orders, which was translated first. Issued by Godfrey Richards in 1663, the success of this venture is attested by the frequent reprintings which were required until well into the eighteenth century.[20]

The last of the great architectural treatises of the Italian Renaissance, Scamozzi's *L'idea della architettura universale* (1615), was studied closely by Jones and Webb, but for the more general architectural reader it was cannibalized regularly for its codification of the Orders, rather than for its theoretical exposition. The most frequently reprinted edition, issued by William Fisher as *The Mirror of Architecture*,[21] was a particularly catchpenny venture, translated, like Peake's Serlio, from the Dutch rather than from the Italian. It illustrated the Orders, as laid down by 'Vincent Scamozzi, Master Builder of Venice', to which were added the 'Principal Rules of Architecture ... made plain to ordinary Capacities', by Joachim Schuym; the description of a joint rule for drawing the architrave, frieze, and cornice of any Order, by John Browne; and a contracted version of Henry Wotton's *Elements of Architecture*. Scamozzi remains untranslated into English.

The stress on the Orders was a recurring feature of English architectural literature from the sixteenth century onwards. The first English architectural book, John Shute's *The First and Chief Groundes of Architecture*, published in 1563, was devoted to illustrating them, and subsequent editions of continental treatises maintained the emphasis. Vignola's *Regole delle cinque ordini* was particularly popular. Published in 1562, it was issued in

[18] Repr. 1982.

[19] Their copies are in the library of Worcester College, Oxford.

[20] R. Wittkower, 'English Neoclassicism and the Vicissitudes of Palladio's *Quattro Libri*', in *Palladio and English Palladianism*, pp. 76–8.

[21] In 1669, with six further editions before 1708; see T. P. Hudson, 'The Origins of Palladianism in English 18th Century Architecture' (University of Cambridge Ph.D. thesis, 1974).

English in a pocket-sized edition by Moxon in 1655.[22] He hoped that he had given the rules of the five Orders 'in a plain and easie way'. 'I have followed (so neer as I could)', he wrote, 'the words of our Author, unlesse here and there I have been a little more large, thereby endeavouring the better to expresse his meaning, and instruct the young Practitioner.' A more faithful version of Vignola, for the benefit of 'all Ingenious Persons that are concerned in the Famous Art of Building' was published by John Leeke in 1669.[23]

Robert Pricke greatly extended the range of references open to the English-speaking practitioner. As well as his version of Vitruvius, he brought out editions of Francini (1669; elevations of gates and arches),[24] Le Muet (1670; elevations and plans of houses, of rather limited relevance for English practice),[25] and Barbet (1670; ceilings, chimneypieces, etc.)[26] He drew on the latter for *The Architects Store House* (1674), where he published many of the decorative features which Jones and Webb, inspired by the original engravings, had employed earlier in the century. Pricke's stress on decorative details was not followed by other writers until the advent of the popular pattern book for builders: these flourished for about fifty years between *c.*1730 and *c.*1780. Books on the Orders, however, having appeared in the 1650s and 1660s, did so again during the early years of the eighteenth century and then from *c.*1725 to *c.*1765 there was a host of books on the subject, all vying to produce ever simpler formulae for the proportioning and construction of these apparently infinitely mutable features.

It is of the greatest importance to note that books of plans for houses, leaving aside the edition of Le Muet, did not begin to appear in English until the eighteenth century, and, apart from the significant exception of versions of Palladio and the works of Campbell and Gibbs, these did not appear in quantity until the mid-century. They immediately became the most important architectural publications, their popularity lasting well into the nineteenth century. Prior to this development, architecture appears to have been seen by many commentators entirely in terms of ornament. Walpole, for instance, as late as 1769, observed that: 'In all Queen Elizabeth's reign there was scarce any architecture at all: I mean no pillars or seldom; buildings then became quite plain. Under James a barbarous composition succeeded.'[27] A rounded knowledge of architectural history was not an inevitable part of the equipment of the cultivated man, any more in the eighteenth century than it is today.

The major appeal of classical architecture, dangerously seductive for the inexperienced or the inept, lies in the great variety which it offers within a basic language. The primary element of that language, the Orders, firstly determines overall proportions and relationships within the structure of the building and, secondly, decorates it (pl. 6). Prompted in part by the availability of books which not only offered a deceptively simple view of the composition of the Orders, but also viewed them in isolation, divorced from their wider context, the attention of the English practitioner generally has been engaged by the secondary, superficial aspects of classicism, at the expense of that proportion,

[22] J. Moxon, *Vignola, or the Compleat Architect.*

[23] J. Leeke, *The Regular Architect: Or the General Rule of the Five Orders of Architecture of Giacomo Barozzio Da Vignola.*

[24] *A New Book of Architecture.*

[25] *The Art of Fair Building.*

[26] *A Booke of Architecture.*

[27] M. Girouard, 'Attitudes to Elizabethan Architecture, 1600–1900', in J. Summerson (ed.), *Concerning Architecture* (1968), 16.

balance, and tension which lie at the heart of all successful classical composition. These qualities cannot be imparted by the mere application of ornament, an act which owes more to sympathetic magic than it does to the difficult art of architecture.

The emphasis on the decorative, swiftly learned and partially understood, is symptomatic of that native English neglect of theory and mistrust of ideology, in favour of an empiricism which is too often devoted to the surface of things, at the expense of underlying meaning. English writers certainly were not slow to produce pattern books to provide models for patrons, architects, and craftsmen, but, even during the highly intellectual phase of early eighteenth-century neo-Palladianism, they eschewed theory, and English architectural training and practice suffered in consequence. James Gibbs was one of the few architects at that time with the ability and authority to strike a warning note:

> it is not the Bulk of a Fabrick, the Richness and Quantity of the Materials, the Multiplicity of lines, nor the Gaudiness of the Finishing, that give the Grace or Beauty and Grandeur to a Building; but the Proportion of the Parts to one another and to the Whole, whether entirely plain, or enriched with a few Ornaments properly disposed.[28]

But Gibbs's *A Book of Architecture* (1728), important though it was, was an impressive collection of his own designs, rather than a treatise. Indeed, there was no coherent, illustrated architectural treatise on the Vitruvian model published by an English architect until 1756, when the second-generation, neo-Palladian Isaac Ware issued his *Complete Body of Architecture*. This was large and influential, but essentially retrospective—more a codification than a prescription. Ware was capitalizing on a century of English experience of Jonesian architecture, as well as on the accumulated wisdom of continental authors, long after the moment of innovation had passed. He was writing, he stated in his preface, about the 'present state of architecture'. He proposed to 'collect all that is useful in the works of others, at whatsoever time they have been written ... and to add the several discoveries and improvements made since that time ... to make our work serve as a library on this subject to the gentleman and the builder; supplying the place of all other books ...'.

It is vain to wonder how far the state of architecture described by Ware in 1756 might have differed if the innovators of the seventeenth century had been more inclined to turn from practice to theory, but it is tempting to do so. Might English architecture have taken a more formally classical route, earlier and more widely, if the treatise upon which John Webb appears to have been working in the 1640s had been completed? Although he did not leave any statement of his programme, enough drawings survive for us to infer some of his intentions. Webb, by both training and inclination, was ideally equipped to produce an expository textbook. Instructed firstly by Jones and then by a detailed private study of the Italian masters, his copious annotations in his copies of Serlio and Palladio, as well as on his own drawings, reveal a system-builder who rejoiced in the resolution of problems after closely comparing authorities. A treatise produced by Webb would have brought these solutions to an audience far greater than that provided by the Court and

[28] J. Gibbs, *A Book of Architecture* (1728), intro.

6 (*above, left*). Claude Perrault's definitive representation of the five Orders, published in Paris in 1683. The influence of Perrault's *Ordonnance des cinq espèces de colonnes* was considerably extended by John James's translation, *A Treatise of the Five Orders of Columns in Architecture*, published in 1708

7 (*above, right*). 'Ornament of the Ionick Order', with additional dentils in the cornice, based on Palladio (cf. Palladio, i. 36)

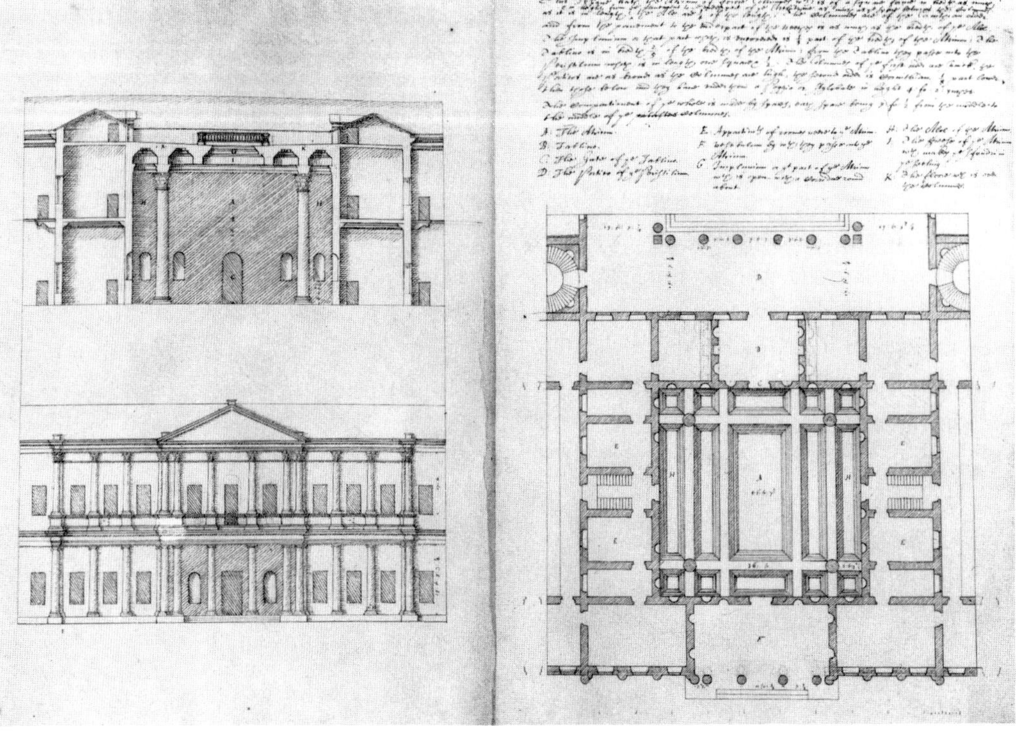

8 (*right*). Reconstruction of the Tetrastyle atrium of the ancient Roman house, based by Webb on Palladio's illustration (cf. Palladio, ii. 27–8)

its immediate circle. Such a treatise would have set the seal on the Jonesian architectural revolution: *Theorica* and *Experientia* would have been united.

There are some two hundred drawings and several sheets of manuscript notes by Webb which have come to be regarded loosely as 'theoretical', in that they did not have a specific, project purpose. However, this is not to suggest that they were all intended for publication and it might be more appropriate to refer to them as miscellaneous. The drawings were first analysed by Colin Rowe, who divided them into four groups:[29]

(i) The Orders; their ornaments and application.
(ii) Domestic buildings; the ancient house and designs from the small house to the palace.
(iii) Miscellaneous urban buildings; drawing upon Palladio's Basilica at Vicenza and an 'Exchange for Merchants' from Serlio.
(iv) Temples and churches.

Rowe suggested that the initial impetus for the proposed treatise probably came from Inigo Jones, but he conceded that the compilation of such a volume perhaps was 'not at first a project easy to associate with Inigo's mind'. As all the drawings are by Webb, Rowe argued that Jones's involvement, maintaining the master–pupil relationship, lay in exercising a controlling interest. In so far as the theoretical drawings represent a continuation of Webb's training, the influence of Jones cannot be ignored. Certainly, the numerous sources consulted by Webb were available to him in Jones's comprehensive library.[30] However, there is no internal evidence within the drawings themselves, and no reference elsewhere, to indicate that the project was the brainchild of anyone but Webb himself. He, unlike Jones, had the appropriate cast of mind.

Those drawings which might be regarded, properly, as theoretical and intended for publication are the highly finished studies of the Orders and the studies of the ancient house (pl. 8). The latter had an application beyond the purely theoretical, as the studies of the houses of the Greeks and the Romans enabled Webb to clarify his own procedures when designing large, domestic buildings: the schemes for Durham House, Belvoir Castle, Whitehall, and Greenwich all benefited as a result. It has been shown that, for his creative reconstructions of the ancient house, Webb used Palladio's illustrations and text, supported by Scamozzi's theory and method of design, referring also to Daniele Barbaro's 1567 edition of Vitruvius, for which Palladio had provided the illustrations.[31] Webb did not merely copy, but made certain alterations to his drawings with the purpose of integrating them into his own comprehensive scheme. During the course of these reconstructions, he took from Scamozzi the method of laying out designs by 'spaces' rather than by the customary classical method of measurement by column width. The spaces were modules, compatible with intercolumniation, which could be varied in size according to requirements in a technique which was applicable to designs as various in size as Hale

[29] Rowe, 'Theoretical Drawings'; see also *Worcs. Coll. Cat.*, pp. 59–93, and *RIBA Cat.*, pp. 26–7.

[30] For Jones's library, see J. Harris, S. Orgel, and R. Strong, *The King's Arcadia* (1973), 217–18.

[31] E. Eisenthal, 'John Webb's Reconstruction of the Ancient House', *Architectural History*, 28 (1985), 7–18; and the same author's MA report, University of London, 1981: 'John Webb's Theoretical Drawings of the Ancient House'.

Lodge and Whitehall Palace. Their use allowed for considerable flexibility within an overall compositional framework, the very hallmark of classical architecture itself. Their employment in the design process made for greater ease in the laying out of the plan and, in the case of reconstructions, enabled Webb to extrapolate façades from drawings where only plans and sections were given.

For his drawings of the Orders, Webb turned to the same Italian sources, considering them critically and combining details from the published versions of Palladio and Scamozzi. The surviving drawings are far from representing a complete set of the five Orders and their ornaments, but the interest displayed by Webb in their possible variations in form (particularly in the Ionic Order, to which he devoted most attention) (pl. 7) suggests that he might have been thinking along the same comparative lines as Fréart de Chambray, whose *Parallèle de l'architecture antique et de la moderne* was published in 1650.[32] Webb's long accompanying text, 'of the Ionick Order', survives in manuscript.[33] This relies heavily on Scamozzi's account and, in being both erudite and repetitive, has much in common with Webb's later published work.

A comparable series of manuscript notes, 'of wyndowes', deals with the various types of window, how they should be made, and where they should be placed.[34] Scamozzi is again called upon, together with Viola Zanini,[35] but in both the text and the accompanying drawings the greatest reliance is placed on Serlio, full page references being supplied by Webb. Comparison with the originals demonstrates that here again Webb used his sources critically, omitting some details and adding others. The drawings are not fully worked up and it is possible that they were drawn either as part of the architectural learning process, or for reference purposes, rather than for publication, although the extensive manuscript notes might suggest the latter.

The sheets of drawings of plans for small houses, villas, and palaces present a similar problem of intention (pl. 9). The majority derives from Palladio's villa designs, taken from the *Quattro libri* and from Jones's collection of Palladio's drawings; others are after Serlio, Rubens,[36] Viola Zanini, and Philibert de l'Orme.[37] The draughting style employed here is unique in Webb's *œuvre*, the lines of the plans being drawn in open hatching, a technique which he took, along with the designs, from some of Palladio's own drawings. It has been credibly suggested that these small sketch plans might have been intended as Office of Works reference sheets, rather than as material for publication, 'providing a quick guide to the old masters of architecture, as well as giving a constant source of inspiration'.[38] In being drawn on scored paper, they would have been particularly easy to enlarge for project purposes.

Some of the larger, finished drawings of houses again derive from Palladio (there is, for example, a close copy of a design for the Villa Pisani) (pl. 10),[39] but others are extrapolations from the centrally planned palazzi published by Cataneo.[40] These achieved

[32] This was translated into English and published by John Evelyn in 1664.

[33] *Worcs. Coll. Cat.* 227C–230H.

[34] Ibid. 231A–233B.

[35] *Della architettura* (1629).

[36] *Palazzi di Genova* (1622).

[37] *Le premier Tôme de l'architecture* (1567).

[38] *Worcs. Coll. Cat.*, p. 61.

[39] Ibid. 169.

[40] *L'Architettura* (1567).

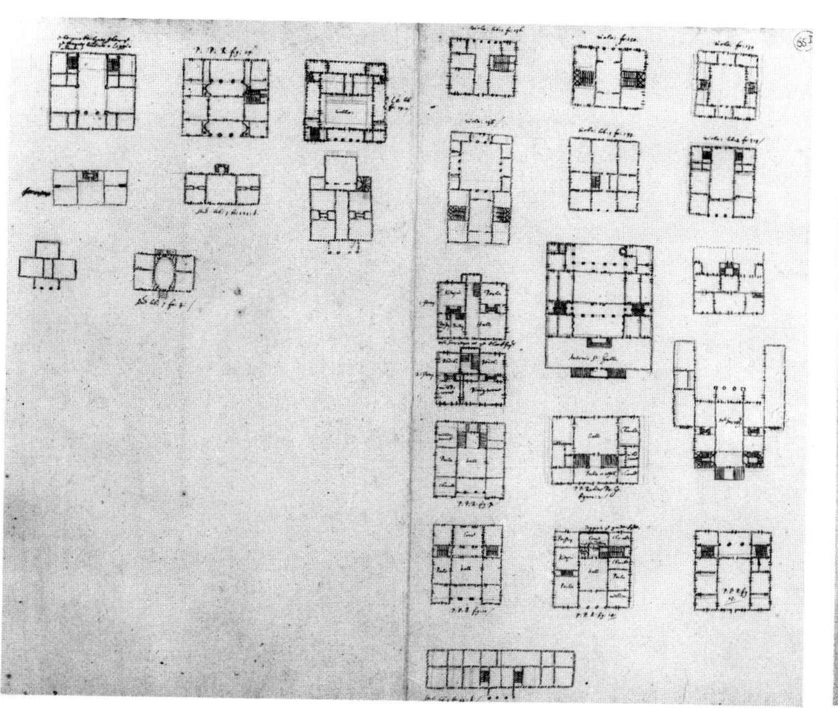

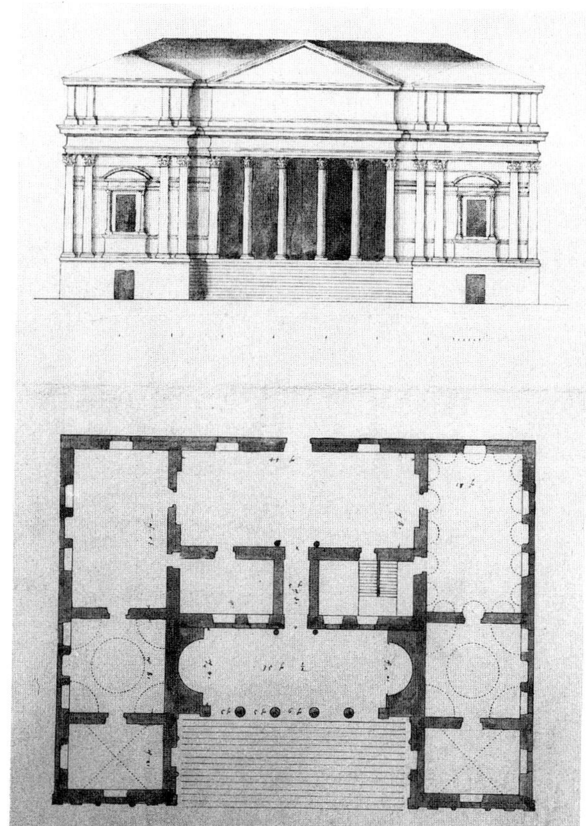

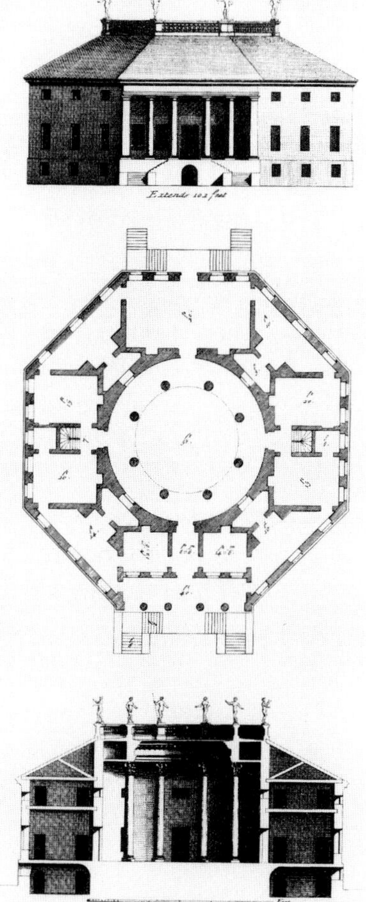

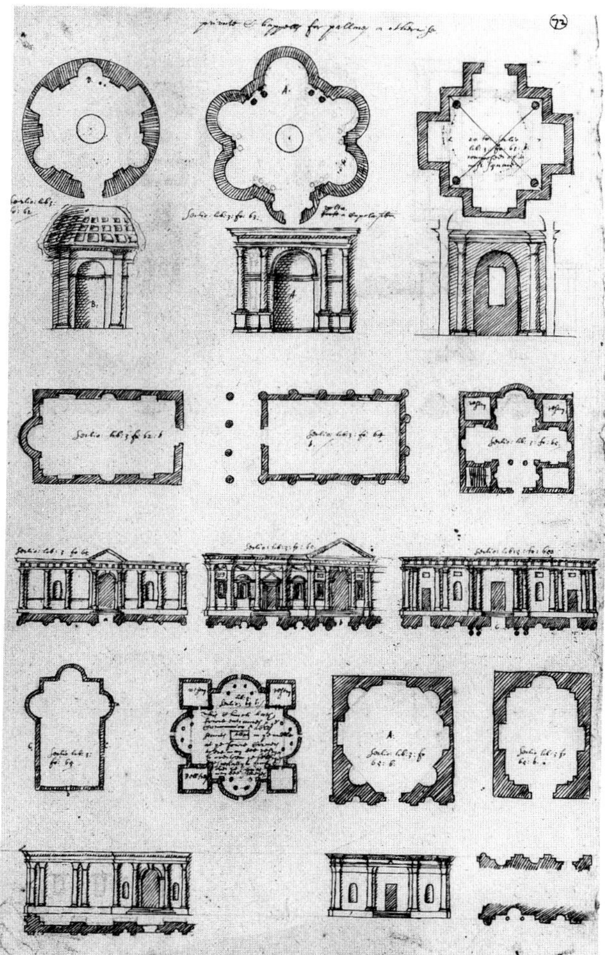

9 (*above, left*). Twenty-five plans for villas and palaces, taken from Rubens, Philibert de l'Orme, Viola Zanini, Serlio, and Antonio da Sangallo. The two plans in the centre of the fourth column are of the ground and first floors of the house in Blackfriars designed by Inigo Jones for Sir Peter Killigrew

10 (*above, right*). A close copy of Palladio's first design (1539–40) for the Villa Pisani at Bagnolo. Palladio's drawing, now in the RIBA, was one of the group purchased in Venice by Inigo Jones in 1614

11 (*far left*). Design for an octagonal house with a central, circular courtyard, based on a plan published by Cataneo; engraved after the drawing by Webb

12 (*left*). Plans and elevations of 'private Chappels for pallaces or otherwise', based on Serlio .

a wide circulation in the eighteenth century through being published by William Kent as *Designs of Inigo Jones* (pl. 11). Their value as reference sheets would have been very limited in an English context and their degree of finish goes beyond the requirements of an academic exercise. Publication must be presumed to have been Webb's intention.

The church designs similarly are divisible into highly finished drawings and small sketches.[41] The sheets of sketches, one of which is entitled 'private Chappels for pallaces or otherwise' (pl. 12), are comparable with the sheets of villa plans and probably were done with the same reference purposes in mind. They are derived from Serlio and include a plan of Bramante's Tempietto and details of the plan and elevation of St Peter's. The finished drawings include a series of essays in the reconstruction of Vitruvian temples, based probably on Rusconi's *Della architettura*; a group of plans, elevations, and sections of small, centralized churches, and a group of longitudinal churches with porticoes and campaniles. Whilst these might have been produced with publication in mind, two other groups of church designs probably were not.

These are for a longitudinal cathedral and for a centralized cathedral. It is tempting to associate both of these schemes with St Paul's, but no direct link can be forged. Webb was associated with St Paul's twice in his career, firstly between 1633 and 1641, when Jones employed him as clerk engrosser during the remodelling of the old Cathedral (pl. 13), with the responsibility for 'double engrossing' the account books and 'for drawing, entering into a ledger book the bargains made from time to time with the workmen, coppying several designs and mouldings and making the tracing according to Mr Surveyor's direction for the workmen to follow'.[42] After the Restoration, Webb was one of the Commission which was constituted in 1663 to investigate and prosecute the repairs which were needed after the depredations of the Interregnum.[43]

After the Great Fire advice was sought from Wren rather than from Webb, and he did not get an opportunity to work on the building again. However, we might speculate on the form which a Webb cathedral might have taken, particularly since his drawings for a longitudinal cathedral cannot be viewed in isolation from Jones's work on old St Paul's. One of Webb's two schemes was for a building which was longer and wider than Jones's, with a high nave, low aisles, and a narrowly based dome, which appears to be only a vertical interruption in the progress of the nave, rather than an emphatic, central space. This, like Jones's Cathedral, was a medieval building in classical dress.[44]

A second, domed design is a similarly improperly synthesized agglomeration of units. its towers suggest Sangallo's scheme for St Peter's, its façade the Gesù, its dome the Pantheon (or Bramante's St Peter's), and its windows and doors, Jones's St Paul's.[45]

[41] All are at Worcester College; M. Whinney, 'Some Church Designs by John Webb', *Journal of the Warburg and Courtauld Institutes*, 6 (1943), 142–50. Whinney did not discuss the designs for the centralized cathedral (*Worcs. Coll. Cat.* 147–50) as at the time of writing she believed them to be by another hand. However, she later acknowledged them as a Webb design (*Wren* (1971), 90–1).

[42] Works Accounts WA 1–15 (Apr. 1633–Sept. 1641), St Paul's Cathedral Library. There is a further volume, for 1639–40, at Lambeth Palace Library (FP 321). For a document relating the *modus operandi* of the restoration, see 'Inigo Jones and St Paul's Cathedral', *London Topographical Record*, 18 (1942), 41–3. Among Webb's drawings for St Paul's was that of a pulley for raising stones, taken from Bartoli's edition of Alberti (see Catalogue and pl. 112).

[43] *Wren Society*, 13 (1936), 13–14.

[44] *Worcs. Coll. Cat.* 152–3.

[45] Ibid. 155.

13 (*left*). The west front of old St Paul's Cathedral, after its remodelling by Inigo Jones

14 (*below*). Sir Christopher Wren's 'Great Model' for St Paul's Cathedral, constructed in 1674

Webb's design for a centralized cathedral is far more assured. This is presumed to be theoretical because it is difficult to imagine a situation in which it would have been remotely possible to build such a liturgically unsuitable, English St Peter's. Clear parallels can be drawn between this scheme and the centralized St Paul's designs produced by Wren in the 1670s, which also were found to be liturgically unacceptable.[46] Webb's scheme was not in the same high class as the Great Model (pl. 14), nor yet the equal of the Greek Cross design, suffering as it did from the same lack of cohesion which marred his longitudinal schemes. It is, however, of considerable interest as the first large centralized church to be designed in England (pls. 15–17). Its plan is related to one which Webb, in another study, derived from Sangallo's San Giovanni dei Fiorentini.[47] A circular space is surmounted by a heavy, Bramantesque stepped dome, carried on eight massive piers. Between this central area and the four projecting chapels, each with subsidiary domes, flows a broad, circular ambulatory. In both plan and section, the design appears to be made up of a series of discrete elements: chapels, ambulatory, and tall, central space, which at upper cornice level is as high as it is wide. These retain their autonomy, rather than making up a harmonious whole, and, as a series of separate, vaulted spaces, have more in common with reconstructions of Roman baths than they do with Wren's St Paul's. Nevertheless, behind Webb's scheme, there lay the idea of the circular, classical temple. The Pantheon (pl. 18), the greatest of Roman temples, and the first to be converted into a church, inspired Bramante's design for St Peter's, and Webb's drawings reflect it, not only in the external form of the stepped dome, but also in the dimensions, of which Webb took note in his copy of Serlio. The 121-*piedi* diameter of the Pantheon's dome (142 ft.) was translated into the 120-foot diameter of Webb's design, the same as the dome of Wren's Great Model.

But Webb was referring back, in his design, to an even more ancient source, for, during the Renaissance, Rome was regarded as the New Jerusalem, with St Peter's its new Temple.[48] By basing his design on Roman precedent, Webb was contributing to a hallowed tradition, underlining both the Antique and the Old Testament character of his conception, by referring to his building as 'ye Temple' on his inscriptions on the verso of the drawings, thus locating his scheme firmly in a historical continuum.

For his imposing portico, Webb looked to more recent, almost equally hallowed precedent, taking his design from Inigo Jones's old St Paul's, whose portico, according to Webb himself, had 'contracted the envy of all Christendom upon our Nation, for a Piece of Architecture, not to be parallell'd in these last Ages of the World'.[49] Webb retained the square angle piers of Jones's design and added a massive pediment. His Corinthian columns (52 ft. 6 ins. high) would have been only marginally shorter than Jones's. Antique in both scale and manner, Webb's cathedral, if built, would have had the spatial austerity which Wren's masterpiece lacks; it would in its own way have been

[46] A link between the schemes may be provided by Edward Woodroffe, whose careful drawings of *c.*1673 for Wren's Greek Cross design are strongly reminiscent of Webb's drawings and suggest that he might have been trained by him. Two of Woodroffe's drawings are published in K. Downes, *Sir Christopher Wren* (Whitechapel Art Gallery exhibition catalogue, 1982), 73–4.

[47] *Worcs. Coll. Cat.* 156.

[48] Cf I. Campbell, 'The new St. Peter's: Basilica or Temple', *Oxford Art Journal*, 4/1 (1981), 3–8.

[49] J. Webb, *A Vindication of Stone-Heng Restored* (1665), 48.

grander, but there can be little doubt that its Roman *gravitas* would have inhibited the sort of affection which Wren's monument continues to inspire.

Of the theoretical drawings, those for the centrally planned cathedral are the ones which demonstrate most clearly Webb's mode of working and his abilities in mid-career. His reliance on precedent, insufficiently synthesized here, is readily apparent, with debts to antiquity, the Renaissance, and Inigo Jones all being revealed. The Scamozzian method of 'comparting by spaces' is explained, precisely, in his accompanying notes: 'ye whole groundplatt is comparted of equal spaces of 12′.' The similarity in terms of both the architectural style (in the setting of aedicules within arches) and the draughting style (pen and wash) with the Whitehall E scheme suggests the mid-1640s as a possible date for the creation of these drawings. This supposition is supported by the watermark of the paper, which shows it to be of the same manufacture as that used for the Durham House designs of the middle to late 1640s. The dating of Webb's drawings by the style employed is problematic, because, although it has been suggested that hatching occurs earlier in his career whilst wash is introduced later, there are dated exceptions to these practices. Of the two, early Somerset House drawings, for instance (1638), one is hatched and the other washed, and towards the end of his career, at Greenwich, Webb again used both techniques. Nor, with the exception of the small, hatched, house plans, can he be said to have fitted style to purpose in a consistent manner. Dating, therefore, must take account of other factors.

The theoretical drawings were made for a variety of purposes: academic, office reference, and publication. The likelihood is that they were all made within the fifteen years between *c.*1635 and *c.*1650; between the period of working on old St Paul's Cathedral, which no doubt prompted his academic studies of the longitudinal church, and the period of the Durham House designs, which are the first to reveal fully his indebtedness to the reconstructions of the ancient house. At the beginning of this period Webb was still working closely with Inigo Jones and studying the books in his library. In following Jones's example, he even went so far as to transcribe some of the notes which the master had made in his copy of Serlio into his own copy of the treatise.[50] Although, like Jones, Webb used his source books over a long period of time, reference being made in his Palladio to work at Gunnersbury (in the later 1650s), his period of maximum usage and annotation would have been during the 1630s and early 1640s, when he was still learning his art. The two dates which are entered in his books are of this period: his Serlio has his address and the date 'Jan:16:1643' (OS; i.e. 1644), and the Palladio includes his dated copy of the sheet of instructions 'for ye payntings in ye seeling of ye Queenes room with glases at Greenwich', sent to Jacob Jordaens in 1639.

With the outbreak of Civil War in 1642 and the ousting from the Royal Works of Jones and Webb in 1643 by Edward Carter, Webb would have found himself with time to develop his theoretical studies. That he was by nature keen to investigate and to publish is demonstrated by his later work on the origins of Stonehenge, and on

[50] The first three books of Jones's 1600 edition of Serlio, acquired in 1986 by the Centre Canadien d'Architecture, Montreal, include several notes which Webb transcribed into his copy (RIBA). I am indebted to John Newman for drawing this to my attention.

15. Plan of 'theoretical' design for a centralized cathedral

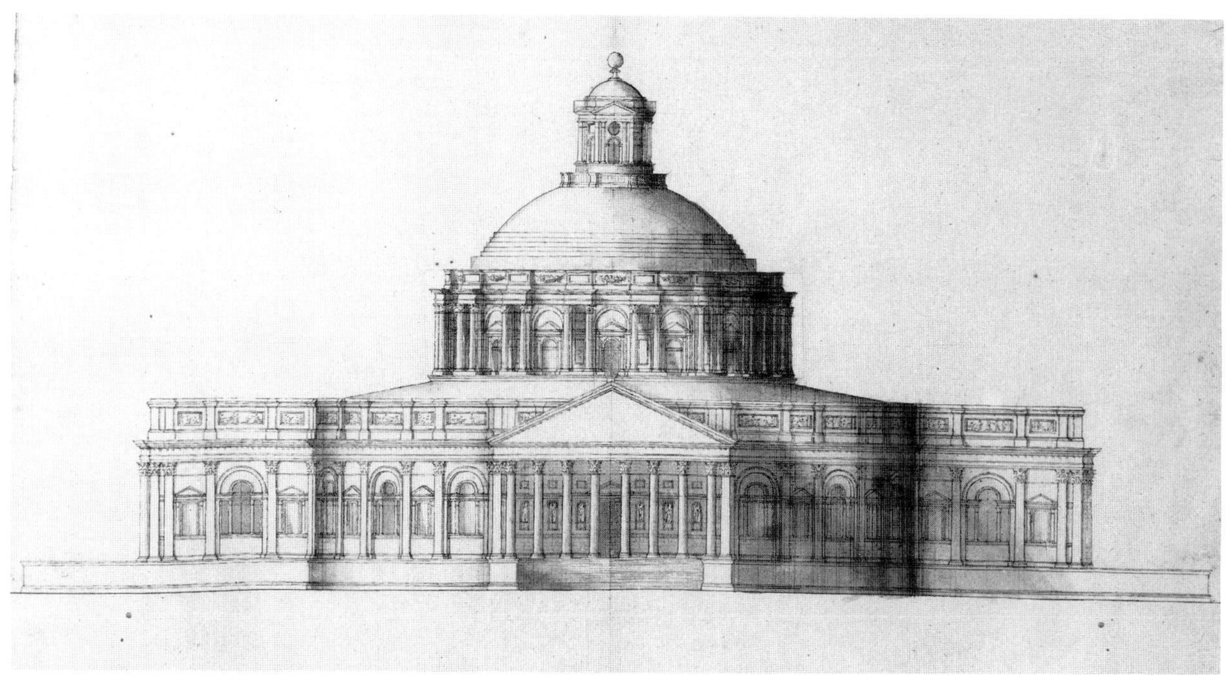

16. Elevation of centralized cathedral design

17. Cross-section of centralized cathedral design

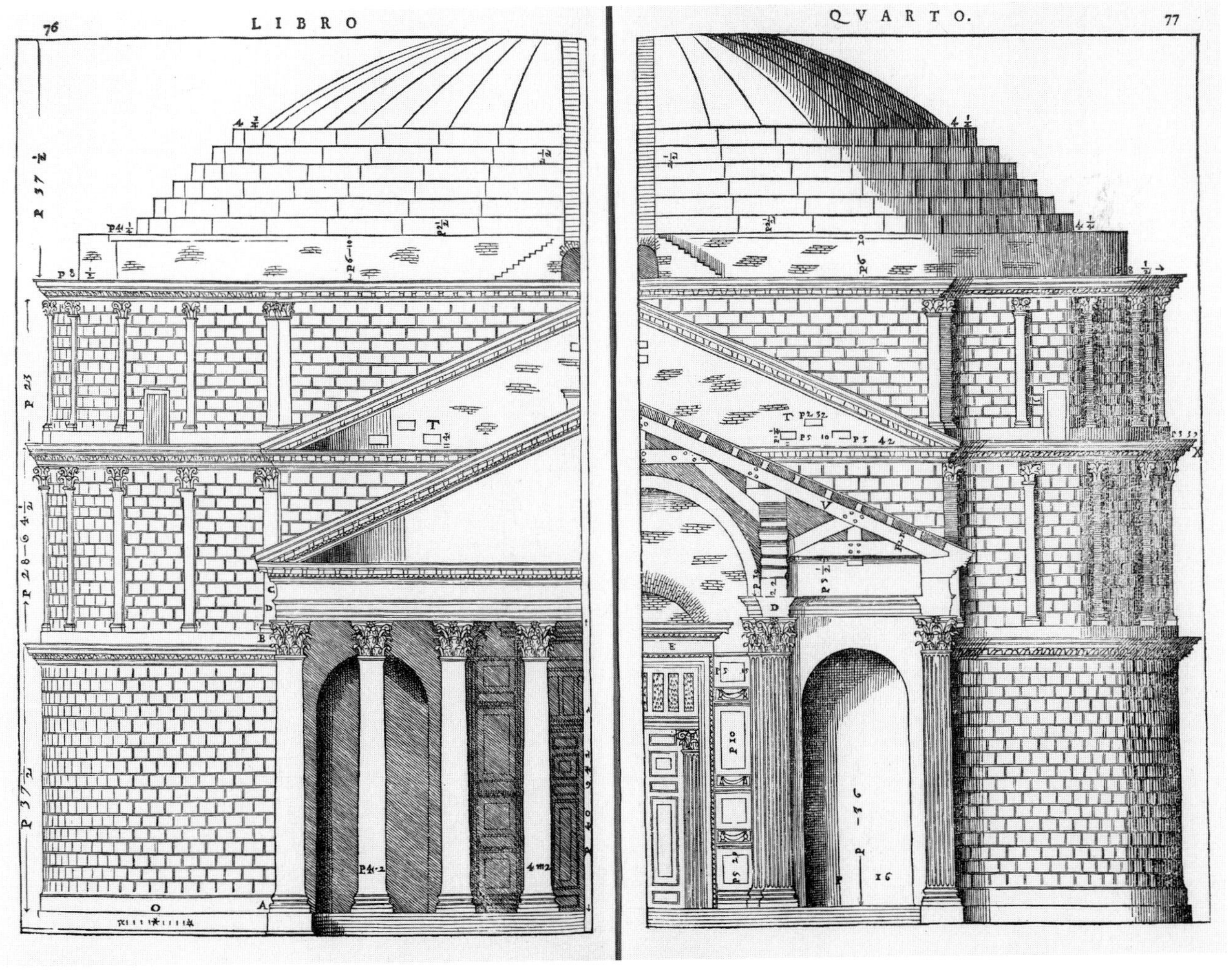

76 LIBRO QVARTO. 77

18. The Pantheon, the most celebrated of the temples of ancient Rome

the Chinese language. The paper evidence of certain of the theoretical drawings, their accompanying notes, and the inferences which can be drawn from them concerning Webb's academic cast of mind, make an architectural treatise a very likely product of the years of training and practice of both himself and Jones. Such a treatise would have placed English architecture firmly in the mainstream of European classicism, with Webb as its prime theoretician. Also, it would have been a memorial to the achievement of Inigo Jones. As it was, Jones's published accolade and the European claims which were made for his architecture had to wait until the advent of neo-Palladianism in the eighteenth century, by which time the individual achievement of Webb had been forgotten.

Whilst it is clear that not all of the theoretical drawings could have been intended for publication, a further group of drawings by Webb, in the 'Book of Capitols' [*sic*],[51] apparently were. On the bottom of a separate sheet of drawings at Chatsworth is the self-conscious note: 'Severall Designes of Composite Capitalls in tender and worke for sundry Noblemen and persons of Quality in England by IW.'[52] The book was recorded by George Vertue as being in the possession of John Talman, from whom it passed to Lord Burlington.[53] It includes designs for Wilton, Sir John Trevor's house, the College of Physicians, Coleshill, Chevening, Gunnersbury, Northumberland House, and The Vyne. The majority of these are finished drawings of good quality, executed mainly in sepia pen and wash. There are some rougher sketch designs, including two by Inigo Jones, pasted in after the main group. On the separate Chatsworth sheet there are more capitals for Gunnersbury and Trevor's house, and one for Amesbury, and at Worcester College there are some more for Coleshill. In addition to these, there are at the RIBA two drawings for capitals for the King Charles Building at Greenwich and seven theoretical sheets comprising forty-one designs, not connected with specific houses (pl. 19).[54]

There are many precedents for the use of composite capitals, not only combining the Corinthian acanthus with the Ionic volute, but also including figures, swags, vegetable forms, and emblematic beasts. Webb appears to have borrowed considerably, although not copied, from Montano's *Cinque libri di architettura*, in Book I of which, *Architettura con diversi ornamenti cavati dall'antico*, are thirty-four capitals with forms suitable to the different gods. He also used sheets of capitals, attributed to Montano and others, which are now in the Ashmolean Museum, having come via Talman from Webb's collection.[55] A further source is suggested by a passage in Wren's *Second Tract on Architecture*:

> I have seen among the Collections of Inigo Jones, a pocket-book of Pyrrho Ligorio's . . . wherein he seemed to have made it his Business, out of the antique Fragments, to have drawn the many different Capitals, Mouldings of Cornices, & Ornaments of Freezes, etc. purposely to judge of the great Liberties of the ancient Architects, most of which had their Education in Greece.[56]

[51] Devonshire Collection, Chatsworth; see J. Bold, 'John Webb: Composite Capitals and the Chinese Language', *Oxford Art Journal*, 4/1 (1981), 9–17.

[52] Chatsworth Album 26, no. 125.

[53] Vertue, I. 94.

[54] RIBA Cat. 151–2, 207–13.

[55] Larger Talman Album, Ashmolean Museum, no. 520:380.

[56] C. Wren, *Parentalia* (1750), 353–8.

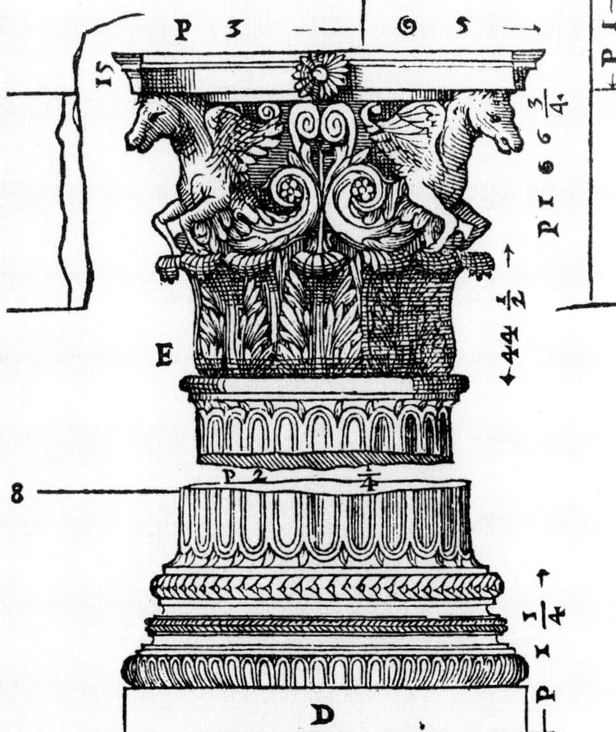

19 (*above*). Designs for composite capitals, based on sheets of capitals attributed to G. B. Montano

20 (*left*). Composite capital from the Temple of Mars, the Avenger

Webb appears to have made direct use of this book, which is now lost, in a capital for Sir John Trevor, the verso of which is inscribed: 'Pirrho 41/not taken'.[57]

Webb's use of composite capitals had a sound, classical pedigree: Jones owned a copy of Torrello Sarayna's *De origine et amplitudine civitatis Veronae* (1540), which recorded antique composites, and Palladio illustrated an example from the Temple of Mars the Avenger (pl. 20).[58] He referred also to further examples which he proposed to publish at a later date.

Webb was a prolific and, after his death, collectable draughtsman. Because so many of his drawings for capitals survive, we should not be seduced into thinking that perhaps he alone was producing such designs in mid-seventeenth century England. Thomas Wilsford noted in his *Architectonice* (1659) that the composite order was 'in all respects varied at the pleasure or fancy of Architects'. But for Webb, the use of composites probably had a significance which was far from fanciful.

In his study of the Chinese language he suggested that the particular quality of the characters lay in their expression of 'Ideal Conceptions'. Composite capitals perhaps were regarded by him in a similar light, employing a comparable language of antiquity, simplicity, and generality to express *concepta* through emblematic means. Many of those in the 'Book of Capitols' and on the separate sheets have a clear heraldic and mythological significance. Thus, the designs for Wilton illustrate the Herbert wyvern; that for the King Charles Building, the lion and unicorn from the royal arms; and that for the Library of the Royal College of Physicians, the torch of life and the Aesculapian serpent.

These capitals were conveying messages of ownership and status which would have been readily understood in educated circles. Inigo Jones's involvement in neo-Platonic doctrine, with its attendant cult of emblems, and his exploitation of this preoccupation in the Court masque, would have been well known to Webb. Henry Peacham, an 'especiall and worthy friend' of Jones, observed that:

> Emblemes and Impresae's if ingeniously conceited, are of daintie device and much esteeme.... How should we give Nobility her true value, respect and title, without notice of her merit? and how may we guesse her merit, without these outward ensignes and badges of Vertue, which anciently have beene accounted sacred and precious ...[59]

The design for the capitals for The Vyne, for the first projecting temple front on an English country house, is of a different type. Rather than being heraldic or mythological, it is pared down, in the manner of certain antique examples. It appears, therefore, to be in keeping with Webb's archaeological approach as manifested in his literary productions. Here, we might suggest, with reference to Vitruvius' romantic account of its genesis, is an early phase in the development of the Corinthian capital, before the leaves had grown fully around the fabled basket, placed on the tomb of the maiden of Corinth.

Such a conceit presents us with a view of Webb at his most erudite and literal. We must presume that the less scholarly Colen Campbell did not appreciate the classical

[57] Chatsworth Album 26, no. 125.

[58] Palladio, iv. 22; cf. M. Lyttleton, *Baroque Architecture in Classical Antiquity* (1974), 56, for antique, zoomorphic capitals.

[59] H. Peacham, *The Compleat Gentleman* (1634), chs. XV and XVII. He refers to Jones as his friend in ch. XIII.

significance of these designs, mistaking them for mere fancies. In his illustrations of Gunnersbury and Amesbury in *Vitruvius Britannicus* he omitted the composite designs, substituting the conventional Corinthian. He thereby compounded his misattribution of the houses to Jones the architect, by the further sin of misrepresentation of Webb, the learned theoretician and diver into causes.

3

LITERATURE

John Webb neither visited China nor understood its language, but these apparent impediments did not prevent his writing the first, extensive, European treatise on Chinese. He consoled himself in the lonely position which he had adopted by comparing himself to those 'that first found out there were Antipodes', and his contemporary 'that first discovered the circulation of the blood'.

An Historical Essay Endeavouring a Probability that the Language of the Empire of China is the Primitive Language appeared in 1669 and was Webb's third published work. His first, a working up of Inigo Jones's 'few indigested notes' on the Roman origins of Stonehenge, had appeared in 1655, and his lengthy *Vindication* of Jones's arguments followed ten years later. In addition to these, he had also, Anthony Wood informs us, made a translation of Giovanni Tarcagnota's *Delle historie del mondo* (Venice, 1562).[1]

An Historical Essay does not appear to have sold well: it was reissued in 1678, six years after Webb's death, by a different publisher, with a new title-page.[2] Webb's expanded 'Essay', completed in 1671, written in response to the unfavourable critical reception of the published edition, remains in manuscript.[3] In it, the author claimed to answer all objections in arguments which had the 'Stamp of Antiquity, the Approbation of Testimony and the Allowance of Authority', the same criteria for the validity of arguments which he employed in his architectural investigations and practice. In bringing his critical and exegetical skills to bear on Biblico-historical problems, with the aim of identifying the nature of mankind's first language, Webb was not pursuing an arcane branch of philological speculation, but was placing himself in the vanguard of contemporary letters: 'There is scarce any subject that hath been more thoroughly scanned and debated amongst Learned men', wrote John Wilkins in 1668, 'than the *Original* of *Language* and *Letters*.'[4] As Webb himself noted, so many writers have treated of the primitive tongue, variously asserting it to be the Teutonic, the Samaritan, the Phoenician, the Chaldean, or the Hebrew, 'with what success I question not'. As a recent commentator has observed, the identity of the first language was obscure, and 'simple solutions did not suggest themselves'.[5]

[1] A. Wood, *Athenae oxonienses*, iv (1813–20), 753–4. Webb apparently translated two of the three volumes of the work.

[2] The 1669 edition was printed for Nath. Brook at the Angel in Gresham College and the 1678 edition for Obadiah Blagrave, at the Bear in St. Paul's Churchyard. Blagrave omitted Webb's 'Epistle Dedicatory' (dated Butleigh, 29 May 1668) but retained both the original page of errata and the map which, according to Webb's manuscript 'Essay', was 'antiquated' and 'published without my consent or knowledge'. Blagrave's edition was retitled *The Antiquity of China or an Historical Essay* ...

[3] Attention was first drawn to this MS, in the Library of Wells Cathedral, by Anthony Wood (*Athenae oxonienses*), iv. 753–4. See also J. Bold, 'John Webb: Composite Capitals and the Chinese Language', *Oxford Art Journal*, 4/1 (1981), 9–17.

[4] Quoted by D. S. Katz, 'The Language of Adam in Seventeenth-century England', in H. Lloyd-Jones, V. Pearl, and B. Worden (eds.), *History and Imagination* (1981), 132–45.

[5] D. S. Katz, 'Language of Adam', p. 132.

21 (*left*). Title-page of Bishop Brian Walton's *Biblia polyglotta* (1657), engraved by Hollar after the drawing by Webb

22 (*below*). Reconstruction of the Temple of Solomon (detail), published by J. Prado and J. Villalpando, *In Ezechielem explanationes* (1596–1604). Villalpando's remarkable reconstruction was re-engraved by Hollar for republication in Walton's Bible and these plates were used again in the Holy Bible published in 1660 by John Ogilby

IENTALIS FACIES SVBSTRVCTIONIS AB IMIS VALLIBVS CVBITOS TRECENTOS ERECTAE AD SVSTINENDOS AGGERES QVIBVS ATRIORVM TEMPLI AREAM SALOMON LAXAND
SVB MINIMA CVBITORVM MENSVRA QVA
ETIAM VNI

Webb notes in the conclusion to his *Historical Essay* that Bishop Brian Walton was one of the 'unquestionable Authors' who had encouraged him to publish his findings on the Chinese language, although Walton himself favoured Hebrew as the primitive tongue. Webb had designed the lavish title-page for Walton's *Biblia polyglotta* (pl. 21), published in 1657, and it might be presumed that he had access to learned polyglot circles at this time.[6] In focusing his attention on China, Webb certainly was drawing on, and contributing to, the increasing literature on a remote and strange land, a country of the mind which held tremendous interest for the European imagination in the seventeenth century.[7]

Father Ricci had reached Peking in 1598, and under his leadership the Jesuit missionaries pragmatically laid aside the garb of priest and assumed that of the scholar. They 'steeped themselves in Chinese culture and sought to assimilate it into Catholic doctine', seeking to justify this 'extreme, if not heretical' strategy by 'praising to the skies the civilisation of their would-be converts'.[8] The great quantity of letters, documents, and books which poured into Europe from the Jesuits in China made the members of the Society for two hundred years the supreme interpreters of the Orient.[9]

However, the Jesuits were not alone in the transmission of knowledge about the East. From 1600, when the British East India Company was organised, England had direct contact with India, Siam, China, and Japan, which not only contributed to the dissemination of knowledge, but also made the English increasingly familiar with oriental products. A vogue for lacquer work was established in the early seventeenth century, and with the Restoration came a considerable taste for Chinoiserie. John Evelyn in 1662 noted the recent proliferation of books on China, after translating one himself: 'I have to the best of my skill translated your relation of China ... in ye mean time, it would be considered whether this whole piece will be to the purpose, there having been of late so

[6] Webb's title-page, engraved by Hollar, is cast in the form of a triumphal arch, flanked by fluted, composite columns and pilasters, with a superstructure supporting the seated figures of St Peter and St Paul. Eight illustrations are applied to the architectural framework: Adam and Eve, Noah and the Ark, the Nativity, the Last Supper, the Nailing to the Cross, the Rising from the Tomb, the Ascension, and, on top, in the centre, the Pentecost (the gift of tongues). A preliminary drawing for the design survives at Worcester College (*Worcs. Coll. Cat.* 106). The drawing carries Webb's faint inscription, 'The Assention of Baronius'. This might imply agreement on Webb's part with the views expressed by Cardinal Cesare Baronius in the *Annales ecclesiastici*, the Counter Reformation reply to the Protestant view of Church history, which, enthusiastically using all available legends and sources, appeared to be in agreement with the hermetic writings of Ficino: see F. Yates, *Giordano Bruno and the Hermetic Tradition* (1978 edn.), 399. Baronius had made a systematic study of the monuments, customs, and liturgy of the Early Church and it has been suggested that this might have had some influence upon the archaeological investigations of Inigo Jones and Lord Arundel (D. Howarth, *Lord Arundel and his Circle* (1985), 49). It is of some interest to note that Walton's Polyglot Bible included re-engravings by Hollar of Villalpando's reconstruction of the Temple of Solomon. These were published again in John Ogilby's 1660 edition of the Bible.

[7] For a further, full discussion of Webb's *Essay* in the context of Chinese studies, and the identification of his sources, see Ch'en Shou-yi, 'John Webb: A Forgotten Page in the Early History of Sinology in Europe', *The Chinese Social and Political Science Review*, 19/3 (Oct. 1935), 295–330. Webb's main sources were:

(i) Father Alvarez Semedo, *Relatione della Grande Monarchia della Cina* (1643; pub. in English in 1655 as *A History of the Great and Renowned Monarchy of China*, and bought by Pepys: 'a most excellent book with rare cuts' (*The Diary of Samuel Pepys*, ed. J. Warrington, iii (1953), 147, 14 Jan. 1668));
(ii) Father Martinus Martini, *De bello tartarico in Sinis historia* (1654); *Novus Atlas Sinensis* (1655); *Sinicae historiae decas prima* (1658).
(iii) Father Athanasius Kircher, *China monumentis* (1667).
(iv) J. Nieuhoff, *Het Gezantschap der Neêrlandtsche Oost-Indische Compagnie aan den grooten Tartarischen Cham* (1665; trans. into French, 1665; trans. into English by John Ogilby as *An Embassy from the East India Company of the United Provinces to the Grand Tartar Cham Emperour of China* (1669)).

[8] W. W. Appleton, *A Cycle of Cathy* (1951), 19–20.

[9] A. W. Rowbotham, *Missionary and Mandarin—The Jesuits at the Court of China* (1942), 243.

many accurate descriptions of those countries in particular.'[10] And two years later, he was shown, by 'Tomson, a Jesuite':

> such a (Collection) of rarities, sent from the Jesuites of Japan & China to their order at Paris ... as in my life I had not seene: The chiefe things were very large Rhinoceros's hornes, Glorious Vests, wrought & embrodered on cloth of Gold, but with such lively colours, as for splendor & vividnesse we have nothing in Europe approches ...[11]

But, despite this sudden growth of knowledge, it was a 'bizarre, romanticised China which impressed itself upon the European imagination—a land sufficiently remote and unreal to encourage the free play of the fancy ... an imaginative world in which strange and unaccountable incidents occurred. Such a world had much in common with the spirit of the court masques.'[12] The various books on China, by praising the country's fertility, prosperity, and social system, and expressing admiration for the industry, politeness, respect for family life, and appreciation of learning shown by the people, 'succeeded in creating the impression that China was blessed with most, if not all, the substantial advantages of Utopia'.[13] Discussion of such a country was an appropriate subject for a man like Webb, with strong archaeological interests and in a state of some disillusionment—passed over for the high office for which his training and his talents had equipped him, and now (in 1671) in retreat in his Somersetshire fastness, 'very fairely at leasure', awaiting the moment when 'his Majesty shall bee gratiously pleased to proceed towards the perfecting of his new Royall Palace at Greenwich'.[14] In the meantime he devoted himself to continuing his examination, not of 'what in Possibility cannot, but what in Probability may be the First Speech':

> Scripture teacheth that the Judgment of Confusion of Tongues, fell upon those only that were at BABEL: History informs, that the CHINOIS being fully settled before, were not there: And moreover that the same Language and Characters which long preceding that Confusion they used, are in use with them at this very DAY.[15]

From the Renaissance onwards, there had been considerable speculation on the nature of the primitive language—that spoken by Adam. This had become coupled with a desire to find a universal language, using, in the words of Bacon, 'real characters' for expressing notions.[16] Pierio Valeriano, in his influential *Hieroglyphica* (1556), had noted that 'to speak hieroglyphically is nothing else but to disclose the (true) nature of things divine and human',[17] whilst, for Marsilio Ficino, the hieroglyphic image did not merely represent the concept but embodied it in Platonic form.[18] These writers were dealing particularly with Egyptian characters, but, up to a point, for Webb, the argument for Chinese was the same: the characters expressed 'Ideal Conceptions'.

The language of Adam also, as Genesis makes clear, precisely expressed things as they

10 Quoted by H. Honour, *Chinoiserie* (1961), 21.

11 J. Evelyn, *The Diary of John Evelyn*, ed. E. S. de Beer (1959), 460–1, 22 June 1664.

12 B. S. Allen, *Tides in English Taste 1619–1800* (1958), ii. 19.

13 Ibid, i. 183.

14 'Essay', address to the reader.

15 *Historical Essay*, Dedication to the King.

16 F. Yates, *The Art of Memory* (1978), 364.

17 R. Wittkower, 'Hieroglyphs in the Early Renaissance' in *Allegory and the Migration of Symbols* (1977), 128.

18 Ibid. 116.

are: 'And out of the ground the LORD God formed every beast of the field, and every fowl of the air, and brought *them* unto Adam to see what he would call them: and whatsoever Adam called every living creature, that *was* the name thereof.'[19]

Biblical enquiry and Renaissance philosophical speculation here come together with a common aim, that of identifying the first language, in the hope that by a process of mystical regeneration it would be possible for Man to regain the dominion over Nature which he had lost at the Fall. Ficino believed that Egyptian hieroglyphs had been invented by the ancient sage Hermes Trismegistus, the supposed writer of the *Corpus hermeticum*.[20] The *Corpus* was translated by Ficino, the Hermetic writings being interpreted by him as Gentile prophecies of the coming of Christ. Many great but conservative thinkers continued to believe in these supposed truths long after Isaac Casaubon theoretically had destroyed the basis of Christian Hermetic thought by demonstrating, in 1614, that the writings dated not from pre-Mosaic times but from late antiquity.[21] The belief appears to have lingered on because of that desire for synthesis and resistance to evidence which characterizes quasi-mystical speculation, and the equally strong, atavistic human desire to hark back to a Golden Age. The Romans, as Webb himself would have appreciated when seeking justification for his own work through ancient precedent, produced their literature in emulation and imitation of Greek models, even to the extent of attempting to demonstrate a relationship when it was manifestly the case that no such relationship could possibly have held. Part of the reason for this appeal to the past lay in the view that humanity was locked into a process of continuous decline from a Golden Age through ever baser epochs; a view which Horace expressed as:

> Time corrupts all. What has it not made worse?
> Our grandfathers sired feeble children; theirs
> Were weaker still—ourselves; and now our curse
> Must be to breed even more degenerate heirs.[22]

If only humanity could identify the primitive language, all subsequent breaches might be healed and the order and harmony of an age of innocence might be recaptured. This order was implicit, in hermetic thought, in the two structures prefiguring the Celestial City, which had been built according to the dimensions given by God: Noah's Ark and the Temple of Solomon. Against these was set the Tower of Babel, which being based on *impietas* and *superbia* was identifiable with Chaos and therefore at a pole from the Ark and the Temple.[23] In his remarkable reconstruction of the Temple of Solomon (pl. 22), Villalpando had sought to demonstrate the compatibility of Christian Revelation with the culture of classical antiquity and, possibly inspired by this, the Jesuit Father Athanasius Kircher produced two books on the other structures which were central to Hermetist concerns: *Arca Noe* (1675) and *Turris Babel* (1679). All three of these structures had significance for Webb. Kircher had also written on China, in a book which Webb drew

[19] Genesis 2: 19.
[20] Yates, *Giordano Bruno, passim.*
[21] Ibid. 398–403.
[22] *The Odes of Horace*, trans. J. Michie (1964), III. 6.
[23] R. Taylor, 'Hermetism and Mystical Architecture', in R. Wittkower and I. Jaffe (eds.), *Baroque Art: The Jesuit Contribution* (1972).

on in his own investigations, *China monumentis* (1667). He was also concerned to identify the primitive language, which, unlike Webb, he believed to have been Hebrew.[24]

The Jesuits' flexible conflation of Catholicism with Confucianism presents us with a model of the way in which the writers we are considering sought to synthesize myth, allegory, hieroglyphic concepts, and Christian thought: Plato and Christ could be reconciled. It is this mode of thought which lies at the heart of Webb's exposition. He never criticizes the 'infallible' scriptures but argues that, as Moses in Genesis was writing only for the Israelites, he omitted much of more general historical interest. By using Chinese histories and later commentaries, Webb demonstrated that Chinese and Biblical chronology were compatible. Such a conclusion might be regarded, generally, as anathema to the pious, but, for the Christian antiquarian and man of letters in the Renaissance tradition—the role in which Webb was casting himself—it was eminently satisfactory.

Webb's argument in favour of the pre-eminent antiquity of the Chinese language was based on two propositions: that the Confusion of Tongues was visited only upon those that were at Babel, and that the Chinese, who were settled already at that time, used the same language both before and after the Confusion. The whole world, Webb argues, was peopled before the Flood, but all its millions upon millions of inhabitants were destroyed save the family of Noah. The question which ultimately he seeks to answer is whether the primitive language survived the Deluge, but he first examines the problem of where the Ark came to rest after the waters had died down, a question of some moment for Biblical scholars. Peter Heylin, in his *Cosmographie*,[25] had subscribed to the view, advanced by Goropius Becanus, that it had landed on top of the Caucasus, but Webb dissented, quoting the Biblical reference that Noah did not travel far and Father Martini's contention that Chinese letters were invented before Babel, and so arguing that China was planted by Noah's race, who came to rest there after the Flood.[26] The Ark must have been made in China, for 'no Countrey in the habitable Earth could better furnish Noah, with all manner of conveniences, and every sort of materials proper for the building of such a Machine than China'. Webb drew on Nieuhoff's account, published in 1665, that 'of all kinds of trees for Carpenters work, such plenty and of such several sorts is to be found within that Empire that the number is beyond admiration incredible'. Furthermore, the Caucasus was not an area noted for its pitch, a substance which Noah had been instructed to use: 'Make thee an ark of gopher wood; rooms shalt thou make in the ark, and shalt pitch it within and without with pitch.'[27] However, China, according to Webb, had pitch in abundance, and he quoted Gonzalez de Mendoza, who had, in his earlier history, noted that this pitch is more tenacious than that employed in England, even to the extent that one Chinese ship will outlast two of England's.[28]

Before the Confusion of Tongues, 'the whole earth was of one language, and of one speech', a unity which encouraged the presumptuous to build a city and a tower 'whose top *may reach* unto heaven'. Seeing this, God feared that 'nothing will be restrained from

[24] For an introduction to Kircher, see J. Godwin, *Athanasius Kircher* (1979).

[25] First published in 1652, an enlarged edition of his *Microcosmos* of 1624. Webb used the 1657 edition.

[26] Ch'en Shou-yi, 'John Webb', pp. 310–11.

[27] Genesis 6: 14.

[28] G. de Mendoza, trans. Parke, *The History of the Great and Mightie Kingdome of China* (1588).

them, which they have imagined to do', so 'let us go down, and there confound their language, that they may not understand one another's speech'.[29] Webb argues that the Lord's displeasure had been directed only at those who had journeyed westward to the plain of Shinar. Those who remained in China, having inhabited it anew after the Flood, were not involved in the building of the Tower of Babel and did not incur His wrath. Their tongue was not confounded.

Having established this point, Webb goes on to argue from historical chronology that the Chinese Emperor Jaus and Noah were one and the same, ruling China both before and after the Deluge. Father Alvarez Semedo had stated that Jaus had come to the throne before the Deluge, which is recorded in Chinese histories, and Webb was following a suggestion of Father Martini in going on to conflate, daringly, the histories and attributes of the two men. He parallels their lives and finds that in all respects they correspond: both were just and righteous; both were accomplished in husbandry; both lived at a time when there were universal floods, the dates of which, according to Webb's reading of the chronologies, agree perfectly; both were blessed with a reprobate son, and so on. Not surprisingly, in the light of this parallel, Webb was at pains to show that there was a correspondence between the religion of Noah and that of the Chinese. Here he was able to enlist further support from the Jesuit commentators, who had found that the Chinese have one God, 'the Monarch of Heaven'; they have a firm belief in immortality and their sense of justice is in keeping with Christian righteousness.

At this point Webb digresses to discuss Chinese cities, towns, geography, and revenues. Drawing on Kircher's *China monumentis*, he notes that there are 150 cities, all built to a square plan, so that 'he that hath seen one of them, may easily comprehend the manner of all the rest'. The houses are made of timber and, although simple on the outside, are splendid within. They are only one storey high but cover a considerable ground area. All this is discussed in laudatory terms because it is indicative of a system which is conducted according to rational principles. The monarchical system is praised for similar reasons: 'if ever any Monarchy in the world was constituted according to political principles, and dictates of right reason, it may be boldly said that of the Chinois is ... their Kings may be said to be Philosophers, and their Philosophers, Kings.'

Implicit in this is a criticism of Webb's own society, and this continues when he praises the Chinese for their laboriousness and industriousness, not only mentioning their inventions—the compass, the manufacture of paper, silk, ink, printing, guns and gunpowder, fireworks, pottery and porcelain—but also stressing that, despite the abundance of raw materials, they collect the vilest and basest rags, in fact, 'all sorts of most filthy and stinking excrements', and make good merchandise of them: they are enemies to sloth and idleness. They delight in agriculture, although their first arts are mathematics, astrology, and astronomy, all of which skills were inherited from Noah. As to poetry, as one would expect, it is morally unimpeachable and a world away from Sir Charles Sedley. Poems are written by the Chinese, according to Webb, on natural philosophy, just government, loyalty, and love. They are chaste, the Chinese having no word for the

[29] Genesis 2: 1–7.

'privy parts'. Noah was, Webb believes, also involved here, the excision of an appropriate vocabulary being a consequence and a reproach for all time for his shaming: 'And Noah began *to be* an husbandman, and he planted a vineyard: And he drank of the wine, and was drunken; and he was uncovered within his tent.'[30] This also could be the reason, he suggests, for the Chinese dislike of wine.

Webb then returns to his main theme and discusses questions of language. He recognizes the truth of Heylin's contention that linguistic change was often a consequence of time, conquest, and intercourse with other nations, and sets out to demonstrate China's isolation, which apparently was such that an ambassador being sent abroad was regarded by his grief-stricken family as going to his death. Not only was Webb incorrect in believing that civilization in China predated that of Egypt and India, but he was also mistaken in arguing for China's historical isolation, as the country came under immense foreign influence from AD 200 to 1000 and it did not achieve the boundaries of *c.* AD 700 again until 1644 (pl. 23). Webb believed that he was faced with the problem of having to explain various divergent dialects, as he did not realize that the sound of a word in Chinese does not necessarily bear any relation to the way in which it is written. He excepted the dialects from the pure, primitive language, saying that they were spoken in colonies which had been corrupted by contact with barbarians. This was an unnecessary strategy, as a written Chinese character is accessible to speakers of different dialects.

Webb was romantically inclined to find immanent in the world a language, and by extension a culture, of absolutely unsullied antiquity and purity. With admirable empiricism, he applied six tests of primitivism[31] (and consequently, from his antiquarian viewpoint, virtue) to his chosen language to demonstrate that it fulfilled certain requirements, but he did not attempt to show how other languages fell short of the ideal. As there is no justification for the assumption that only one language could pass the tests, we must presume that the victory of Chinese was in the class of self-fulfilling prophecies, despite the overlay of logical and scientific arguments and the underpinning of weighty scholarship which informed Webb's approach to the problem.

The first of the six tests, antiquity, presented no problems, as this was well established by various authors and was unquestionable. The second point, simplicity, was harder to demonstrate, because the language appears to be difficult. It is, however, simple, because it is monosyllabic and hieroglyphic, differing crucially from Egyptian hieroglyphs, because they were designed to conceal *Arcana* from the people whereas the Chinese communicated *Concepta*. Further, the language is free from all the artificial niceties of grammar and the characters can all be formed, despite their numerousness, by only nine strokes of the pen!

The next test, generality, is easily demonstrated: the language has been in use for over 3,700 years and is common to 200 million people. Modesty of expression, the fourth test, is easily shown. The absence of a word for the 'privy parts' is reiterated, the absence of obscenities is noted, and the honourable and modest modes of address applauded. Here Webb does compare Chinese with a rival primitive language, Hebrew, dismissing it on

[30] Genesis 9: 20–1.

[31] These tests were taken up by Webb after being proposed by other writers; see Ch'en Shou-yi, 'John Webb', p. 320.

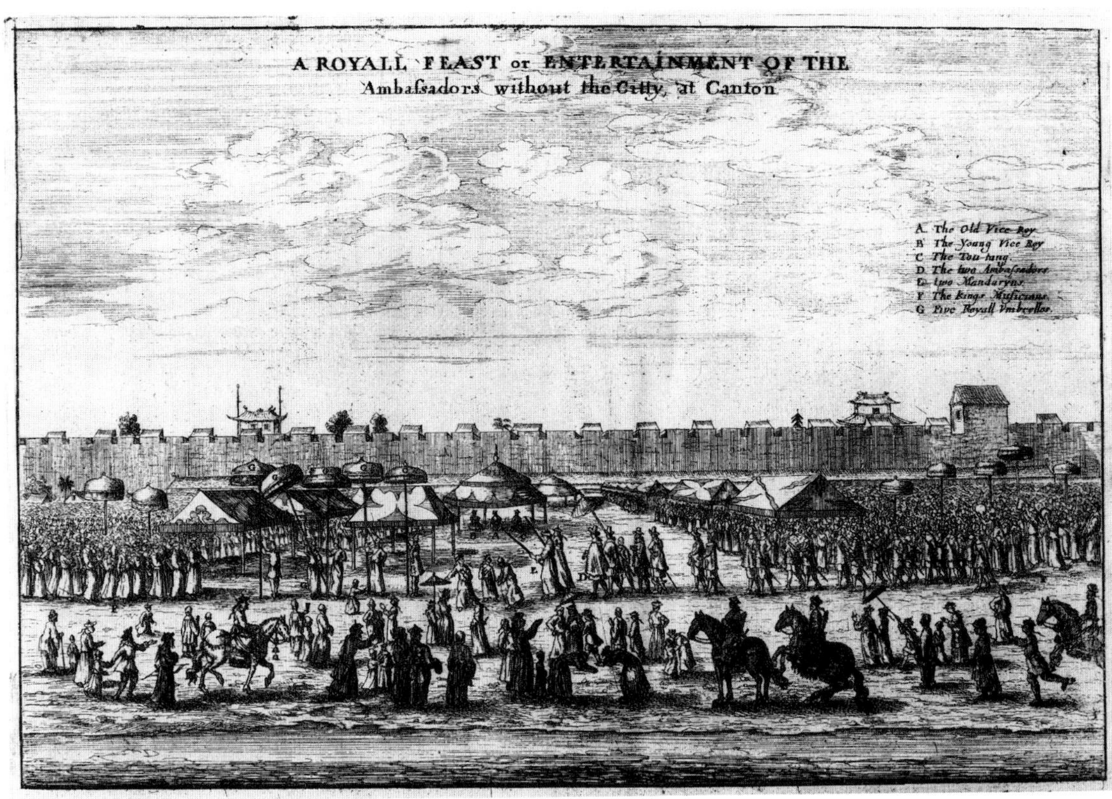

23. The entertainment of the ambassadors outside the city walls at Canton, the chief commercial city and port of southern China; from John Ogilby's edition of J. Nieuhoff's *An Embassy from the East India Company of the United Provinces* (1669). The two ambassadors, P. de Goyer and J. de Keyser, are depicted in the centre of the illustration, walking behind the two mandarins

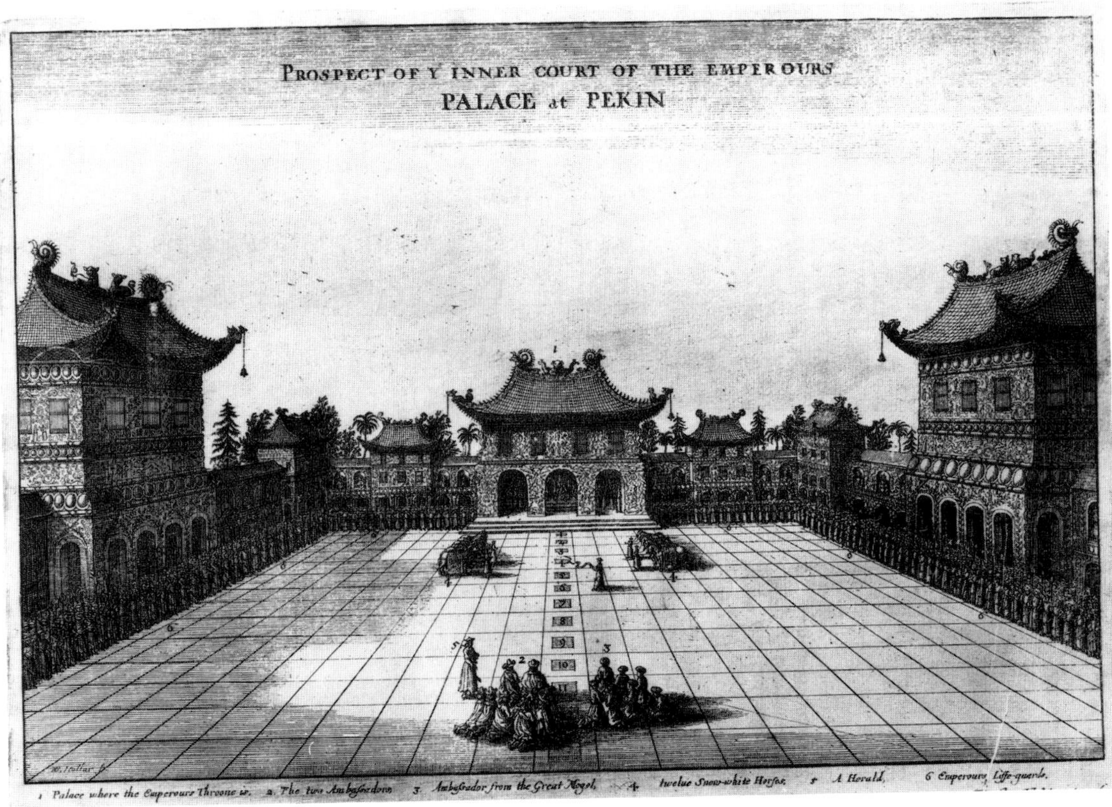

24. The inner courtyard of the Emperor's Palace at Peking, from John Ogilby's edition of J. Nieuhoff's *An Embassy from the East India Company of the United Provinces* (1669)

the grounds that it is presumed by all learned men that the primitive tongue must be harmless and Hebrew contains much that is licentious. Lastly, Chinese is possessed of both utility, affording us the knowledge of one true God, and brevity.

Webb, having gained the consent of both 'sacred scripture and unquestionable Authors', thus shows to his satisfaction that 'the Language of the Empire of China is the PRIMITIVE Language'. In the climate of the time, this was eminently defensible, for, although Robert Hooke, addressing the Royal Society in 1686, considered that the relations he had met with concerning the Chinese language were written 'by such as did not well understand it',[32] William Whiston in 1696 accepted that China was peopled by the posterity of Noah, and Samuel Shuckford in the 1730s suggested a connection between Noah, China, and a primitive language.[33] Hooke, despite not having been able 'to procure sufficient helps to inform myself of the whole Art of Writing and Reading the Chinese Character', was acute enough to grasp the important point that 'the Pronunciations had no affinity with the stroaks of the Character'—that is, the language had another base which is now recognized as being associative and metaphoric.

Webb's approach to the subject of the Chinese language and the methods he employs in marshalling the evidence tell us a great deal about the man and his preoccupations. The stability and morality of Confucian government had a great appeal for those who had lived through turbulent times. Webb, whose career had suffered because of political unrest, appreciated the value of a great, morally organized, hierarchical empire. China was sufficiently remote to be all things to all men and, as a source of subject-matter, it was capable of affording a large and divergent number of exempla. Webb was able to select what he required from the evidence available and mould it to his design. Throughout, he protested the historicity of his approach and the certainty of his conclusions, but it is not the validity or invalidity of his arguments, still less the truth or falsity of his conclusions, which should concern us here. Rather, it is the manner in which the problems are identified and addressed, for 'in the final analysis the prolongation of the effort to prove the Chinese the possessors of the primitive tongue has an emotional basis. On men of sensitively keyed imagination the mysteries of China exercised a continuing fascination.'[34] The fascination which the subject held for Webb is clear. He returned to it in his expanded 'Essay', a closely written, bound manuscript of 325 folios, far longer than the 212-page octavo published edition. The Dedication to the King is dated 29 May 1671: Charles's birthday.

The manuscript is divided into six books which are themselves subdivided into chapters. Book One deals with the 'First Age of the World'. It was wholly peopled, with a common language. Noah's Flood was universal. The colonies established by Noah and his sons, particularly in China, are discussed and the book closes with a consideration of Babel and the alteration of languages through commerce and intercourse. Book Two is devoted to other pretenders to the primitive language, particularly Hebrew. According to Webb,

[32] R. Hooke, 'Some Observations and Conjectures Concerning the Chinese Characters', *Philosophical Transactions*, 16/180 (1686), 63–78.

[33] W. Whiston, *A New Theory of the Earth* (1696), and S. Shuckford, *Sacred and Profane History of the World* (1731–7); cf. Appleton, *Cycle*, pp. 33–4.

[34] Appleton, *Cycle*, p. 36.

there is no mention of Hebrew in the scriptures until the time of Abraham, who learned the language after his arrival in Canaan. Old Hebrew was not the primitive tongue and, moreover, it was corrupted before the captivity of the Jews in Babylon.

Book Three returns to China, its antiquity, its Deluge, the Ark, and the Noah–Jaus parallel. Puoncuus, the First Governor of China, believed by Isaac Vossius to be Noah,[35] seems rather to Webb to be Adam. The next book treats of China's magnificence, populousness, and fertility, and its government and religion. The personal qualities of the Chinese are described and their 'divers ingenuities' listed. Another new section is added here on Chinese architecture and painting.[36]

Webb's received descriptions of Chinese architecture are of great interest because they come clearly straight from the heart of one who, having been frustrated in his own grand, palatial designs, would not have despised the opportunity to essay comparable prodigiousness. The Governors of the Provinces of China have, he writes, palaces which are

> nothing inferiour either in magnificence of building or costly furniture, to the noblest structure of most of the Princes in Europe. They have each of them four or five stately courts and houses in front of every court, with spatious Halls, Places of Judicature, roomes for visits and entertainements, all of them ordered in severall apartments distinctly by themselves, the innermost Court being for the habitation of the Governor, his wives and children.

Later, Webb qualifies his comments, deciding that much Chinese public architecture is 'stupendious and prodigious rather than magnificent and great'. Whilst not equal to European piles for 'nobleness, perpetuity and splendour', they are nevertheless generally superior in 'capacity, commodiousness and neatness'. The Emperor's court at Peking is of a different degree entirely, surpassing 'whatever undertaking of ours, whether the vastnesse or the singularity of ornaments bee respected' (pl. 24). The court is bounded by three high walls, the inner alone extending 4 or 5 miles. The Emperor's quarters comprise apartments, gardens, woods, and lakes: 'although I call it one palace, in effect it contains divers all disposed by accurate and due symmetry and proportion.' The greatest palace is for the Emperor, the Empress, and the young Princes. 'Every one of the Royall-Issue having passed his childhood, hath a Palace to himself,' and there is another palace for 'old men who have well deserved of the Commonwealth.' Fifteen thousand people live and are maintained within the palace. It is of no mean workmanship: marble and stone arches, porticoes and terraces, columns and statues, yellow tiles which appear golden from a distance, provide what is clearly an arcadian setting.

The abundance, magnificence, and sheer weight of numbers involved in the description of the Court allow it to stand as a metaphor for Webb's view of China as a whole. He is overwhelmed, so he curtails the discussion:

> And if I should here speake of the lakes, fishponds, parks, gardens, orchards, woods, with the other ornaments and appurtenances of the Palace, it would be the work of an entire volume to relate them all. ... nothing that is beautiful, nothing almost that is good which can be found

[35] I. Vossius, *Dissertatio de vera aetate mundi* (1659).

[36] 'Essay', iv. 12.

throughout the whole Chinese Empire; nothing that is rare, which cann be brought from forraigne nations, but is continually carried into the Pallace, but never anything brought forth.

Webb does not attempt to reconcile this commerce with his arguments on the purity of language. In his description, China, despite all his protestations of historicity, becomes once more a country of the mind and his only defence is that this is the way his sources tended to view it as well.

With regard to the art of painting, Webb finds that the Chinese are lagging behind Europe, and it is interesting to see his reasons, as an informed connoisseur, for thinking this, as they demonstrate those qualities of painting upon which he placed a premium: 'they know neither the reasons nor rules of shadowes, nor how to use oyle colours', although, since the arrival of Europeans, some new techniques have been acquired. The chief claim of the Chinese to artistic admiration is their use of 'dry colours' in which they represent 'Birds, flowers, trees and the like ... naturally to the life.'

Book Five of the manuscript deals with China's relations with the rest of the world and Book Six returns to the question of language, rehearsing the published arguments and concluding that, 'untill more full consent, and greater certainty bee produced for any other', the 'Language of the Empire of China is the PRIMITIVE Language'.

Webb's work on China ought to be viewed, along with his other literary efforts, as a manifestation of his desire to search into roots. His conclusions are false, but the book has much more than curiosity value. At a time when the dividing line between science and magic was unclear, his comparison of his achievement with that of Dr William Harvey was not as far-fetched as it now appears. It must not be forgotten that, although during the post-Restoration period the animistic interpretation of the universe was giving way to the mechanistic, the evolution was gradual. Magic was unfashionable in the Royal Society, but this did not inhibit the continued publication of books on alchemy in the later seventeenth century. John Evelyn, in 1680, was still capable of keeping a foot in both intellectual camps when he noted the appearance of comets, 'which though I believe appeare from natural Causes ... yet I cannot despise them; They may be warnings from God.'[37] Webb's *Historical Essay* is rooted in a comparable ambivalence.

It is on the *Historical Essay* on China that any claim of Webb's to being a historian must rest and, bearing in mind that he was writing before the advent of stricter methods of comparison and classification, and that it was not until the nineteenth century that real English Sinology began, his claim must be supported. His underlying fault, an over-ambitious attempt at synthesis, was not his alone but ran through a large part of Renaissance exegesis. Webb was fully aware of the pitfalls of historical enquiry: 'in the intricate, and obscure study of Antiquity it is far easier (as Camden very well observes) to refute and contradict a false, than to set down a true and certain resolution.'[38] In discussing China, he was at least setting down his own resolutions. In the earlier books on Stonehenge, he was acting, initially at least, as witness to the ideas of his master.

[37] Evelyn, *Diary*, p. 702, 12 Dec. 1680.

[38] J. Webb, *The Most Notable Antiquity of Great Britain, Vulgarly Called Stone-Heng* (1655), 1.

In *The Most Notable Antiquity of Great Britain, Vulgarly called Stone-Heng*, published in 1655, Webb writes as if in the person of Inigo Jones:

Being naturally inclined in my younger years to study the Arts of Designe, I passed into forrain parts to converse with the great masters thereof in Italy; where I applied myself to search out the ruines of those ancient Buildings, which in despight of Time itself, and violence of Barbarians are yet remaining.

According to Webb's account, King James I, whilst at Wilton on a Progress in 1620, summoned Inigo Jones and commanded him to 'produce out of mine own practise in Architecture and experience in Antiquities abroad, what possibly I could discover concerning this of Stoneheng'.[39]

The problem seems to have occupied Jones for some years and his conclusion, arrived at by the application of an 'Architectonicall Scheam', was that Stonehenge was a Roman temple of the Tuscan order, open to the sky, dedicated to the god Coelus, the Heaven. He found that its plan, which he reconstructed, was based on four, intersecting equilateral triangles, inscribed within a circle, the basis, according to Vitruvius, of the ancient theatre (pls. 25 and 26). Jones's interpretation, that Stonehenge was a hexagonal temple with an inner, open-aired Cella, was unprecedented, finding no parallel in either antiquity or classical theory. John Aubrey put forward a criticism of the argument which was very much to the point:

In 1655, there was published by Mr. Web a Booke intituled Stonehenge-restored (but writt by Mr. Inigo Jones) which I read with great delight. There is a great deale of Learning in it: but having compared his Scheme with the Monument it self, I found he had not dealt fairly: but had made a Lesbian's rule, which is conformed to the stone; that is, he framed the monument to his own Hypothesis, which is much differing from the Thing it self.[40]

Until the advent of scientific methods of dating, and even after, the origins and purpose of Stonehenge provided a rich seam for fantasists. Given the reliance which both Jones and Webb placed upon antique precedent, their conclusion should not come as a surprise, despite their unusually uncritical examination of the sources. In the *Historical Essay* on China, Webb was to display a well-developed ability for pointing out the divergences in argument of different authors, and his demonstrable unease over the analogy between Stonehenge and a theatre caused him to introduce the Temple of Le Galluce, illustrated by Palladio, as the source from which Jones took 'his first Hint, for finding out the original Form of our Antiquity'. It has been argued, convincingly, that 'the parallel in Jones's mind between Le Galluce and Stonehenge was an intellectual rather than a physical one', the former being based upon a 'scheam' which had a great appeal for Jones and which he very much wished, despite its non-explanation of rational purpose, to impose upon the latter.[41]

The Most Notable Antiquity of Great Britain was brought out in a small edition and its

[39] The King was the guest of William, 3rd Earl of Pembroke. Webb dedicated the book to Philip, the 5th Earl. For a discussion of *Stone-Heng* and the image cast by the monument in the imagination of Jones, see F. Yates, *Theatre of the World* (1969), 176–85.

[40] J. Aubrey, *Brief Lives*, ed. O. Lawson Dick (1972), 55.

[41] A.A. Tait, 'Inigo Jones's "Stone-Heng"', *Burlington Magazine*, 120 (1978), 155–8.

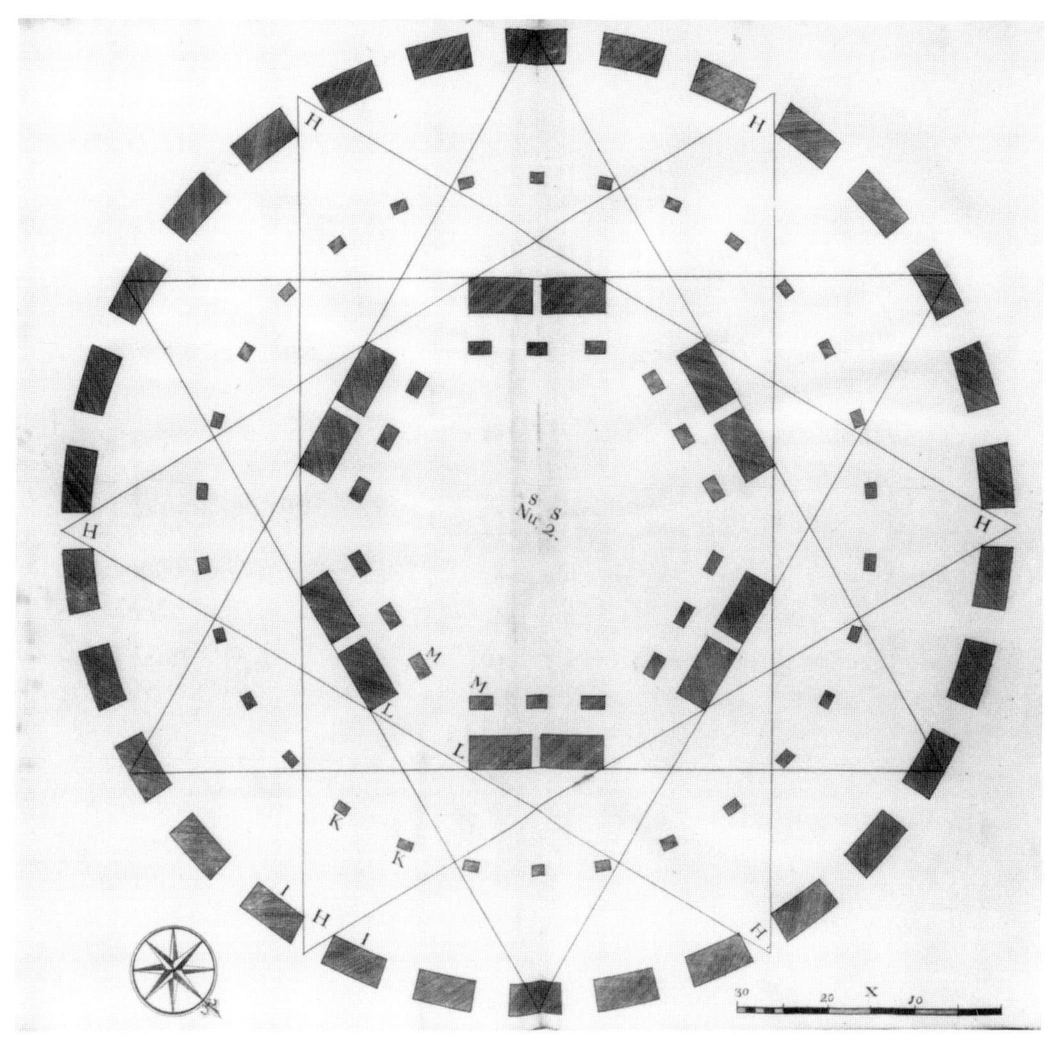

25 (*left*). Inigo Jones's reconstruction of Stonehenge, published by Webb in 1655 in *The Most Notable Antiquity of Great Britain*: 'The Ground-plot of the Work, as when first built ... with the four equilateral Triangles making the *Scheme*, by which the whole Work was composed'

26 (*below*). Inigo Jones's reconstruction of Stonehenge, published by Webb in 1655: 'The whole Work in *Prospective*, as when entire, whereby the general Composure of the particular Parts of the Uprights, are together all seen: and, by which also, the stately Aspect, and magnificent Greatness thereof, are fully, and more apparently conspicuous'

sales were few and slow. There had, however, been sufficient reaction to it to prompt Dr Walter Charleton, Physician in Ordinary to King Charles II, to argue in 1663 in *Chorea gigantum* that Stonehenge had been built by the Danes as a site for the election and inauguration of their kings. In doing so, he made the mistake of criticizing Inigo Jones, suggesting that Jones was imagining and imposing a Vitruvian plan at Stonehenge, a matter which Webb, who had at first regarded Charleton's opinion as merely a 'capricious Conceit',[42] could not ignore. The impugning of his master's integrity spurred him into the attack, and *A Vindication of Stone Heng Restored* was published in 1665.

A Vindication is almost twice as long as the first two Stonehenge books put together.[43] In it, Webb presents a vindication of Jones's argument, based on literary sources rather than on any re-examination of the monument, and supplies a spirited, lengthy, yet partial account of the character, life, and work of 'the Vitruvius of his age', a man 'neither arrogant nor ambitious'. Indeed, so self-effacing was Jones that, according to Webb, his conclusions regarding Stonehenge would not have been revealed at all if Webb had not been pressed to publish them, after Jones's death, by 'the best Antiquaries then living' and by such 'Lovers of Antiquity' as Sir Justinian Isham of Lamport, for whom Webb was working at the time.

The *Vindication* continues with a discussion of the architecture of ancient Rome and, for the benefit of Charleton, 'an Historical Narration of the most memorable Actions of the Danes in England'. Jones, Webb tells us, had not arrived at his solution to the problem of Stonehenge without detailed analysis of the evidence. Far from being superficial in his survey, he had 'digged throughout all the Foundations', in much the same way as Palladio had done when investigating the surviving temples of antiquity in Italy: 'What was truly meant by the Art of Design', Webb continues, 'was scarcely known in this Kingdom, until he [Jones] ... brought it in use and esteem among us here'. As we have seen, these were early days in the development of the architectural profession, and Webb, as the legatee of the man who had done more than anyone else to establish the position of the architect in England, clearly was offended by the intervention of Charleton in an area in which he had neither professional interest nor knowledge: 'As for my own part, as I intend not to write of Physick, being not within my Sphere; So, I would advise others, not to intermeddle with Architecture, unless they knew better what belonged to it.'[44]

The *Vindication* offers further, substantial proof of Webb's learning. Historians as well as architectural theorists are cited. Vitruvius' definition of architectural decorum is noted and endorsed: 'When the Thing built is agreeable to the Quality of the Person, for whom it is built'; 'When the Parts of the Work correspond unto the whole'; 'When the Structure hath a Situation proper for the Use to which it was intended'. Wotton, Serlio, Palladio, Scamozzi, and Vignola are all brought forward as witnesses. The conclusions which Webb reaches in his defence of Jones's hypothesis that Stonehenge was built during the later years of the Roman occupation are incorrect, but his arguments do have a certain internal consistency. Having decided that the Romans were the builders, it was not difficult to

[42] J. Webb, *A Vindication of Stone-Heng Restored* (1665), 1.

[43] All three were reprinted in one volume in 1725; a reprint was issued by Gregg Press in 1971 with an introduction by S. Piggott.

[44] Webb, *A Vindication*, p. 125.

find in the monument the proportions, elegance, and stateliness of Roman architecture: 'Stone-Heng was and could be founded by no other Nation than the magnificent, powerful, and great Masters of Art, and Order, the Romans.'[45] Certainly, academies of design, Webb points out, were unknown to the Druids and there is no evidence to suggest that they were students of architecture. The early Britons also could be discounted as its builders, being rude and barbarous, and Geoffrey of Monmouth's account of Merlin's transporting the stones out of Ireland was, as far as Jones or Webb could see, a ridiculous conceit. The Danes were similarly improbable candidates as builders of such a monument, being 'Barbarians' who came to 'cast down, and destroy', unlike the Romans who 'came hither to build, and propagate'. Besides, 'Mr. Jones living so long in Denmark as He did . . . would never have omitted the taking notice of the Monuments in that Dominion, had they either been worthy taking notice of, or any way resembling our Stone-Heng'. Charleton's Danish attribution is scornfully dismissed, Webb not wishing 'to perplex you more with these Gothick Names'.

It is ironic, in the light of these arguments, that recent writers on the subject have suggested, firstly, that the ruin of Stonehenge might be due in part to deliberate destruction by the Romans and, secondly, that Geoffrey of Monmouth might have been much nearer the truth than Webb thought, if we interpret his comments as being about the removal of a sacred site from the west to Salisbury Plain: from Wales rather than from Ireland.[46]

But, in assessing John Webb's literary output, the essence of appreciation lies in travelling hopefully, for it is clear that his conclusions are of rather less importance than his arguments, particularly when these arguments offer incidental information about other aspects of his work. To a large extent, all historical writing is implicitly autobiographical, as the writer who attempts to recapture and reinvent the past stands revealed by his choices and selections, of subject, of example, and of mode of discourse. Webb's arguments reveal once more the system-builder, the erudite comparer of authorities, and the searcher after precedent, already familiar from other contexts. They reveal also a man who appears to have been at odds with his times, searching for remedies for contemporary ills in the close examination of vanished civilizations and distant lands. For Webb, ancient Rome and modern China were equally accessible through the literature, equally inaccessible physically, and equally incorruptible.

[45] Ibid. 228. [46] G. Daniel, *Megaliths in History* (1972),

4

DOMESTIC WORKS

JONESIAN classicism was a Court-based architecture. Webb's chief hope and ambition lay in the designing of royal palaces, an activity to which he devoted a considerable amount of time, but in which ultimately he was to be frustrated by his times. In the absence of Royal Works during the 1640s and 1650s, he took the Court style to the country in a large number of domestic projects. Times of political uncertainty are perhaps not the most propitious for architectural design, but Webb nevertheless was able to build up a considerable practice, claiming in 1660, not without rhetorical flourish, that there were 'scarce any of the greate Nobility or eminent gentry of England but he hath done service for in matter of building, ordering of meddalls, statues and the like'.[1] It might well have counted against him at the Restoration, despite his strenuous efforts on behalf of the King in the early 1640s, that not all of these men were of unimpeachably Royalist persuasion. Philip, the 4th Earl of Pembroke, Webb's patron at Wilton and Durham House, had been a favourite of James I, but during the 1640s he deserted the King as his allegiance shifted towards the Parliamentary opposition. In the later 1640s and 1650s Webb's patrons included the Parliamentary soldiers Lord Fairfax (Nun Appleton), Colonel Ludlow (Maiden Bradley), and Colonel Harley (Ludlow), as well as figures active in the support of the Commonwealth: Sir George Pratt (Coleshill), Chaloner Chute (The Vyne), Sir John Maynard (Gunnersbury), and Sir John Trevor (Wrexham). Although he worked for Royalists during this period as well—the Duke of Lennox and Richmond (Cobham), the Countess of Rutland (Belvoir), the Earl of Peterborough (Drayton), Sir Justinian Isham (Lamport), and the Marquess of Hertford (Amesbury), Webb did not allow his own political allegiances to determine his acceptance of commissions. In 1657 his name was put forward for nomination as a Commissioner for the regulating of building in London and he expressed the view to his 'Honored Freind Christopher Hatton Esq', the owner of Kirby Hall, that 'I thinke it improper to neglect so faire opportunity whereby I may bee further enabled to expresse my Selfe.'[2] This statement sums up precisely Webb's approach to his profession. It was inevitable that, during a period of Parliamentary ascendancy and confidence, commissions from those of an anti-Royalist persuasion would be more numerous than those from supporters of the King in exile. Webb probably could not afford to spurn the work, although it was to cost him dearly in the longer term.

Webb's first important, independent design, for 'a Lodge in a Parke', was made for

[1] PRO SP 29/5 74.1 (see App. II).

[2] BL Add. MS 29550, fo. 297. No more is known of Webb's involvement here. An 'Act for the Preventing the Multiplicity of Buildings in and about the Suburbs of London' was passed in June 1657 (C. Firth and R. Rait, *Acts and Ordinances of the Interregnum*, ii (1911), 1223–34).

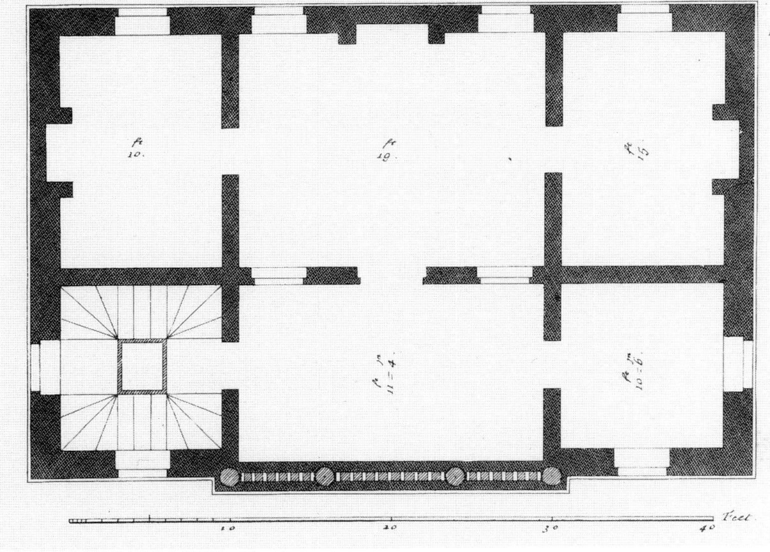

27. Hale Lodge: plan and elevation; engraving published by William Kent after one of Webb's three, closely related schemes

28. The Queen's House, Greenwich: elevation of the south front; designed by Inigo Jones; begun 1616–19 for Queen Anne of Denmark and completed 1630–5 for Queen Henrietta Maria

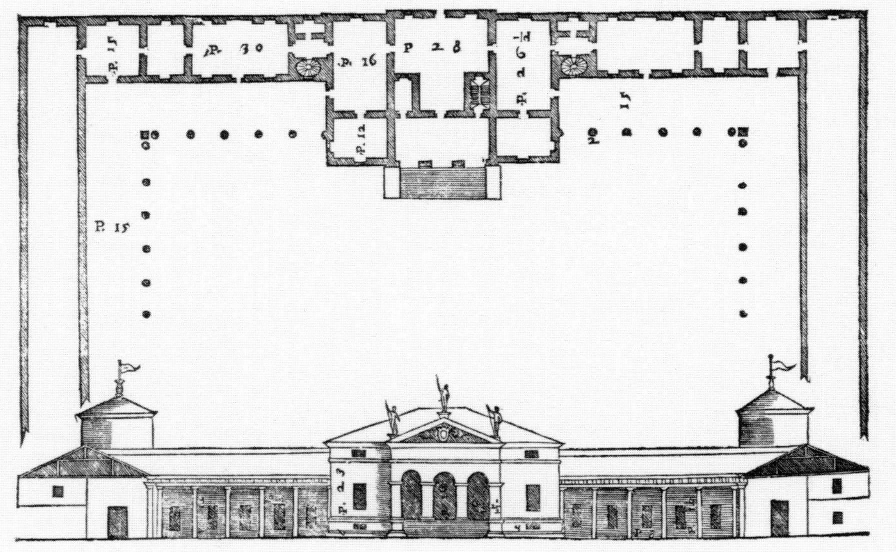

29. The Villa Saraceno: plan and elevation; designed and built by Palladio for Biagio Saraceno *c.* 1545–8

John Penruddock, whose estate at Hale in Hampshire was close to Wilton, where Webb was working in the later 1630s (pl. 27). Three designs exist for the Hale Lodge and they demonstrate an approach which was to become characteristic: firstly, the production of alternative, closely related schemes; secondly, the borrowing from Inigo Jones: from the Queen's House (pl. 28); and, thirdly, the basing of the plan on a Palladian prototype: the Villa Saraceno (pl. 29).[3] There is no evidence that the lodge was built, but its seminal importance for English Palladianism was recognized by Burlington and Kent in the early eighteenth century when it was published as one of the *Designs of Inigo Jones*. Webb's designs propose a rectangular building between 42 feet and 52 feet in width, of five bays, with a first-floor loggia. The chief concern in the alternatives appears to have been the assessment of the most desirable shape for the main, central room, and the positioning of the stairs in relation to it. Thus we find Webb experimenting with an almost square room and with rectangular rooms aligned across the building or going into its depth, the stairs being variously placed at different corners of the house.

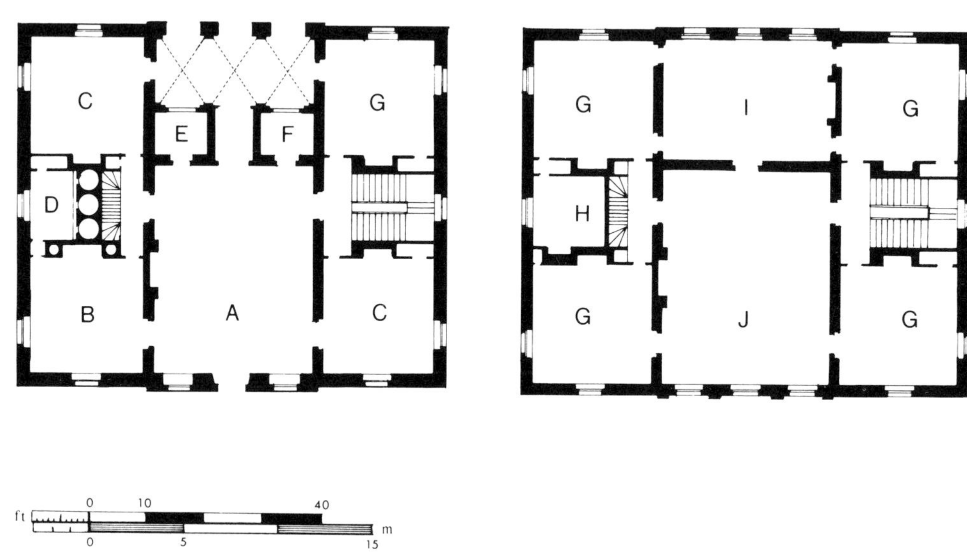

FIG. 1. DESIGN FOR MAIDEN BRADLEY: PLANS OF GROUND AND FIRST FLOORS
A Hall; B Kitchen; C Parlours; D Pastry; E Larder; F Pantry; G Bedchambers; H Study; I Withdrawing Room; J Dining Room.

Webb's next small-house design is known only through plans which are endorsed for 'Colonel Ludlow at Mayden Bradley, Wiltshire' (fig. 1). Ludlow was made Colonel in 1644 and elected to Parliament two years later. Webb's design appears to have been intended as a replacement for his existing house, but it probably was not built. It holds considerable interest for its innovative planning. The choice of direction offered by the nexus of interconnecting rooms, a feature typical of Palladio's villas, offers here a freedom

[3] Palladio, ii, 56.

of circulation unusual in the English house. The design shows a development from the Hale plan in the provision of more accommodation and further borrowing from the Villa Saraceno in the creation of a vaulted, arcaded vestibule on the ground floor. This would have had considerable practical value since it is likely that this house, in being sited on a farm, was intended, in the true manner of the Palladian villa, to be the focal point of a working estate. The sense in which the term 'villa' came to be understood in the eighteenth century—as a country retreat—was more applicable to Webb's later essays on this theme at Lamport, Gunnersbury, and Amesbury, all three of which were designed in the 1650s.

Webb's work at Lamport was partial, involving the designing of a new range to front older buildings, but Gunnersbury and Amesbury were complete and self-sufficient houses. It is remarkable, given the extent of Webb's work, that these two commissions provided him with the only opportunities of his career to design and build complete houses from start to finish. In their creation, he successfully married ideas from Palladio with themes adumbrated by Inigo Jones to produce solutions of timeless elegance to the problems of villa design; solutions moreover which, thanks to eighteenth-century publication, achieved a wide circulation.

As a palace designer *manqué*, Webb was also involved throughout his career in the designing of palatial houses for the aristocracy. His work in this area, particularly at Wilton and at Belvoir Castle, also achieved a wide circulation through publication by Campbell and Kent in the eighteenth century. His involvement at Wilton, one of the best known as well as one of the most architecturally significant of English country houses, ought to have ensured Webb's place in the front rank of English architects, but the history of the house is complex and the roles of the principal protagonists in its design are only beginning to be understood.

Webb's major, published house designs, attributed as they were by later commentators to Inigo Jones, provided, along with the actual works of the master, the foundations and exemplars for the eighteenth-century Inigo Jones revival. Webb's individual architectural achievement lay in his ability to synthesize from his Jonesian and Italian Renaissance sources to make accessible to a larger clientele the sophisticated and learned classical language of the Caroline court. His further, and by no means lesser, achievement was to do this in a manner which prefigured modern architectural practice.

It is customary to speak of the classical language in terms of rules and systems of proportion, but, having been educated by Jones in both theory and practice, Webb recognized that such rules and systems did not represent absolute values. His critical approach to his sources is evidenced frequently in the annotations which he made in his copies of Palladio and Serlio: 'Observe that in this Cornice Palladio differs wholy from the rule of all others';[4] 'I doe well approve of Scamozzi's reason but not in all places';[5] and, most revealingly for the builder of the first projecting temple front on an English country house, he noted at the end of his copy of Serlio's Book VII on domestic architecture: 'In all this booke of houses there is not one fayre loggia with a frontispiece the

[4] Palladio, i (1601), 50 (Webb's copy, at Worcester College).

[5] S. Serlio. *Tutte l'opere d'architettura et prospetiva*, 1619, contents; Webb's copy, RIBA, repr. Farnborough 1964.

wch Palladio so much affected and it may bee the Ancients did not use them but in Temples and Publique works . . .'[6]

Webb's flexible marriage of theory and practice was essentially and necessarily pragmatic. He would no doubt have agreed with the spirit of James Stirling's remark that 'compromise is the essence of architecture. Compromise with the site, with user requirements, costs and technology.'[7] Webb was an architect for whom there was always a gap between the ideal scheme of the drawing board and its realization by others on the building site. The ideal was achieved by drawing, revising, and drawing again, but it was always a stage rather than an end in itself: the end, not always reached, was the building. Architecture, unlike painting or sculpture, requires collaboration. In correspondence concerning the building of Lamport, we find that, although Webb visited the site and sent numerous instructions and drawings, he relied heavily on the contractor in charge of the works for information and for the implementation of his ideas.

A letter which he sent to Colonel Edward Harley in October 1655 offers further evidence of a pragmatic approach. In view of the time of year and his other commitments, Webb found himself unable to make the journey from London to Ludlow in Shropshire, to discuss 'some buildings you intend there', but, he goes on,

> let me advise you that if you intend a new building . . . with all those accommodations convenient for a Country habitation, send mee but word thereof by letter what manner of scituation you have . . . and what you intend to bestow thereon, and I doubt not to satissfie you without the charge or labour of my cominge down. Or else if you intend any new addition to some formerly erected house . . . (employ a workman to) draw out the said house with straight lines onely . . . set downe the heights of the stories . . . the thicknesse of the floores & walls, and the bignesse of the roomes . . .

Such a drawing, Webb concludes, together with an indication of the required additions and the money available, 'shall be as sufficient as if I came downe my selfe', although, failing that, 'I shall endeavour to visitt you accordinge to your desire'.

Nothing more is known about this house, but the letter alone offers clear proof of a businesslike approach to design. His letters and his practice alike proclaim Webb's concern with quality. He produced designs for the smallest of workaday details as well as for imposing, architectural set pieces. He endeavoured to have these works carried out by the most skilled and experienced craftsmen. Webb was, in short, a professional. He brought to domestic practice the architectural style, the quality of construction and organization, and the intellectual integrity of the Jonesian Royal Works. The proof of this lies in the houses themselves.

[6] Serlio, *Opere*, vii, fo. 243^{v}. [7] D. Sudjic, *New Architecture: Foster, Rogers, Stirling*, (1986), 167.

WILTON HOUSE

Webb worked on Wilton during both of the major periods of construction in the seventeenth century which caused this house, above all others, to become the symbol of English Palladianism. Early in his career he assisted Inigo Jones in making designs for ceilings and doors, which were executed by Isaac de Caus. After the fire of 1647, which gutted the south-side state rooms, he was in sole charge of their refitting.

The Wilton Abbey buildings and estates had been granted after the Dissolution to William Herbert, later the 1st Earl of Pembroke, who, having begun his expenditure on building works in 1543, was said by 1565–6 to have newly constructed all the houses, gardens, orchards, and other appurtenances at a cost of more than £10,000 (pl. 30).[8] It was this quadrangular house which Philip, the 4th Earl of Pembroke, began to alter and enlarge in the 1630s. The genesis of these building works is well known. Aubrey relates that King Charles I 'did love Wilton above all places: and came thither every Sommer', and it was the King

> that did put Philip ... Earle of Pembroke upon making this magnificent garden and grotto, and to build that side of the house that fronts the garden, with two stately pavilions at each end, all *al Italiano*. His Majesty intended to have had it all designed by his own architect, Mr Inigo Jones, who being at that time, about 1633, engaged in his Majesties buildings at Greenwich, could not attend to it; but he recommended it to an ingeniouse architect, Monsieur Solomon de Caus, a Gascoigne, who performed it very well; but not without the advice and approbation of Mr Jones ...[9]

Inigo Jones is known to have visited Wilton during the time of the 3rd Earl, a personal friend, most memorably in 1620 when he was summoned there by Pembroke and King James I to carry out his investigation into the origins of Stonehenge.[10] The recommendation of Jones, as Surveyor to the Crown and as a man familiar with the house, was a natural one for the King to make. Equally, it was to be expected, given the tremendous amount of official work which he had to do, that Jones, whilst retaining an interest, should pass the commission on to another. As Howard Colvin has demonstrated, that other was not Solomon de Caus, but his son or nephew Isaac, who had worked already with Jones at the Banqueting House and who in 1633–4 was acting as the Surveyor's executant architect at Covent Garden.[11]

Surviving account books show that work on the garden at Wilton began in 1632–3, with a high point of expenditure in 1634–5. Work on the house began in 1636, when de Caus was instructed to 'take downe ... that side of Wilton house which is towards the Garden and such other parts as shall bee necessary and rebuild it anew with additions according to ye Plott which is agreed'.[12] The garden executed and later published by de Caus was laid out symmetrically to the south of a proposed new range which was to extend 400 feet (pl. 31).[13] This grand front, with a central, hexastyle pedimented portico,

[8] 'Survey of the Lands of William, 1st Earl of Pembroke' (*c.*1565–6), Wiltshire CRO 2057/S3; privately printed for the Roxburghe Club, (1909), ed. C. R. Straton.

[9] J. Britton (ed.), *The Natural History of Wiltshire* (1847), 83–4.

[10] J. Webb, *The Most Notable Antiquity of Great Britain, Vulgarly Called Stone-Heng* (1655).

[11] H. M. Colvin, 'The South Front of Wilton House', *Archaeological Journal*, 111 (1954), 181–90.

[12] A. A. Tait, 'Isaac de Caus and the South Front of Wilton House', *Burlington Magazine*, 106 (1964), 74.

[13] I. de Caus, *Wilton Garden* (*c.*1654; repr. 1982); his drawings for the garden and the long south front, *Worcs. Coll. Cat.* 109–10.

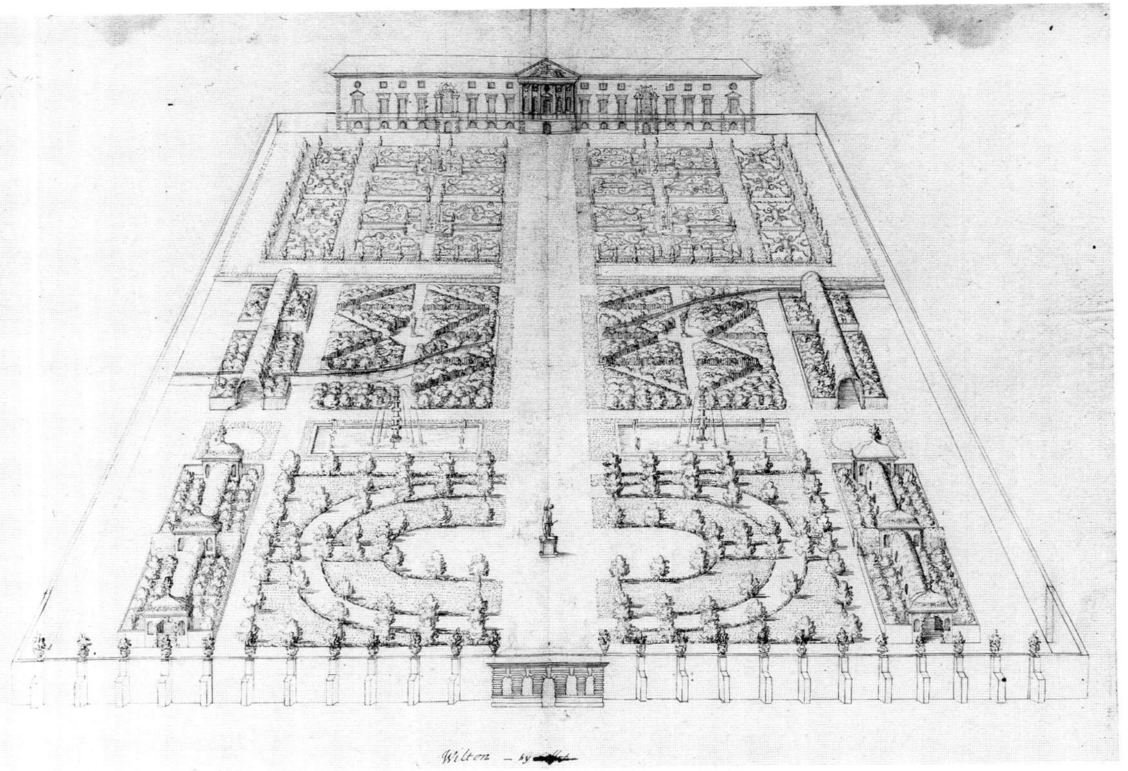

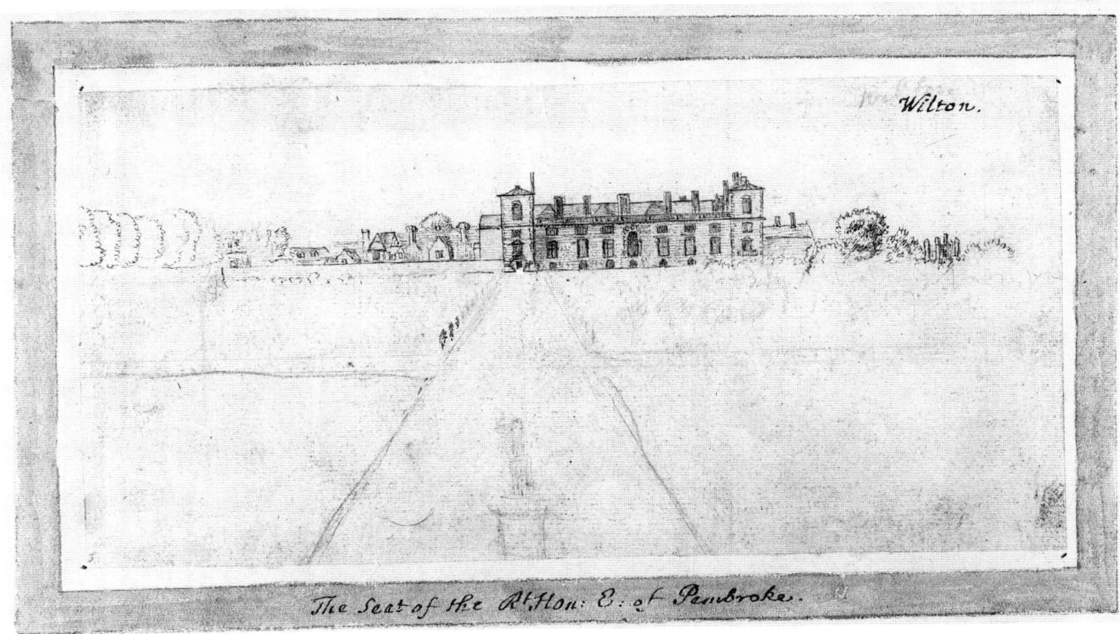

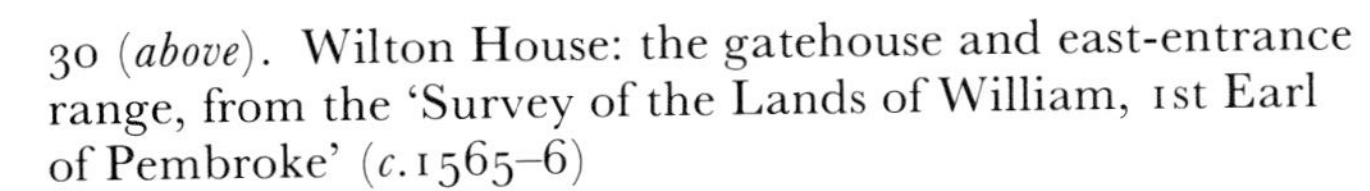

30 (*above*). Wilton House: the gatehouse and east-entrance range, from the 'Survey of the Lands of William, 1st Earl of Pembroke' (*c*.1565–6)

31 (*above, right*). Wilton House: Isaac de Caus's proposal for the grand, south front, aligned on the central avenue of the formal garden

32 (*right*). Wilton House: the south front as built, showing the pyramidal roofs on the towers which were replaced after the fire of 1647

33. Wilton House: the south front

which aligned with the central avenue of the garden, was begun but was then drastically reduced, perhaps as a result of the financial difficulties which the 4th Earl was suffering, notwithstanding his large income.[14] Its place was taken by the curtailed scheme which substantially survives today. In effect the initial revision involved retaining the eastern half of the grand design, placing an additional bay at its west end in place of the pedimented centrepiece, and adding an enlarged achievement of the Herbert arms over the central Venetian window to reinforce its position as a focal point. The 'two stately pavilions at each end, all *al Italiano*', Wilton's most distinctive and emulated features, were an afterthought which was not only dictated by the need to provide vertical emphasis to the façade, but was also required because of the presence of the Tudor towers at the ends of the east-entrance range (pl. 32). To effect a satisfactory marriage of the new south wing with the existing range to the east, it was necessary either to demolish the Tudor towers altogether or to rebuild them in a style in keeping with the new south front. De Caus's grand scheme and his drawing for the curtailed scheme[15] imply the demolition of the Tudor towers, and we may infer from this that the 4th Earl initially intended the new south range, even in its curtailed form, to be merely the first in the total rebuilding which proved to be beyond his means (pl. 33).

Italian precedents for the design of the towers can be found not only in the work of Palladio, but also more directly in that of his pupil Scamozzi (pl. 34).[16] It was perhaps here, initially, that de Caus received some 'advice and approbation' from Jones, who had met the aging Scamozzi in Venice in 1614. De Caus's drawing for the curtailed scheme displays in its hipped roof with dormers and its *œil-de-bœuf* windows a decidedly Francophile appearance, but, as built, the south front was purely Italianate, with towers rather more *al Italiano* than they are today. Prior to their rebuilding after the fire of 1647, they were terminated not by the familiar, pedimented gables but by hipped, tiled roofs.[17]

The 1647 fire was caused, according to Aubrey, 'by airing of the roomes'. In 1648, he continued, 'Philip ... re-edifyed it, by the advice of Inigo Jones; but he, being then very old, could not be there in person, but left it to Mr Webb ...'.[18] In fact, it is highly improbable that the aged Jones would have been involved at all in these further works. By this time the 4th Earl was inclined towards the Parliamentary cause and the 5th Earl, who succeeded his father in 1650, made his views clear when he referred later to 'Iniquity Jones': His Majesty's Surveyor was clearly *persona non grata*.[19] Webb's involvement is demonstrated not only by drawings, some of which are dated 1649, but also by the accounts which cover the years 1650 and 1651, which show that he was in charge at an annual fee of £40.

The extent of the fire has been discussed by Howard Colvin and his conclusions have been supported by recent structural investigation which confirms that the south range was damaged severely, but that the masonry shell survived. Webb's work involved him

[14] J. Aubrey, *Brief Lives*, ed. O. Lawson Dick (1972), 302–5.

[15] *Catalogue of the Drawings Collection of the RIBA: C-F* (1972), p. 80 and fig. 56.

[16] V. Scamozzi, *L'idea della architettura universale* (1615) I. iii. 284 (repr. Farnborough, 1964).

[17] G. Popper and J. Reeves, 'The South Front of Wilton House', *Burlington Magazine*, 124 (1982), 358–61.

[18] Britton, *Wiltshire*, p. 84.

[19] Vertue, v. 26.

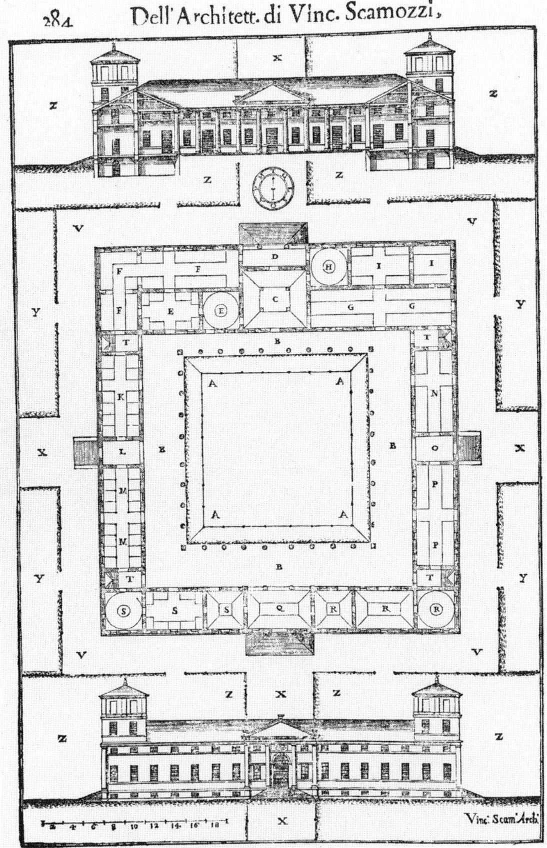

35 (*above*). Wilton House: design for the ceiling of the Countess of Pembroke's Bedchamber (probably situated in the south-west tower, above the Hunting Room). The inscribed title on the left is in Inigo Jones's hand; the other inscriptions are by Webb

34 (*left*). Design for a palace published by Scamozzi

36 (*above*). Wilton House: design for the ceiling of the Cabinet Room, dated 1649

37 (*left*). Wilton House: design for a door in the King's Bedchamber. The inscribed title is in Inigo Jones's hand; the other inscriptions are by Webb

in rebuilding the upper stages of the towers, which he redesigned, and in refitting the state rooms. By May 1652 these were complete: Lodewyk Huygens was conducted around the 'nouvelle bastie a l'Italienne' and he found the ceilings 'tout peint d'une assez bonne main'.[20] Two years later John Evelyn was equally impressed by the 'Dining-roome in the modern built part towards the Garden, richly gilded, and painted with story by De Creete, also some other apartments, as that of Hunting Landskipps by Pierce: some magnificent chimny-pieces, after the French best manner . . .[21]

In his later work at Lamport, Webb was to advise his patron against employing French carvers for statuary because of the 'fantasticall' nature of their designs, but, following Jones, he considered a measure of extravagance to be entirely appropriate for the more exuberant features of interior decoration: ceilings and chimneypieces. This taste for extravagance was first indulged by Webb in the ceiling designs which he made as Jones's assistant for Wilton before the fire (pl. 35). These drawings have been attributed to Jones himself, and, in view of his reported reluctance to participate in the design of the 1630s house, it has been suggested that they might have been produced for his friend the 3rd Earl for the old house. However, Webb in the later 1630s was already 'copying several designs and mouldings' for Jones at old St Paul's Cathedral, and the evidence suggests that he was doing the same at Wilton. The ceiling designs are unique in the surviving corpus of drawings by Jones and Webb, but they have more in common with other drawings by Webb than they have with others by Jones, being marked out fully with a stylus, with ruled pencil lines, and without the strong outline and freehand verve which one would expect from Jones, but which one would be surprised to find in the young Webb.[22]

The drawings are titled in ink by Jones, but their measurements and, on two of them, the provisional black chalk titling, are in Webb's hand. A comparison of this group of ceiling designs with one of Webb's dated ceiling designs of 1649 (pl. 36) is instructive, for, although the dated drawing is styled rather differently, the drawings have much in common: the full use of the stylus, the black chalk underdrawing, the manner of the pen-and-wash handling of the schematic swags and garlands, and the method of noting measurements. Further, the idiosyncratic faces which appear in the border of one of the designs lack the liveliness which could be expected from Jones, even at this scale, whilst Webb's tentative approach to figure drawing is apparent throughout his career. As designs, these ceilings are rather sophisticated for the Webb of the 1630s. They rely heavily on the designs of Jean Cotelle, whose contemporary ceiling designs for Parisian *hôtels* appear to have been available in the Office of Works,[23] and Jones's inscribed titles may be read as evidence of the Surveyor's direction and approval of the pupil–assistant's efforts. A comparable endorsement occurs with a group of designs for doors (pl. 37). Drawn and annotated by Webb, and titled by Jones, these also are datable to the later

[20] Colvin, 'South Front', p. 189.

[21] J. Evelyn, *The Diary of John Evelyn*, ed. E. S. de Beer (1959), 342–3, 20 July 1654.

[22] G. Higgott, 'The Architectural Drawings of Inigo Jones: Attribution, Dating and Analysis (University of London, Ph.D. thesis 1987).

[23] Ashmolean Museum, Cotelle Album; see also J. Cotelle, *Livre de divers ornemens pour plafonds* ... (*c.*1640), and P. Thornton, *Seventeenth Century Interior Decoration in England, France and Holland* (1978), 38, 405.

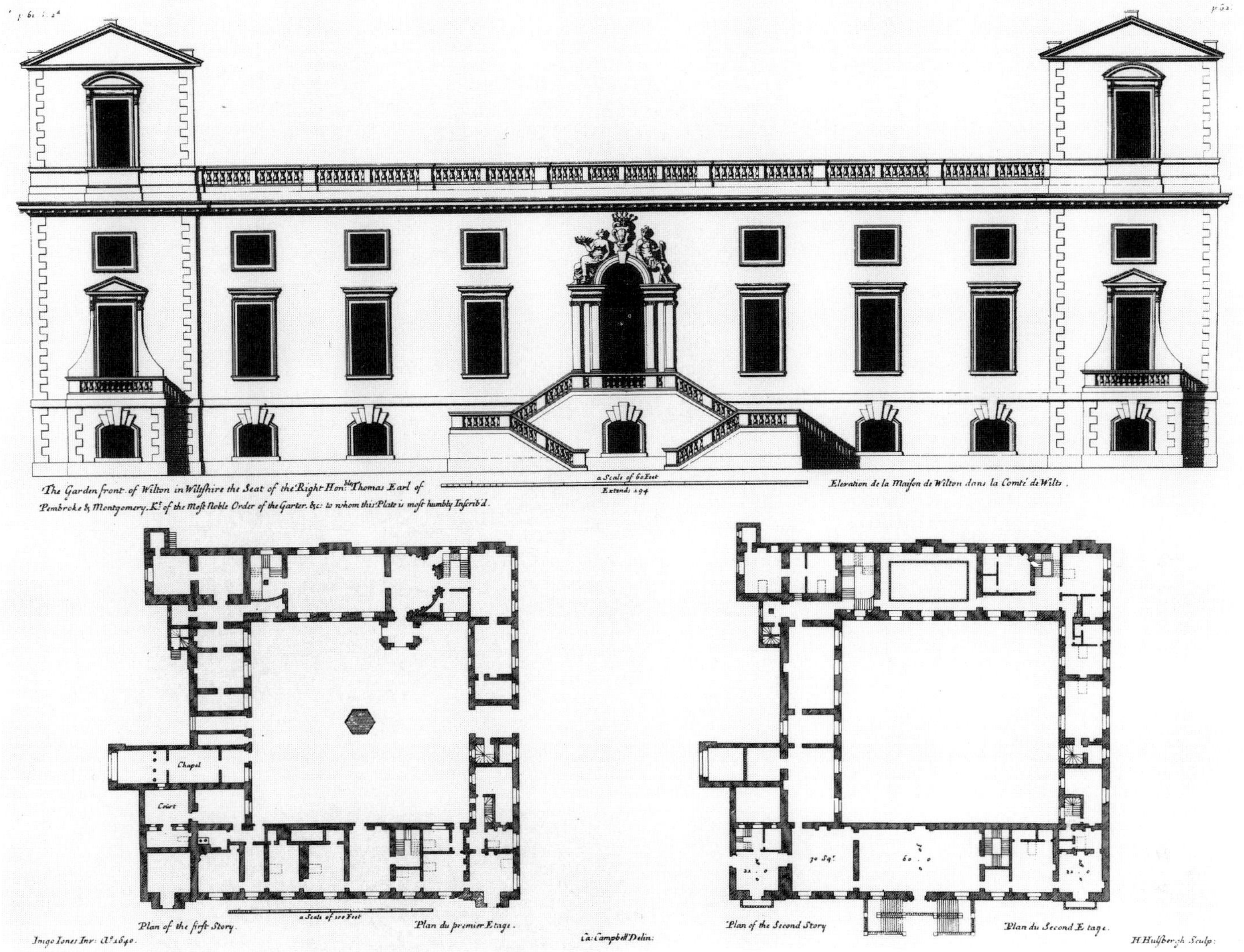

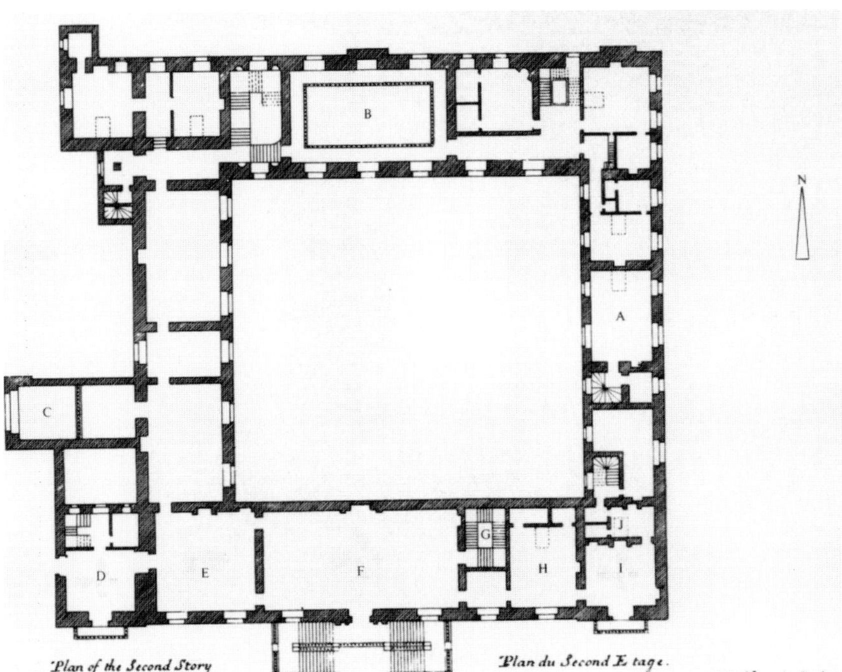

38 (*above*). Wilton House: elevation of the south front and plans of the ground and first floors

39 (*left*). Wilton House; first-floor plan showing layout of state rooms

A Bedchamber over the entrance to the courtyard
B Upper part of the Hall, with gallery around
C Chapel and chapel gallery
D Passage Room or Hunting Room
E Withdrawing Room or Single Cube Room
F Great Room, Dining Room, or Double Cube Room
G Geometrical Staircase; later, with the adjoining passage, this became the Ante Room
H King's Bedchamber; later, the Colonnade Room
I Cabinet Room or South East Corner Room
J Little Ante Room

40. Wilton House: the Single Cube Room, looking towards the north-west corner

41. Wilton House: the Double Cube Room; Van Dyck's magisterial portrait of the Herbert family, commissioned by the 4th Earl of Pembroke, is on the west wall

1630s, although there is evidence to suggest that Webb reused them after 1647.[24] They present designs for almost all the doors on the main floor of the south range, including the blind ones, thus confirming the involvement of Jones and Webb in the original laying out of the state rooms, producing the designs in London which de Caus executed on the site, and demonstrating that Webb's refitting after the fire did not involve any changes to the plan of the south range.

Wilton suffered very considerably in the early nineteenth century at the hands of James Wyatt, who made alterations in all four wings of the house, with the apparent intention of transforming it back into a medieval abbey. Following a fire in 1705, the north range had been rebuilt, and, after Wyatt's further attentions, it has become impossible to assess the extent to which Webb might have been involved in works apart from those in the south range, which Wyatt fortunately altered least of all (pl. 38). All of Webb's surviving, titled drawings relate to the south-side rooms and the attention of visitors has always been directed, rightly, towards the state suite in this range, whose rooms provide an indication of what might have been if Webb's Whitehall Palace had been built, or his King Charles Building at Greenwich completed. The editor of the 1748 edition of Defoe's *Tour* was typical in his expression of boundless admiration:

> It is universally acknowledged, that the Apartments called the Salon, and the great Dining-room, are the noblest Pieces of Architecture, that have been hitherto produced: the first is a Cube of 30 Feet; the other is a double Cube of 60 by 30; and both of them 30 Feet high.
>
> When you are entered these grand Apartments, such Variety strikes upon you every Way, that you scarce know to which Hand to turn yourself first . . .[25]

Access to the house before the intervention of Wyatt followed the route laid down by the 1st Earl (pl. 39). Passing through the grand entrance in the east range, the visitor progressed across the north-east corner of the internal courtyard to the 'Holbein porch', which is resited now in the garden, then, via a screens passage, entered the north-side hall. Beyond the hall, a grand staircase gave access to the main floor, the level of the south-side state rooms. Passing through the west range, past the chapel built by de Caus, the visitor entered the Single Cube Room (pl. 40). This, and the adjoining Double Cube Room (pl. 41)—a domestic version of the Whitehall Banqueting House—are the most complete survivals at Wilton from the Webb period, the decoration of both of them dating from after 1647. Their original flat ceilings, with upper windows set within the friezes, were destroyed by the fire, and in his reconstruction Webb replaced them with deep, painted coves. Both rooms retain their painted decoration by Emanuel de Critz, Matthew Gooderick, and Edward Pierce;[26] their richly carved swags and garlands set on to the wall panelling, and their Francophile chimneypieces, designed by Webb after the engravings of Jean Barbet.[27] Webb incorporated the Herbert wyvern in the idiosyncratic composite capitals of the Cube rooms' overmantels (pl. 42) and in the cartouche over the

[24] One of the drawings carries the apparently later inscription by Webb, 'For Mr Kennard', possibly the Thomas Kinward who from 1660 until his death in 1682 was Master Joiner of the King's Works.

[25] D. Defoe, *A Tour thro' the Whole Island of Great Britain*, i (1748), 332–6.

[26] E. Croft Murray, *Decorative Painting in England 1537–1837*, i (1962).

[27] Cf. J. Barbet, *Livre d'architecture, d'autels, et de cheminées* (1633).

42 (*above*). Wilton House: the Double Cube Room—the chimneypiece and overmantel. The statues of Ceres and Bacchus frame Van Dyck's portrait of Charles, James, and Mary, the three children of King Charles I

43 (*above, right*). Wilton House: the Double Cube Room—the great door to the Ante Room. This originally gave on to the Geometrical Staircase. A drawing by Webb, dated 1649, survives for the central coat-of-arms cartouche. This is surmounted by wyverns, emblematic of the Herbert family, supporting a ducal coronet

44 (*right*). Wilton House: the Colonnade Room. Originally the King's Bedchamber, this room was remodelled *c.*1735 when the closets at the north end were removed and a colonnade inserted, probably to the design of the 9th, 'Architect', Earl of Pembroke

magnificent great door of the Double Cube Room (pl. 43). There was emblematic significance also in his inclusion of cornucopias in the overmantel capitals of the Double Cube Room—the ceremonial Dining Room—and in the flanking figures of Bacchus and Ceres.

The Double Cube Room as recorded by Colen Campbell, in the plan and section published in *Vitruvius Britannicus*, is symmetrical, but here, as elsewhere, Campbell was correcting what he found. In his engraving, the fireplace in the centre of the north wall faces a central Venetian window from which entry to the garden could be made down a double flight of steps. In fact, the window opened on to a balcony, the steps being situated asymmetrically at the west end of the south range. The window and chimneypiece also are off centre and the side windows are not equidistant from their respective corners, but the size of the room is such that this asymmetry does not disturb. These internal peculiarities can be explained only by the replanning which was made necessary by the curtailment of the original grand scheme after work on it had already begun.

Sir William Chambers, who worked at Wilton in the later eighteenth century, was perhaps the first to cast an informed, critical eye over the Double Cube Room and, although he did not mention its asymmetry, he certainly was not blind to its infelicities. He considered the room to be ill lit, with a coving which was too deep, the painting indifferent, and the carving clumsy.[28] One does not have to agree wholeheartedly with Chambers's purist, neo-classical view to acknowledge that, despite its grandeur and its significance as a rare survival from its period, the overall effect of the Double Cube Room is spoiled by the decorative painting, which, in the words of more recent commentators, 'is unworthy of the architecture and carving with which it was conceived and, compared with the work of contemporary painters in Italy, France and Holland, lamentably provincial'.[29]

Beyond the Double Cube Room in the seventeenth-century layout was the Geometrical Staircase, described by Evelyn as 'artificial winding stayres of stone'. Such stairs were normally on a circular or elliptical plan, Inigo Jones's Tulip Staircase at the Queen's House being an example, but the square plan was not unknown.[30] The stair rose from the ground to the first floor. It had a coved ceiling for which a drawing by Webb survives, and its walls were later painted 'in Arabesco' by Andien de Clermont, who was employed at Wilton in the 1730s.[31] This staircase and the adjoining passage room were removed by Wyatt in his creation of the Ante Room. The new ceiling then was painted in a conscious pastiche of the de Clermont manner.

The next two in the sequence of state rooms retain their Webb chimneypieces after Barbet, the magnificent chimneypiece in the King's Bedchamber incorporating the Herbert wyvern in its decorative carving. This room was remodelled *c.* 1735 to form the Colonnade Room (pl. 44), the closets at its north end being removed and a colonnade

[28] RIBA MS CHA 1/13.

[29] M. Whinney and O. Millar, *English Art 1625–1714* (1957), 291.

[30] R. Neve, *The City and Country Purchaser and Builders Dictionary* (1726), 246.

[31] Croft Murray, *Decorative Painting*, ii (1970); I. Roscoe, 'Andien de Clermont: Decoratve Painter to the Leicester House Set', *Apollo*, 123 (Feb. 1986), 92–101.

inserted, probably to the design of the 9th, 'Architect', Earl of Pembroke. The singerie ceiling was painted during the same period by de Clermont. Wyatt contemplated the destruction of this room but he settled eventually for decorative embellishments. The panelling is ill-fitting and appears to have been tampered with, whether during the 1730s or the 1800s is unclear.

Among Webb's surviving ceiling designs, four represent alternative schemes for the Cabinet Room at the south-east corner of the house. One of these dates from the later 1630s and the others from 1649. Two of the later, dated drawings are quarter plans presenting alternative schemes, one for a *quadratura* treatment and the other showing a proposed layout for a painted scheme with a coving. The present ceiling, above the seventeenth-century cornice, has a surround painted by de Clermont, with a splendid inset central painting by Giordano, *The Conversion of St Paul*, which was placed here in the 1730s.[32]

The adjoining small room, the Little Ante Room, positioned to the north of the Cabinet Room within the south-east tower, retains its very free plasterwork of *c.*1650, possibly inspired by the engraved designs of Le Pautre, which now frames Sabbatini's *Birth of Venus* which was placed in this position after 1731.

At the west end of the south range, within the south-west tower, the original Passage Room to the garden, with wooden steps leading down, and its adjoining staircase, have been remodelled to form the Hunting Room. The drawing for its ceiling decoration shows that it was slightly wider than the Cabinet Room at the east end, a detail which Campbell ignored in his quest for symmetry when preparing his plan. The small difference in width in the two, apparently identical towers was yet another consequence of the adjustment which was needed when the original grand rebuilding scheme was curtailed: the new end wall of the west tower was built 3 feet further west than perfect symmetry would dictate, to bring it into closer alignment with the central avenue of the garden which had been laid out already to align with the central portico of the original grand scheme. The double staircase at this point, since removed, in projecting still further beyond the line of the end wall, helped to foster this illusion of axial alignment.

The present ceiling in the Hunting Room is of the Wyatt period. It is probable that the original 1630s ceiling, for which Webb's drawing survives, was replaced after the fire by the ceiling which was described by Celia Fiennes as depicting sporting scenes.[33] The present double order of panelling in the room frames inset panels of hunting scenes by Edward Pierce which alternate with hunting trophies attributed to de Clermont. The room was remodelled and the panelling reset by Wyatt when he replaced the adjoining staircase with a new stair in a stair tower and extended the Hunting Room into the space made available.[34] The new ceiling was painted in the same de Clermont pastiche style as his new ceiling in the Ante Room.

It remains to consider three further ceiling designs by Webb, for the Countess of Pembroke's Bedchamber and the Countess of Carnarvon's Bedchamber and Withdrawing

[32] Sidney, 16th Earl of Pembroke, *A Catalogue of the Paintings and Drawings in the Collection at Wilton House* (1968), 89.

[33] C. Morris (ed.), *The Journeys of Celia Fiennes* (1947), 9.

[34] Wilton House archives 2057 H1/6, H3/22.

Room. Comparisons of approximate dimensions suggest the upper rooms in the south-east and south-west towers as probable locations for these. The Countess of Carnarvon's Withdrawing Room is given the same dimensions on Webb's drawing as the Cabinet Room and could have been positioned above it with a Bedchamber above that. Both these rooms retain their seventeenth-century chimneypieces. The Countess of Pembroke's Bedchamber was, according to Webb, the same width as the Hunting Room, and therefore could have been positioned above it with a Withdrawing Room between the two. No ceiling design survives for a Withdrawing Room and we must presume that it is lost, along with the other drawings which must have been made for the state rooms.

The handsome, straight-headed doorways which give on to the flat roof from both of the south-range towers suggest a further functional purpose for them, beyond the provision of accommodation. In de Caus's published account of the layout of the extensive and splendid gardens, he makes much of the points of view from which it might be seen to advantage; clearly, walking on the leads would have provided the best view of all.

Wilton, through the elegance and understatement of its towered south front and the grandeur of its Jonesian, cubed rooms, was to become the archetype of many of the great houses of the eighteenth century. The two greatest neo-Palladian houses, Holkham (pl. 45) and Houghton, were indebted to it in their massing, and its towers were a major source of inspiration until beyond the mid-century. But Wilton was by no means a pure or a copyable design in all particulars. The south range evolved piecemeal out of compromise and necessity, providing a particular solution to a particular problem rather than a model for others to follow. Its single-depth sequence of rooms must have been inconvenient in an age in which privacy and convenience were becoming increasingly the desiderata in house planning. In the mid-eighteenth century, proposals were made for a courtyard cloister walk, but it was not until the arrival of Wyatt that this idea was realized and the system of circulation improved. The two-storey cloisters in the internal courtyard remain as his most useful contribution to Wilton.

For Webb, Wilton was crucial. It provided him as a young man in the late 1630s with the practical opportunity to learn, under the direction of Inigo Jones, the intricacies of a sophisticated, contemporary, decorative style which was new to English domestic architecture. It further provided him, after the fire, with his first opportunity, not merely to design the decoration for a major sequence of rooms, but also to see those designs implemented.

DURHAM HOUSE

Wilton provided Webb with his first opportunity to decorate an interior; Durham House provided him with his first opportunity to put the experience of his theoretical studies to practical use in the designing of a major house. This would have been, in effect, a Wilton in the city, a palace of imposing size and scale designed for the 4th Earl of Pembroke.

In 1641 the Bishop of Durham had agreed to King Charles I's proposal that the old Durham House in the Strand should be granted to the Earl of Pembroke in return for an

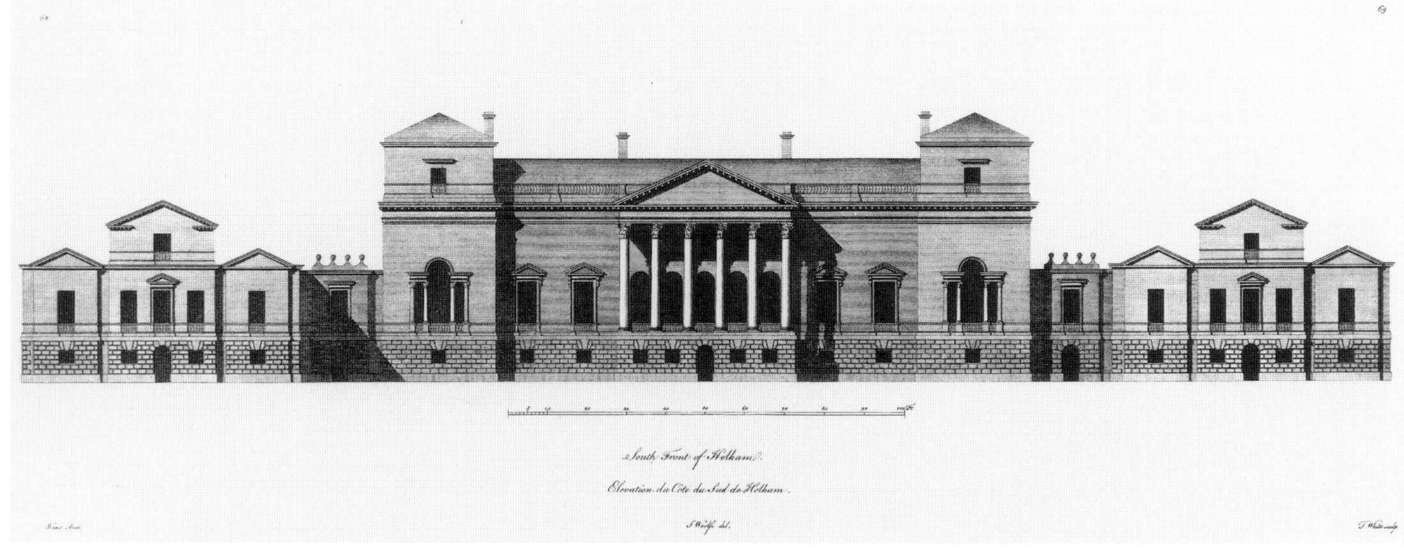

45. Holkham Hall, Norfolk; begun in 1734 for the Earl of Leicester, to the designs of William Kent, this house, one of the pre-eminent monuments of eighteenth-century neo-Palladianism, is clearly indebted to Wilton for the massing of its central block and for its towers

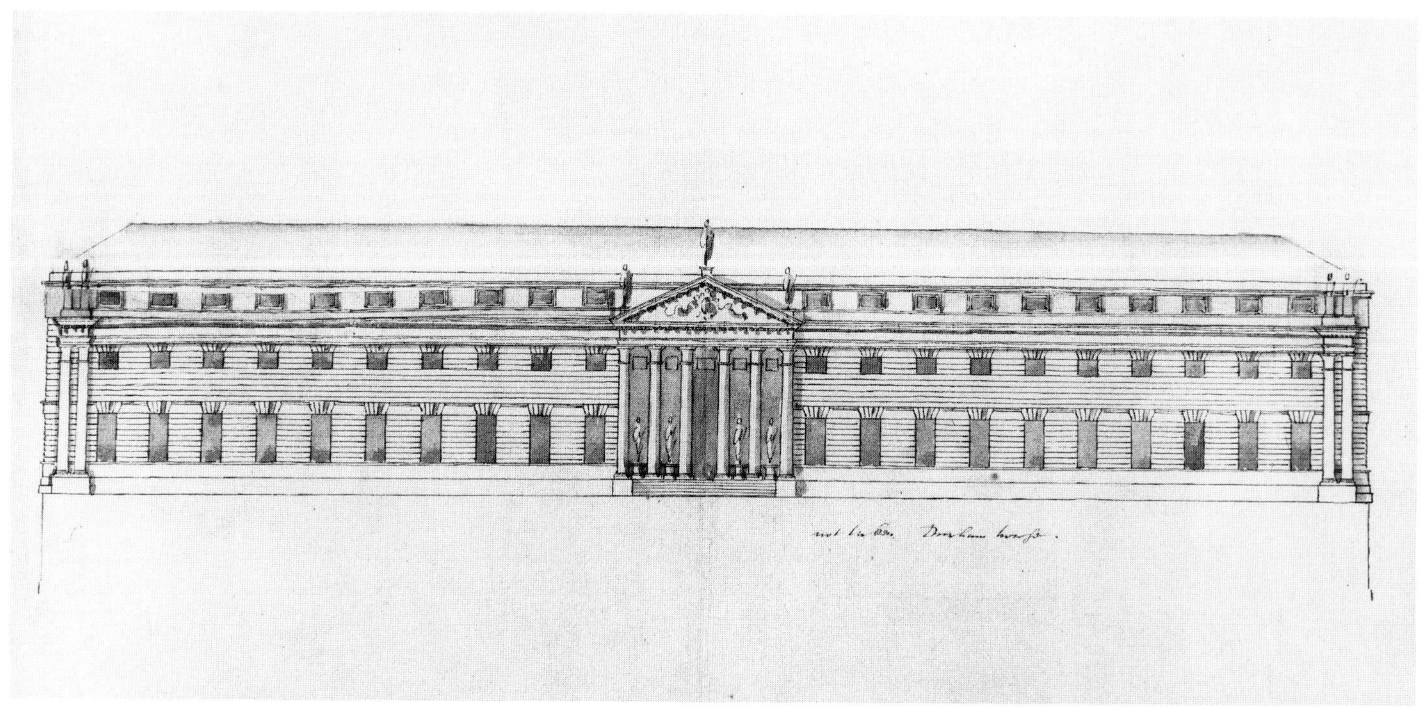

46. Durham House: elevation of the Strand front of the proposed palace for the Earl of Pembroke, inscribed by Webb, 'not taken'

annual payment of £200.[35] Pembroke was, at this time, still a royal favourite, although his choleric temper was beginning to lose him friends and towards the end of the decade his alienation from Court circles would be complete. Despite the expense of Wilton, he surprisingly entertained the idea of building a new riverside mansion which would have rivalled the nearby Northumberland House in grandeur and greatly outshone it architecturally. In 'Painting and Building', he had, Aubrey tells us, 'singular Judgement, and had the best Collection of any Peer in England'.[36]

Six drawings by Webb survive for the new house: plans of the ground and main floors of the second and third designs, the elevation of a design which is similar to, but does not quite accord with, either set of plans, and a much smaller elevation. Both of the large schemes were 'not taken', but the third design, dated 1649, had the word 'not' inserted as an afterthought by Webb, which suggests that it was not until after the death of the 4th Earl of Pembroke in January 1650 (still 1649, OS) that the idea for a large new house was abandoned. The 5th Earl perhaps briefly considered going ahead with the smaller scheme, which is represented only by the undated elevation drawing, a fairly literal translation by Webb of a design by Scamozzi. However, 1650 was not a propitious time for building: later that year, Parliamentary soldiers were quartered in the old house, and after the Restoration it was taken down and the land leased for building plots.

The basic plan of the two large schemes proposed by Webb for Durham House was the same: two grand fronts over 300 feet in length, two shorter side ranges, and a central 'passage gallery' or 'entrata' dividing the central open space into two courts. This, in block form, approximated to Webb's later 'Small' scheme for Whitehall Palace. Both Durham House designs had a double range of rooms to each block, with the service rooms to the north, including a two storey kitchen at the north-east corner, and the 'Rooms of State' overlooking the River Thames. Two galleries, to house the extensive picture collection, were proposed for the second floor of the east and west ranges (figs. 2 and 3).

In the layout of the various vaulted, coved, and columned rooms in both designs, Webb borrowed heavily from the reconstructions of the ancient house made by Palladio and Scamozzi, to which he was indebted also for his contemporary Whitehall Palace 'Taken' scheme of *c.*1647–8.[37] The later plan represented a distinct improvement on the earlier: the state rooms, so far as can be judged from the plan alone, appeared to be more imposing in both size and arrangement, and the plan in general was improved in efficiency, having more subsidiary staircases and being generally tauter in concept. The Thames-side entrance, designed after the model of the tetrastyle hall of the ancients, was doubled in size to eight columns, extending the full width of the five-bay frontispiece. To the west of this were servants' rooms (including a self-contained ground-floor suite for the estate receiver general, or auditor), and, to the east, a chapel and library. The two main staircases beyond the hall were realigned in the later design for both convenience and effect. Thus, having crossed the single-storey hall, the visitor would have found himself in a cross-vaulted space with a choice of stairs to left or right. These led to the vestibule

[35] *Survey of London*, xviii (1937), 93.

[36] Aubrey, *Brief Lives*, ed. Dick, p. 304.

[37] Cf. E. Eisenthal, 'John Webb's Reconstruction of the Ancient House', *Architectural History*, 28 (1985), 7–18.

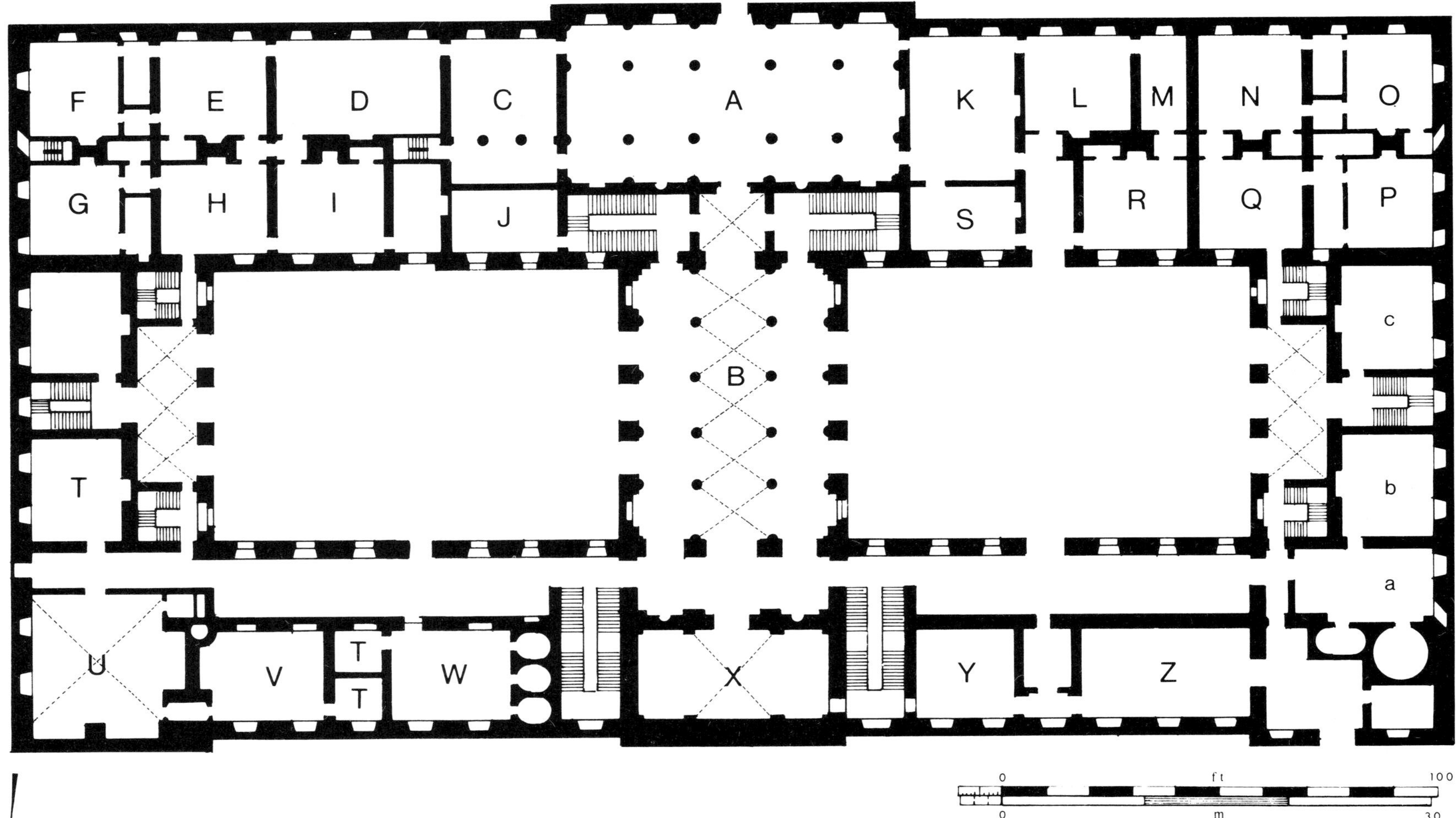

FIG. 2. DESIGN FOR DURHAM HOUSE, 1649: GROUND-FLOOR PLAN

A Hall; B 'Entrata'; C Chapel; D Library; E Secretary's Chamber; F His Study; G Surveyor's Chamber; H Antechamber; I Chaplain's Chamber, and Study adjoining; J Bottle House; K Waiters' Dining Room; L Steward's Dining Room; M Steward's Study; N Receiver General's Chamber; O His Study; P Receiver of the House or Auditor's Chamber; Q Antechamber; R Steward's Chamber; S Pantry; T Larders; U Great Kitchen; V Privy Kitchen; W Pastry; X Wine Cellar; Y Ale Cellar; Z Beer Cellar; a Bakehouse; b Milkhouse; c Under Housekeeper's Room.

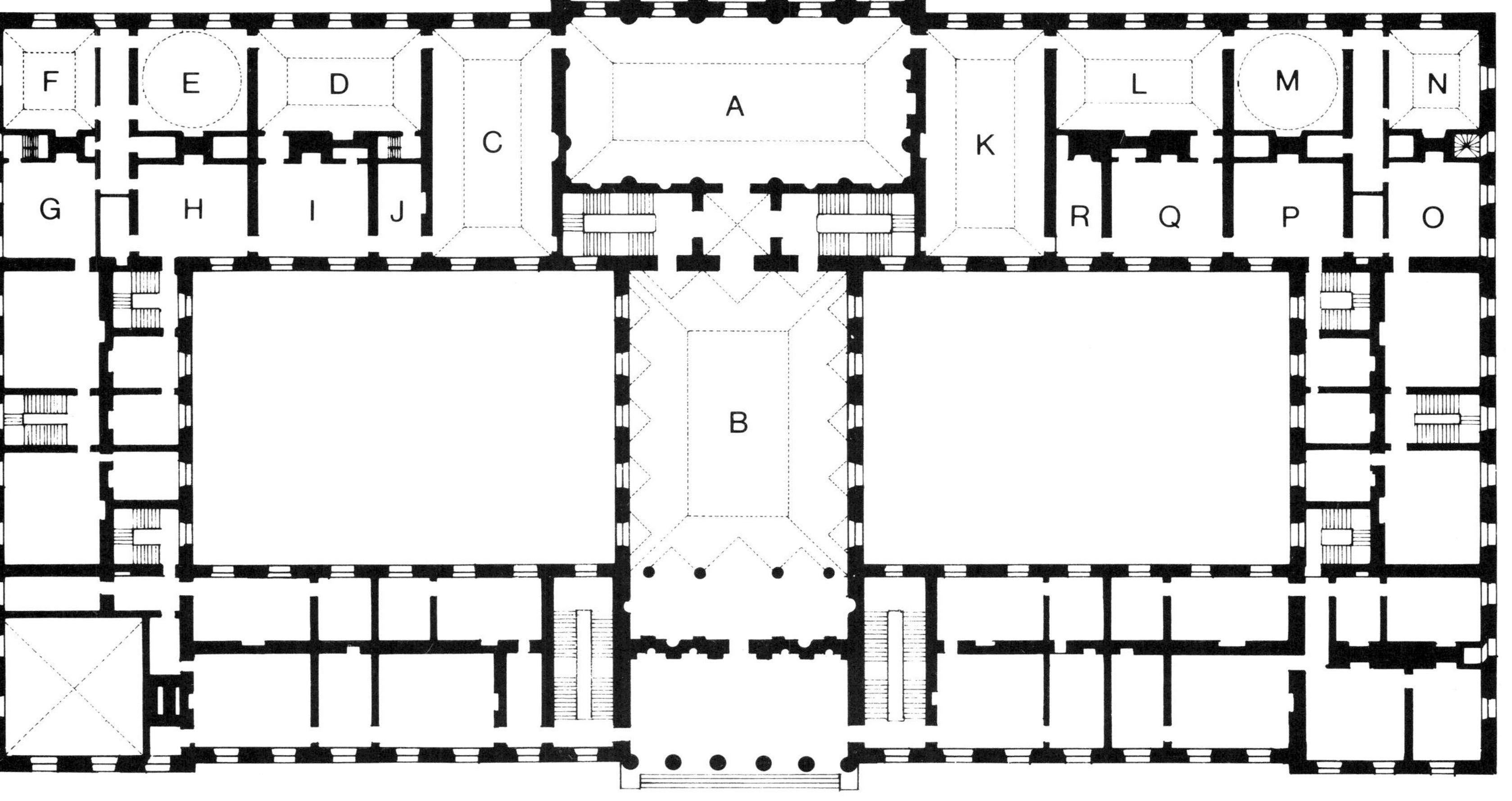

Fig. 3. DESIGN FOR DURHAM HOUSE, 1649: FIRST-FLOOR PLAN

A Great Chamber; B 'Entrata'; State Rooms—Lady's Side: C Presence Chamber; D Privy Chamber; E State Bedchamber; F Cabinet; G Waiting Room; H Backstairs Room; I Bedchamber; J Dressing Room; State Rooms—Lord's Side: K Presence Chamber; L Privy Chamber; M State Bedchamber; N Study; O Waiting Room; P Backstairs Room; Q Bedchamber; R Dressing Room.

on the upper floor which gave on to the coved Great Chamber over the hall, a double cube room of 40 feet by 40 feet by 80 feet, designed at the same time as Webb was receiling and redecorating the Double Cube Room at Wilton. To each side of this grand, ceremonial space, symmetrically disposed, were Presence Chambers, also of two-storey height, aligned across the depth of the range, with Privy Chambers next to them on the river front and State Bedrooms beyond; a remarkably palatial arrangement.

The central, spinal range between the north and south fronts, referred to as the 'Passage Gallery' in the earlier design, became in the second the coved 'Entrata', a massive room of 50 feet by 70 feet, positioned over a vaulted and arcaded room of basilican arrangement. Around the courts in both designs were arcaded, vaulted vestibules of the type which Webb was to build later in his career at Greenwich. The whole effect of Durham House, particularly if we presume that a decorative scheme along the lines of Wilton House was intended, would have been one of incomparable antique splendour: an aristocratic palace of monarchical intent. The extent of Pembroke's power and influence would have been expressed visibly by the grandeur of the state rooms. It would have been underlined further by the extent of the accommodation provided not only for the family but also for the secretary, the chaplain, the steward, the surveyor, and the receiver general.

The surviving elevation drawing, for the Strand front, offers further evidence of the grand design's palatial pretensions, as well as demonstrating, here as in the 'Taken' scheme for Whitehall Palace, how far in the later 1640s Webb was moving away from the style of Inigo Jones towards the Baroque (pl. 46). Because of the sloping site, ground level at the river became basement level at the Strand, so entrance therefore was made up a short flight of steps directly through the portico to the main floor. The ground floor on the Strand side, being partly below ground level, is expressed on the elevation drawing as a plinth, apparently unfenestrated, although high windows at ground level might have been intended. The combination of plinth, channelled rustication and deep cornice with attic storey above gives the façade a predominantly and assertively horizontal aspect, which is broken only by the giant hexastyle portico and the coupled columns which are placed hesitantly, almost but not quite at the ends of the façade. This front represents a restatement by Webb, in considerably more sophisticated and dramatic terms, of Isaac de Caus's first grand elevation for Wilton. Indeed, the whole of the abortive Durham House project can be read as a statement of how Webb might have approached Wilton if he had been given the opportunity to rebuild completely, rather than just to refit one range.

The Durham House designs were worked out fully, as a practical proposition rather than as a theoretical exercise, so we can be sure that the project was contemplated seriously; but, given the financial constraints which appeared to have hampered the Earl of Pembroke in the Wilton House work, it is hard to see how he could ever have contemplated affording to build such a palace in London.

BELVOIR CASTLE

Belvoir provides us with an eloquent example of the gap between architectural theory and practice. Webb drew on the experience of his theoretical studies of the ancient house, on the experience of Durham House, and on his knowledge of the work of Inigo Jones, particularly at Newmarket, to produce designs for the first, great neo-Palladian mansion in England, sixty years before Colen Campbell's Wanstead. The significance of Belvoir was recognized in the eighteenth century, when the designs were published by William Kent, but the house as built bore only a small relation to Webb's grand conception.

Belvoir, a Royalist garrison during the Civil War, capitulated to the Parliamentary forces in 1647, and on 3 April 1649 the Council of State 'ordered that it is for the service and safety of the Commonwealth that the Castle of Belvoir be demolished'.[38] The sum of £2,000 was proposed as compensation to John Manners, 8th Earl of Rutland, but this was amended later to 'not exceeding the sum of £1500'.[39] The rebuilding was said to have been prompted not by the Earl, who would have preferred to live at nearby Croxton, where his grandson afterwards built, or at Haddon Hall, his family home, but by Frances his wife. Webb visited the 'slighted' Castle and produced his optimistically palatial proposals for rebuilding in 1654. These were not executed, but between 1655 and 1668 £11,730 was spent on new buildings and Webb's continuing involvement is attested by a drawing of 1667 for 'The Architrave Freeze and Cornice that goes about the roome'.

The house was rebuilt to its existing ground plan, some of the Tudor buildings surviving sufficiently to be retained in recognizable form. Fuller noted in 1662 that 'some part of it is rebuilding', but he suspected that it 'will not be so full and fair as the former'.[40] Webb's Castle was the third on the site. It was swallowed up in the early nineteenth century, first by James Wyatt's remodelling, then by a great fire in 1816. Its appearance is preserved in a model made in 1799, in surveys made in 1779, and in Badeslade's and Rocque's views of 1739 which show it on the summit of the precipitous hill which overlooks the Vale of Belvoir (pl. 47). The main entrance front is short and faces north. Webb's rejected schemes proposed a major realignment, retaining a north entrance but placing the main entrance in the centre of the long east front (pl. 48).

Many of the antique features with which Webb had experimented at Durham House recur in his alternative schemes for the ground plan of Belvoir. The framework, a large, symmetrical H plan with double-pile central range and angle pavilions, was established early, but the layout of the central state rooms evolved during the design process (figs. 4 and 5). Entrance, as at Durham House, was proposed initially into a hall of eight columns, aligned across the central five bays of the building, with two identical staircases behind, which would have led to a first-floor Great Chamber or Saloon. These rooms were realigned in the finalized scheme, which Kent subsequently published, in which entrance was made into a columned hall extending through the depth of the central range of the building, with the identical staircases which flanked it giving access to a double cube

[38] HMC, 12th Report, App., Pt. v, Rutland MS ii (1889), 4.

[39] I. Eller, *History of Belvoir Castle* (1841).

[40] T. Fuller, *Worthies* (1662), 126.

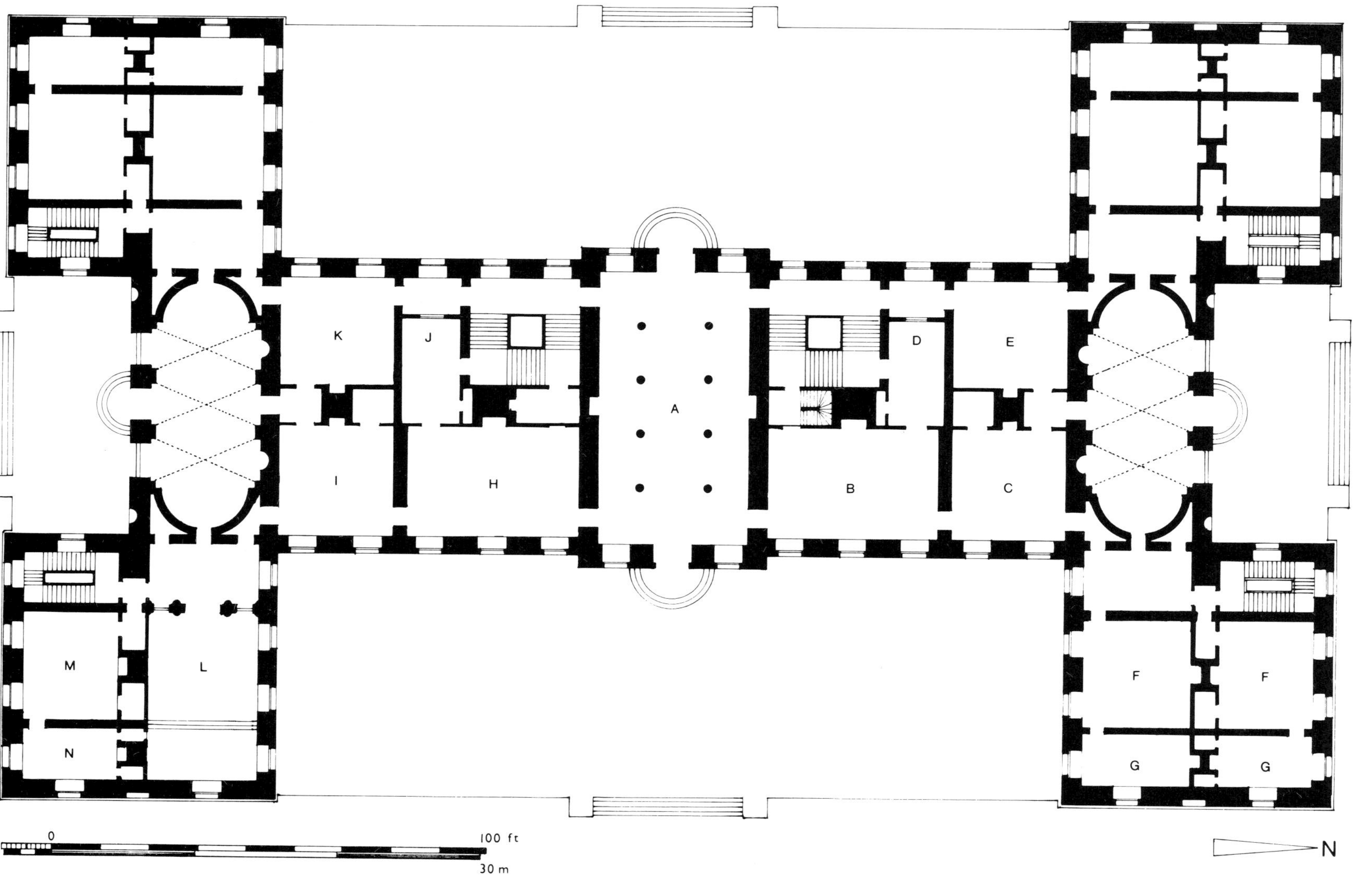

Fig. 4. DESIGN FOR BELVOIR CASTLE: GROUND-FLOOR PLAN

A Hall; B Great Parlour; C Withdrawing Room; D Closet; E Little Parlour; F Bedchambers; G Studies; H Servants' Dining Room; I Steward's Dining Room; J Pantry; K Steward's Bedchamber; L Chapel; M Chapel Chamber; N Chapel Study.

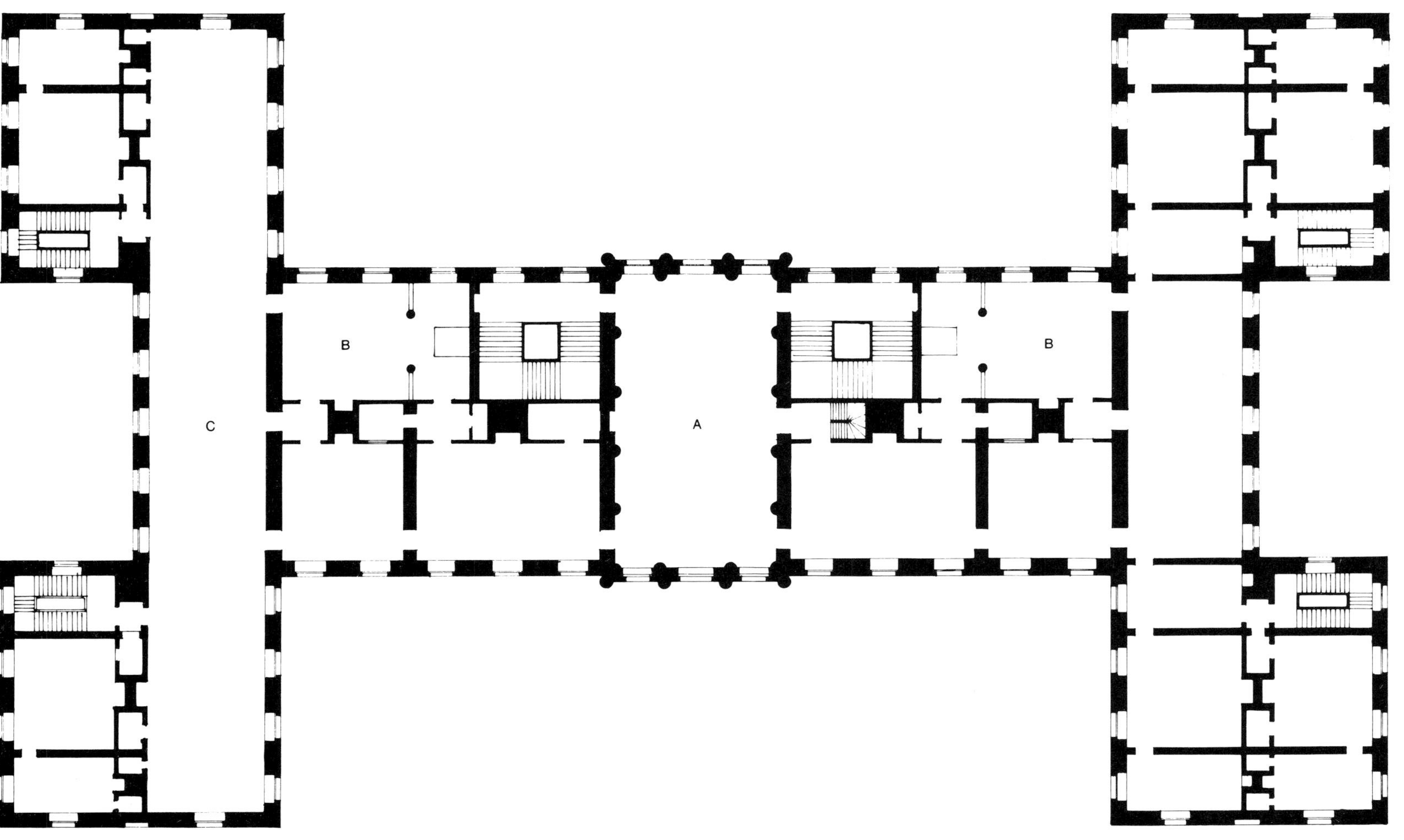

FIG. 5. DESIGN FOR BELVOIR CASTLE: FIRST-FLOOR PLAN
A Great Chamber or Saloon; B Principal Bedchambers; C Long Gallery.

room of 60 feet by 30 feet by 30 feet on the upper floor. This sequence of grand rooms of parade—hall, stairs, and saloon—prefigures the arrangement at Gunnersbury, and a version of it was incorporated into Belvoir as it was rebuilt.

Webb probably was indebted to Jones's Newmarket (pl. 49) for his layout of the grand sequence of rooms and for the design of the applied, pedimented centrepiece which fronted it, but the extension of the long east front to 272 feet owed nothing to Jones. By Webb, out of Scamozzi, the Belvoir design represented a Palladian solution to the problem of composing a long façade, in contrast to the proto-Baroque solution of Durham House. Durham's treatment to some extent had been conditioned by the exigencies of the sloping site, the rusticated first and second floors appearing on the Strand front to be the ground and first floors. At Belvoir, Webb was able to adopt the Palladian rusticated ground floor with one and a half storeys above, which relates the design to the proposed smaller elevation for Durham. The design shares with the grand Durham House scheme an unfussy, rectilinear severity, with decorative emphasis only at the centre and towards the ends, at the applied portico and at the central, first-floor windows of the framing pavilions.

For the north and south entrances, Webb proposed recessed centrepieces with apsidal, vaulted vestibules within. This was a favourite room shape of his, learned from both ancient Roman and modern Italian practice; essayed, without the apses, at Durham House, and finally achieved at the King Charles Building a decade later.

In exterior appearance, the reconstructed Belvoir owed little to Webb's palatial scheme, having more in common historically with Nottingham Castle, which was rebuilt in the 1670s by Samuel Marsh for the 1st Duke of Newcastle on a similar site. The connection between the two is clear: Marsh was paid for masonry work at Belvoir in 1654–5 and in 1667, and it is quite possible that, for at least part of the rebuilding period, he was the man in control on the site.[41] In charge of the joinery in the 1650s was Thomas Kinward, later Master Joiner of the King's Works, who had already worked with Webb on the post-fire refitting of Wilton.

Within the confines of his piecemeal rebuilding of Belvoir on the existing, irregular, courtyard plan, Webb nevertheless endeavoured to create grand effects, particularly in the north range. Entrance was made here into a large hall which extended across the central, five bays of the front. An Imperial staircase, which vies with the one at Gunnersbury for the distinction of being the first to be built in England, provided a triumphal approach to the great dining-room on the first floor. Elsewhere, other grand rooms were fitted up, notably a Long Gallery in the west wing, and an Eating Room, a Drawing Room, and a Music Room in the east wing. These were placed behind the long, undistinguished elevation which had about it rather more of the artisan Marsh than the Palladian Webb.

[41] Belvoir Castle archives, Acct. 461 and Misc. MS 67.

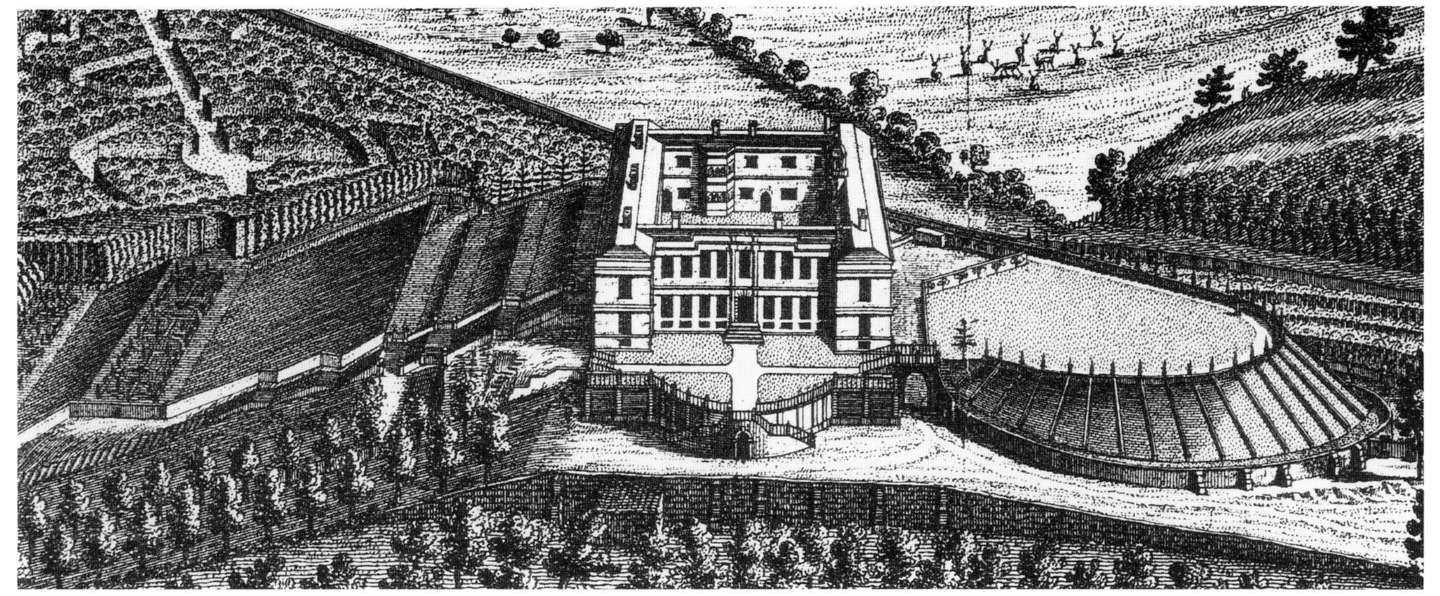

47. Belvoir Castle: bird's-eye view from the north (detail), showing Webb's rebuilt entrance front of *c.*1655–68

48. Belvoir Castle: the east front of Webb's proposed new house

49 (*right*). Prince's Lodging, Newmarket: alternative designs by Inigo Jones for the façade, designed *c.*1619–21, demolished *c.*1650

50 (*below*). Lamport Hall: Webb's five-bay west front, framed by the wings added by the Smiths of Warwick in the early eighteenth century

LAMPORT HALL

A particular error to which the seventeenth-century English gentry was said to be prone, was the refronting of old buildings in a manner 'such as shall give an idea of somewhat very fine to be expected and no whitt of it to be found'.[42] Such a 'deceiptfull disposition' was risked by Sir Justinian Isham in his improvements to his Tudor house at Lamport. He rejected proposals made by David Papillon for a completely new house and instead commissioned Webb to make additions, a course which Papillon, a very partial critic, considered 'si fort repugnant aux reigles de l'art'.[43] Webb succeeded in avoiding the usual pitfalls by providing an entirely new block which proclaimed itself as such. It was not self-sufficient, but, although it was linked at the rear to the older buildings, it was intended to be seen as being distinct from them. The house is of unusual interest because, unlike many of Webb's designs, it was built and it survives, and also because it is the most fully documented of his buildings.

Isham embarked upon the improvements to Lamport soon after his marriage in 1653 to Vere Leigh, a daughter of Thomas, Lord Leigh of Stoneleigh. In February 1654 he informed his friend Bishop Brian Duppa that 'my chiefest employment at present seems to me as naturall as to the very birds and crowes about mee, to be busy in building my nest against my wife lies downe'.[44] The circumstances of his employing Webb for the new work are not known, but he might well have been introduced to the architect by Henry Cogan, one of the overseers of Inigo Jones's will. Like Webb, Cogan came from a Somersetshire family. Isham had stayed in his house in Charing Cross in 1649, 1651, and 1653 and was the subject of the dedication of his translation, *The Court of Rome*, published in 1654.[45]

In effect, Webb provided Isham with a compact, five-bay villa, which now forms the centre of the west front of the house, wings having been tactfully added to it by the Smiths of Warwick in work which began in 1732 (pl. 50). Webb's front remains as built, save for the replacement of the mullion and transom windows by sashes, the addition by Henry Hakewill in the nineteenth century of the inscription 'IN THINGS TRANSITORY, RESTETH NO GLORY', and the addition, also by Hakewill, of the awkward, stilted pediment which replaced that by Francis Smith, which in its turn had replaced Webb's own rather curious afterthought, a dormer-like pediment of 1657.

Webb's Lamport must have been surprising in its Northamptonshire context (pl. 51). It was far more purely Italianate than Peter Mills's contemporary Northamptonshire house, Thorpe Hall, which once was attributed to Webb. The two-storey façade, although astylar, owed a great deal to Inigo Jones's Banqueting House, in its rustication and in the employment of alternating segmental and triangular pediments over the ground-floor windows. Within, Webb provided a two-storey 'High Roome', fit for the reception of 'des personnes d'honneur', together with two further ground-floor rooms and two bedrooms

[42] H. M. Colvin and J. Newman, *Of Building: Roger North's Writings on Architecture* (1981), 145.

[43] G. Isham, *The Architectural History of Lamport* (1952); Papillon's letter of 12 May 1652: Northants CRO IC 312.

[44] *The Correspondence of Bishop Brian Duppa and Sir Justinian Isham 1650–60*, ed. G. Isham (1955).

[45] Ibid. 71.

51. Lamport Hall: elevation of the west front

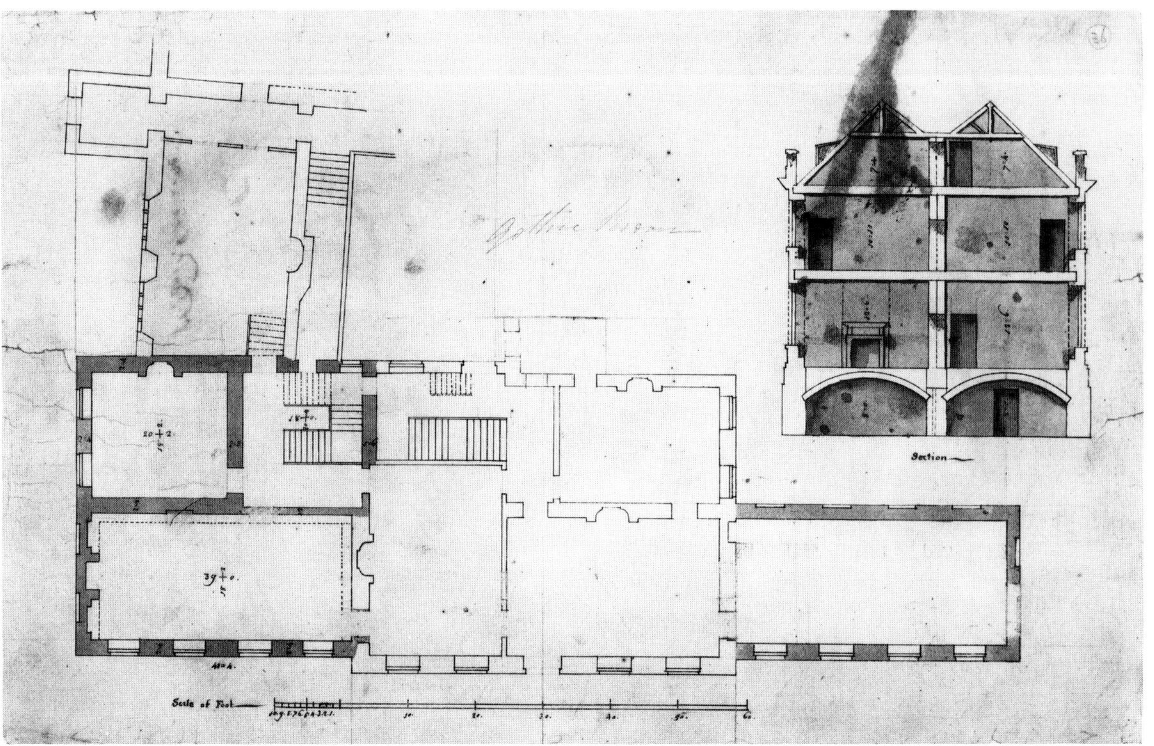

52. Lamport Hall: ground plan and section of the west range, at the time of the Smiths' addition of wings to Webb's house

above (pl. 52). This high entrance hall, three bays long, now known as the Music Hall, was entered not in the middle but close to one end, an asymmetrical arrangement which enabled the architect to combine a grand hall of 30 feet by 20 feet by 25 feet with more intimate, smaller rooms, within a block whose overall dimensions were only 55 feet by 42 feet by 27 feet. The Royalist Isham, having had to pay £1,000 to compound for his delinquency, and having moreover to find dowries for the four daughters of his first marriage, was in no position to build on a large scale. Webb supplied him with greatness in little in a compact amalgamation of one- and two-storey spaces: the two-storey hall and grand staircase (pl. 53 and 54), and the single-storey parlours and bedrooms. Webb's staircase was replaced in the nineteenth century, but some of its panels with foliage scrolls survive and its original appearance can be reconstructed.[46]

The survival of many of Webb's drawings and letters to Isham, as well as letters from the contractor Thomas Sargenson of Coventry and the mason John Greene, written to the owner during the period of his detention at St James's Palace during the summer of 1655, makes Lamport a particularly well-documented building. The letters are of interest not only for their chronicling of the progress of the building work, but also for the insights which they give into the conduct of an architectural practice, and the impression which they give of the personality of the architect. Webb wrote from his office in Scotland Yard to his patron, sending him not only general designs but also full-size details of the mouldings. These were then relayed to the contractor, who acted as an intermediary between the masons and carpenters and the owner. All the contractor's questions and proposals were addressed to the owner rather than to the architect and the latter's responses returned by the same indirect method.

In some respects, the Lamport correspondence might be untypical of the normal dealings between architect and patron. Isham was an informed client, one of the gentry who had 'some knowledge in the Theory of architecture',[47] and this clearly would have had a bearing on the correspondence. Furthermore, the generally accommodating tone of Webb's letters, his advice to Isham on buying pictures and his passing references to other work on which he was engaged at Belvoir, Drayton, and Chevening all contribute to an agreeable informality which is not only indicative of the rising status of the architectural profession, but is also suggestive of a degree of personal friendship between the two men. It is unfortunate that only one side of the correspondence survives.

The first three letters, written in June and July 1654, were concerned with the design of the front and its details, particularly the windows and the proposed portico. Webb demonstrated his concern with 'gracefulnesse' in reducing the height of the upper windows from 6 feet to 4 feet and he also revealed himself as reassuring and pragmatic: 'As for the falling out of ye Rusticks against the dore it matters not, smale things must give way to great ...' Isham himself was not always so flexible. Webb failed to convince him of the desirability of building a portico. He was, following Palladio, an enthusiastic designer of porticoes although he recognized that there was a good deal of special pleading in

[46] RCHME volume on the Country Houses of Northamptonshire, forthcoming; I am indebted to John Heward and Robert Taylor for advice on Lamport.

[47] Cf. 'A Breife ..., (see App. II).

53. Lamport Hall: the Music Hall, originally the entrance hall. The panelling is of the later seventeenth century and the plasterwork of the eighteenth century. A version of Paul van Somer's full-length portrait of Queen Anne of Denmark, painted in 1617, hangs on the north wall

54. Lamport Hall: the first-floor gallery above the staircase, which incorporates some of the carved panels of Webb's original stair

Palladio's justification for using the form—that they were used by the ancients on houses after the model of temples. He succeeded in 1655 in building the first projecting temple front on an English country house at The Vyne, the year after Isham had turned down the proposal for Lamport precisely because he thought that it would appear too temple-like. Webb, undaunted, then offered a design for a porch, praising it for adding variety to the façade as well as for being useful (pl. 55). This too was rejected. Given the emphatic plasticity of the window pediments which press against the sills of the windows above, even a porch would have been a tight fit.

By the time of the next letter, February 1655, the house had progressed as far as the raising of the walls. One bay of the older building had to be demolished where the new structure joined it.[48] Webb sent designs for all the mouldings of the outside wall and he also mentioned the hall's splendid chimneypiece, for which a fine drawing survives (pl. 56). He recommended that the lower part of this should be of Weldon or Portland stone and 'because of ye enrichments I would wish it were wrought here in Towne by Mr Marshall'. This was Edward Marshall, who worked for Webb at The Vyne, Northumberland House, and Gunnersbury. In his reply, Isham seems to have suggested that the chimneypiece could be carved in Weldon stone and plaster by Pierre Besnier, who had been appointed as successor to his brother Isaac in 1643 as Sculptor in Ordinary to King Charles I. Besnier was employed to carve the coat-of-arms cartouche over the entrance doorway at Lamport. In a letter of 12 July he informed Isham that 'yor building goeth on verie well according to yor plott and for my part the Pictures and sheilds I shall have finished the nexte weeke'.[49]

Webb advised that the upper part of the chimneypiece would be better of 'Joyners work than plaister for it will stand much neater, and not bee so subject to casualties'. He disapproved of the idea of 'yor French workman' as 'I desire alwaies to employ our own countrimen', as it is only 'want of encouragement' which 'makes them negligent'. 'Howsoever', he continued, 'if the man be able in gods name employ him rather than bee at charge to bring one from London.' These sentiments were echoed forty years later by Wren in a letter to Mr Treasurer Hawes of Christ's Hospital: 'our English Artists are dull enough at Inventions but when once a foreigne patterne is sett, they imitate soe well that commonly they exceed the originall ... this shows that our Natives want not a Genius, but education ... in designing or drawing ...'[50]

The Lamport chimneypiece design is recognizably from the same hand as the chimneypiece designed by Webb for the Earl of Peterborough at nearby Drayton in 1653, but it is more powerfully modelled, with a triangular pediment and cartouche bursting through a broken, segmental pediment. The decorative pendants and garlands are compact and bulbous and the ensemble is completed by two swans, emblematic of the Isham family. The lower part only is of stone, and the upper, as Webb advised, of wood. The carving appears to have been the work not of Besnier but of Caius Gabriel Cibber, who was to be employed again at Lamport in the designing of a wall tomb slab for the church.[51]

[48] Northants CRO IC 4957.
[49] Northants CRO IL 3956.
[50] Whinney and Millar, *English Art*, pp. 318–19.
[51] A document discovered by Sir Gyles Isham refers to the carving's being done by 'Mr Kays' (i.e. Caius); see also Northampton Museums and Art Gallery, *Sculpture in England in the 17th Century* (1968), no. 10.

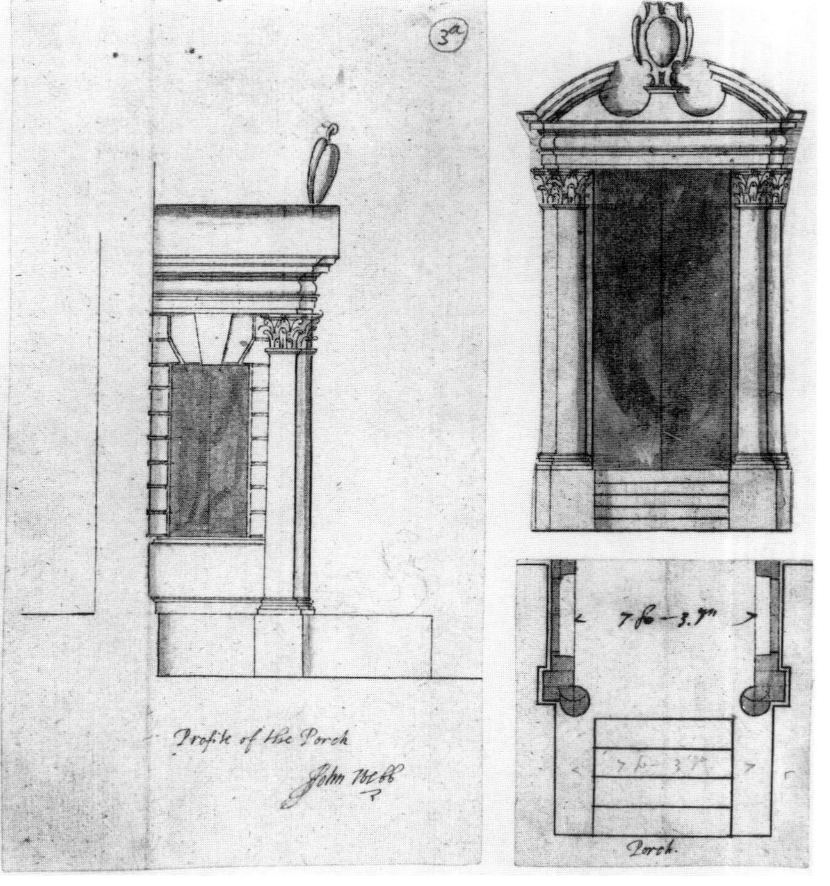

55 (*above*). Lamport Hall: unexecuted design for the porch, 1654

56 (*right*). Lamport Hall: the chimneypiece and overmantel for the entrance hall. This was executed by Cibber according to Webb's design (see pl. 53)

It is clear from the correspondence that Webb had no great faith in provincial workmen and, when they questioned the proportions of the front, he was quick to advise Isham: 'for the moulds lett not the masons trouble themselves ... but take care they worke them truly as they are made', before going on to make some basic points about laying the courses of stonework. Such information probably was superfluous, for in Sargenson Isham seems to have had a reliable contractor, who was well able to make his own pertinent suggestions. In April 1655 he wrote that, although continuing lame and unable to stir, 'I had much thought upon your building, to haue ye insides, both of Hall and Parler, to be as uniforme in the windowes as may be', and he further proposed: 'make ye 2 end walls thicker than ordinary, and the middle wall between Hall and Parler as thinn as may be, as of a foote thicke at most.'[52] Webb advised Isham to follow 'Mr Sergency's' advice and gave detailed instructions for the construction of relieving arches within the stone work at frieze level to take the weight of the cornice and balustrade, a technique which Webb had learned from Inigo Jones at old St Paul's Cathedral.[53]

Whilst in London in the summer of 1655, under guard from mid-July until October, Isham received regular progress reports from Lamport. Both Sargenson and John Greene kept him informed of the day-to-day developments in the laying of floors, the making of windows, and so on, as well as reminding him of how much stone would need to be bought to enable an early start and rapid completion during the following spring. On 19 July the contractor wrote:

> Before we can appoynt the floore for the platform of led on the top of the house we desire to know your minde how you will have it whether as my Lord St. John's house [i.e. Thorpe Hall] (which I went purposely to see) which is lead and plaine on the toppe with small gutters under the lead to carry the water to the greater gutters on the sides to be by pipes conveyed to the ground.

One week later he wrote to say that he would do 'the roofe for the leads like my Lord St. Johns', which indicates that Isham had approved the suggestion with such speed that he had scarcely had time to consult Webb. Despite all the good intentions on the parts of both Sargenson and Greene, Isham returned home to find that progress had not been all that he had hoped. He wrote on 2 November to his former fellow prisoner at St James's, Sir Ralph Verney, to say that his house was 'not yet all covered in'.[54]

The only interior for which Webb's designs survive is the entrance hall, which was altered considerably in 1686 and 1738 (pl. 57). Isham must have expressed doubts about the dimensions of this room, but Webb, in his letter of 16 April 1655, allayed his fears by saying that Lord Dacre's room (at Chevening) 'is very noble ... but I am confident yors wilbe more proportionable'. He had promoted the cause of English workmen in an earlier letter, and he advised Isham that, if he used the 'French workman', he should have him cast the statues for the niches out of 'Antique moulds', French fashions being 'fantasticall'. The statues in question were to occupy straight-headed niches on the short sides of the room. Over these were panels containing reliefs. Masks and swags adorned the frieze with busts on pedestals above. Isham appears to have taken Webb's point about French

[52] Sargenson's letters: Northants CRO IC 4968–4979.

[53] *King's Works*, iii. 151.

[54] Claydon House MS, quoted by Isham, *Architectural History of Lamport*.

57. Lamport Hall: elevation drawing for the east wall of the entrance hall, signed by Webb

59 (*above*). Lamport: unexecuted design for the Isham depository, the family mausoleum, which was to have been built next to the Church of All Saints, to the north of the Hall

58 (*left*). Lamport Hall: alternative designs for the rusticated gatepiers, one of which is surmounted by a swan, emblematic of the Isham family. The impression of the swan in the sealing wax in this drawing provided Webb with a guide for his subsequent drawing of the gatepiers in which the Isham emblem is represented more accurately

workmen: 'Phillipps the stone cutter ... furnished us with black marble for the inlays',[55] and Andreas Kearne, 'a German sculptor, brother in law to Nicholas Stone senr ... carved many statues for Sr Justinian Isum'.[56] Whether Webb's design was fully carried out is unclear. Only thirty years later the room was being wainscoted by a local joiner, possibly the better to accommodate the growing Isham picture collection. The present elaborate decoration of the room's attic storey and ceiling is eighteenth century.

There is a gap of two years in the surviving correspondence between May 1655 and June 1657, when the last three letters were written. By this time the building of the house had progressed far enough for the design of the internal doors to be under consideration. It is interesting to note that the architect's responsibility stretched even to such points as these, but, equally, it says a great deal for the variations which were expected to occur between the drawing of the designs in London and their provincial execution: 'the moving dores of your House cannot be designed until I receive from you the iust heights and bredths of them ...'[57]

The remainder of the correspondence was devoted to the gates and to the 'depository'. Rustic gatepiers were recommended as 'for the gathering of some greene it is not amisse, it being a symptome of Antiquity' (pl. 58). The gates were surmounted in Webb's design by the Isham swan. They do not survive.

The Church of All Saints, Lamport, stands close to the Hall. Sir Justinian rebuilt the chancel in 1651, not altering the medieval appearance which it retained until its classical rebuilding by William Smith in the eighteenth century.[58] Webb's depository, of 1657, a family mausoleum for the Ishams, was to be positioned next to the chancel with access through an iron, grated door (pl. 59). Externally, the depository was to be a heavily rusticated cylinder of 18 feet in diameter, articulated by blind lunette windows, surmounted by a brick dome of Pantheon-like profile and top lit by an open oculus. There was a massive severity in this design which for Webb encapsulated the necessary Roman *gravitas*: 'The outside should be rustick as I have drawne it for so the Ancients used, but it may bee made plaine if you will. ... I shall desire to know how you like it, being as it is rarely new and will take well.'

Within, the depository was to be octagonal, with a central obelisk surmounted by 'an Urne most proper for your intention'. At the base of the obelisk a step was provided 'to kneel or sett on'. Isham's suggestion that the interior might be articulated by pilasters was met by Webb's pointing out that this would increase the cost. In fact, the depository was not built at all and it was not until 1673 that a family vault was completed. This, of much more orthodox form, adjoins the chancel of the church. It was built by Henry Jones of Walgrave in a style in keeping with Webb's work on the house.

[55] Northants CRO IC 4960.

[56] Vertue, I. 98.

[57] It is interesting to compare this with the equally professional practice of John Carr in the eighteenth century. When Carr's Basildon House was being restored in the 1950s, a consignment of fittings brought from his Panton Hall included doors which fitted straight on to the Basildon hinges (*Country Life*, 161 (1977), 1299).

[58] G. Isham, *All Saints' Church, Lamport* (1950).

60. Gunnersbury House: S. Wale's view of the south front, published in 1761

GUNNERSBURY HOUSE

The proliferation of the suburban villa in the eighteenth century was one of the most significant developments in the whole history of English architecture. All around the capital in the 1720s, Defoe found evidence of the building boom as the 'present encrease of wealth in the city of London, spreads itself into the country, and plants families and fortunes'. Few of the new houses were tied to estates; rather, they were

> gentlemen's meer summer-houses, or citizen's country-houses; whither they retire from the hurries of business, and from getting money, to draw their breath in a clear air, and to divert themselves and families in the hot weather ... in short all this variety, this beauty, this glorious show of wealth and plenty, is really a view of the luxuriant age which we live in, and of the overflowing riches of the citizens ...[59]

Gunnersbury House was the suburban villa *par excellence*. For this, in retrospect perhaps the most important commission of his career, John Webb drew on the work of Palladio and Inigo Jones to produce a design of great typological significance. Begun in the late 1650s for the advocate, Sergeant John Maynard, the house became a fashionable centre in the eighteenth century when it was owned successively by the Joint Secretary to the Treasury, Henry Furnese, who was an art collector of some distinction, and then by the third daughter of King George II, Princess Amelia.[60] She held receptions 'of a most brilliant description' at the house for 'Kings, Princes, Statesmen, Poets', as well as 'people of humble birth', all of whom were 'cordially welcomed'.[61]

Gunnersbury was recognized in the eighteenth century as a house of archetypal importance. Campbell published it as a design of Jones and at least three further engravings and one group of watercolours were made of it during the course of the century (pls. 60 and 61). Defoe himself did not mention the house specifically, because 'it would take up two or three volumes ... to describe the county of Middlesex', but it appeared in the expanded, later editions of his *Tour*: 'built by Mr. Web ... the building is as plain as possible, yet there is a simple Boldness in it ...'[62] William Angus, in 1797, in his *Seats of the Nobility and Gentry*, commended especially the view from the loggia which commanded 'a fine prospect of Surry, of the Thames, and of all the Meadows on its Banks for a great extent, even to London'. Just as the Palladian villas of the Veneto looked on to the Brenta, so did the neo-Palladian villas of the home counties look over the Thames. Regrettably, the loggia did not survive long into the next century. Mr Morley, a speculator and manufacturer, demolished the house in 1800–1 and disposed of the land in lots.[63]

In the planning of Gunnersbury, Webb contrived to combine a central sequence of grand spaces for parade with more intimate suites of rooms at the angles of the building for less formal occasions (pl. 62). The grand spaces would have provided Maynard with the 'handsome and well adorned places to walk in', which Palladio recommended for the

[59] D. Defoe, *A Tour thro' the Whole Island of Great Britain*, i (1724–6), 168.

[60] Documents at Ealing Town Hall, ref. DP 119, relate to Gunnersbury and its owners.

[61] F. Turner, *History and Antiquities of Brentford* (1922).

[62] Defoe, *A Tour thro' the Whole Island of Great Britain*, iii (1742).

[63] D. Lysons, *Environs of London* (1810–11). Gunnersbury Park Mansion, the present Museum, was built on a site to the west of the demolished house.

61. Gunnersbury House: the north front and forecourt, painted *c.*1792–3 by W. Payne

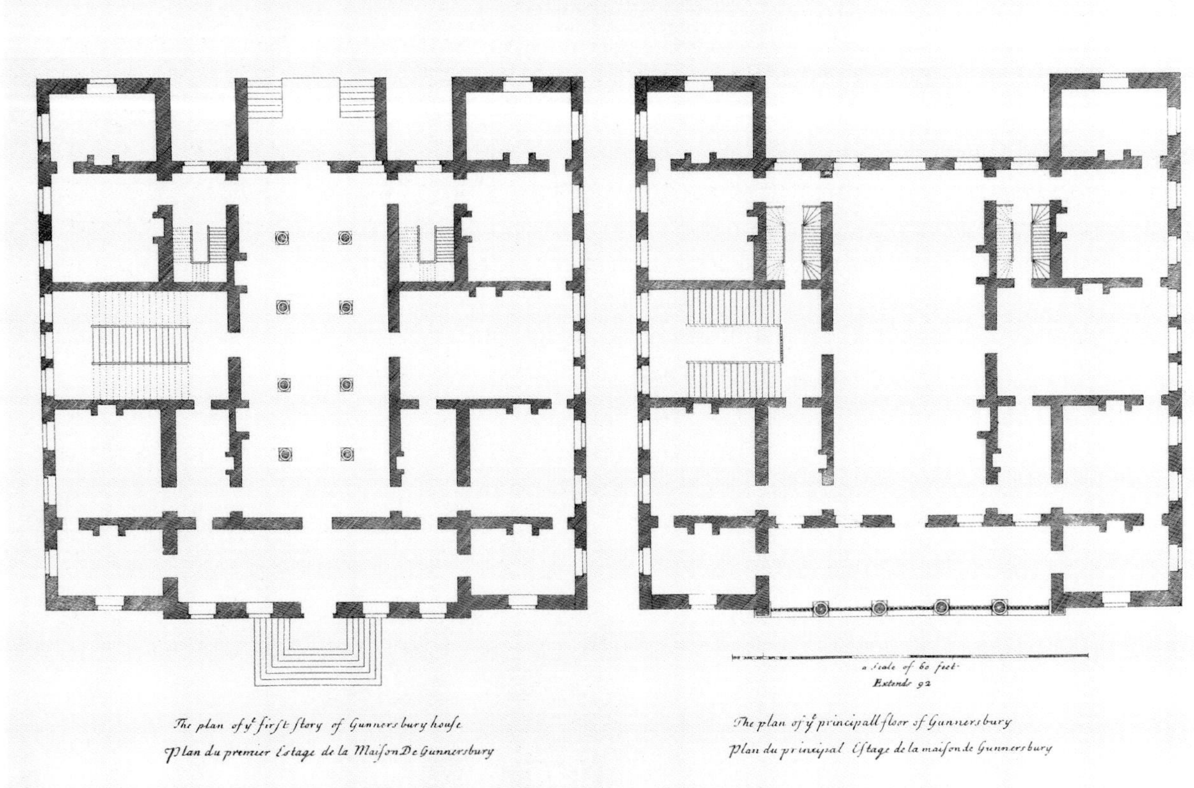

a scale of 60 feet
Extends 92
The plan of ye first story of Gunnersbury house
Plan du premier Estage de la Maison De Gunnersbury
The plan of ye principall floor of Gunnersbury
Plan du principal Estage de la maison de Gunnersbury

62. Gunnersbury House: plans of the ground and first floors (north is at the top)

houses of advocates.[64] Entry from the north was made into a paved, stone hall of eight columns, which, in the manner of Palladio's Villa Badoer, effectively divided the building into two, symmetrical halves.[65] Such columned halls had occurred before in Webb's theoretical studies and in his designs for Durham House and Belvoir Castle, but this was the first to be built and as such surely would have impressed with its unprecedented classical grandeur, although Sir Roger Pratt was probably right to complain about the lack of light in a room which was very long and relatively low with windows only at its north end.[66]

The division of the columns in the entrance hall into two groups of four gave emphasis to the central doorways, one of which gave on to the grand staircase. This, together with the example at Belvoir, introduced the Imperial staircase to English architecture. The significance of the Imperial type lies in its combination of an open well with three parallel flights, a design which first appeared at Philip II's Escorial, a building which was of some importance in the background of the Whitehall Palace designs.[67] At Gunnersbury, at the top of the first flight, the stair offered a choice of direction, dividing into two flights which returned to give access to the first-floor saloon which was aligned directly over the hall. This grand, coved room, a double cube of approximately 50 feet by 25 feet by 25 feet, was clearly in the line of descent from Newmarket, Wilton, and the Durham House and Belvoir designs. Furnese was said in 1742 to be fitting up the room 'in a most elegant Taste', proposing to hang it with his 'fine Collection of capital Pictures', which 'will render it one of the finest rooms in England'.[68] Roger North, writing in the late seventeenth century, had been less admiring, for the same reasons as Sir Roger Pratt. He was, he wrote, 'a great friend to portico walks abroad', but he found the saloon at Gunnersbury 'most unpleasant because it hath no light but from that covered walk'.[69] Pratt had been rather more sweeping in his criticism, observing that the builder ought not to 'proceede to a rash and foolish imitation' of foreign models, 'without first maturely weighing the conditions of the severall climes, the different manner of living etc. and the exact dimentions, and other circumstances of the building, especially the lights, etc. in all which thinges the Hall and Portico at Gunnersbury are verry faulty'. Pratt, however, was not an impartial critic; he was a fellow architect. He was, like North, concerned with the interior aspect, whereas the eighteenth-century critics of Gunnersbury were more inclined to praise the portico for the possibilities which it afforded for viewing the 'very delightful' prospect.[70]

The portico was the climax of Gunnersbury's grand, processional route from the ground-floor hall, up the stairs, and through the saloon. Here, Webb was building on Palladio's ideas for columned halls and saloons with loggias, and on the precedents provided by Inigo Jones at both Newmarket and the Queen's House, where he had built a similar south-facing loggia with a hexastyle portico *in antis*.

[64] Palladio, ii (1738), 37.

[65] Palladio, ii. 48.

[66] R. T. Gunther, *The Architecture of Sir Roger Pratt* (1928), 37.

[67] Cf. C. Wilkinson, 'The Escorial and the Invention of the Imperial Staircase', *Art Bulletin* (Mar. 1975).

[68] Defoe, iii.

[69] Colvin and Newman, *Of Building*, p. 130.

[70] There were exceptions: 'The portico is too large, and engrosses the whole front except a single window at each end. The staircase and salon are noble, but destroy the rest of the house; the other chambers are small, and crouded by vast chimneypieces, placed with an Italian negligence in any corner of the room' (H. Walpole, *Anecdotes of Painting in England*, iii (1763), 152).

According to the sale catalogue which was produced in 1787 after the death of Princess Amelia, there were at that time, in addition to the saloon on the principal floor, her card-room, library, billiard-room, morning sitting-room, four bedchambers, and two dressing-rooms.[71] The functions of some of the rooms can be expected to have changed after a century of use, but Webb's basic plan, as recorded by Campbell, appears to have remained. His provision of discrete, separable clusters of interconnecting rooms, disposed around the grand, formal spaces, was indicative of a new impetus in English architecture towards spatial separation and privacy.

Webb at Gunnersbury revealed himself to be a master of architectural synthesis. He took elements from the inherited classical vocabulary and skilfully balanced them against the requirements of function to produce a type of building which was new to England. The Palladian villa at its best could provide grand, formal spaces and informal rooms, without significantly sacrificing either one to the other. Webb was to refine this mode of planning further at Amesbury.

AMESBURY ABBEY

Amesbury has been described, justly, as John Webb's 'triumph in country house design'.[72] Themes adumbrated at Gunnersbury are here brought to fruition in an ensemble whose 'uncommon grandeur', C. R. Cockerell tells us, 'fills and occupies the mind'. Cockerell, visiting the house in 1823, recognized the triumph but not its author, following Colen Campbell in supposing the design to be by Inigo Jones, his genius being 'in few examples more conspicuous'.[73]

Webb's Amesbury (pls. 63 and 64), built on the site of an older Priory, was designed before 1660 for the Marquess of Hertford. Hertford died in October 1660 shortly after being restored to the Dukedom of Somerset and the title passed to his grandson who was only eight years old. The Marquess's death left his widow in some financial confusion and in letters written in 1664 she referred to debts, 'whereof there hath beene no interest paid since the Duke's death' and to 'moneys owing to the workmen for the building at Amsbury'. She feared that land would have to be sold to clear these commitments.[74]

For the sources of the Amesbury design, we must look again to Palladio and Inigo Jones. It has been suggested that the house is an elaboration of an early Palladio design, the Villa Godi at Lonedo (pl. 65), where there is a comparable symmetry about a central axis and an elevation which might have provided a model for the rear of Amesbury.[75] However, the front of Amesbury is Jonesian rather than Palladian, in the line of descent from Newmarket, although it is stamped with Webb's own distinctive mannerisms: the

[71] Copy of sale catalogue: Gunnersbury Museum.

[72] By J. Harris, in J. Harris, S. Orgel, and R. Strong, *The King's Arcadia: Inigo Jones and the Stuart Court* (1973), 207.

[73] J. Harris, 'C. R. Cockerell's "Ichnographica Domestica"', *Architectural History*, 14 (1971).

[74] Wiltshire CRO 1300/227A & B.

[75] J. Summerson, *Architecture in Britain 1530–1830* (1970), 146; Palladio, ii, 65.

dramatically heavy keystones and the alternating rusticated and ashlar masonry. In plan, the house is far subtler than the Villa Godi, and more integrated in its elements, and it is perhaps more productive to see it as a development from Gunnersbury. At Gunnersbury, the discrete clusters of interconnecting rooms were placed around the grand, formal spaces. Amesbury is smaller and tauter, the idea of interconnecting groups of rooms being retained, but communication between the suites being more direct because of the provision of corridors on both of the main floors through the centre of the house. This was made possible by the alignment of the ground-floor hall and first-floor saloon across the front of the house, rather than being placed transversely as they were at Gunnersbury.

It was the planning of Amesbury which drew the highest praise from Cockerell:

> Plan regular and remarkably elegant. Saloon above stairs delightful with handsome dressings to doors, chimney pieces and ceiling—contrivance of the staircase with backstairs in the newel the most convenient and elegant that can be conceived.... There are offices below as well as abundant bed Ro: above & I consider that for economy of convenience with proportion & effect, it may challenge any Ho: in England ancient or modern.

For his remarkable staircase arrangement, Webb could have been indebted to designs published by both Serlio and Rubens.[76] The main stair rose through two storeys to the chamber floor, whilst the central, oval service stair continued up to the cupola. This very sophisticated arrangement inspired both Sir William Chambers and James Paine to the sincerest form of flattery in their respective designs for Lord Bessborough's villa at Roehampton[77] and for Belford Hall, Northumberland.[78] In neither did the device appeal to the owners as much as it did to the architects: the servants perhaps were too close for comfort.

The disposition of the stairs appears to have been Webb's starting-point in his planning of the house. The neatness of the contrivance, allied with the provision of the corridors, enabled him to make the rear rooms especially usable as self-contained apartments, comprising bedchambers and accompanying dressing-rooms, separate from the formal sequence of hall, main stair, saloon, and portico. The saloon achieved grandeur despite its relatively modest size; its coved ceiling, accommodated within the chamber storey, recalling the Cube rooms at nearby Wilton, not only in architectural form but also in its painted decoration (pl. 66).

Amesbury was held in high regard in the eighteenth century. Although, being in Wiltshire, it is unlikely to have been known to as many people as fashionable Gunnersbury, its design did achieve a wide circulation through being published by both Colen Campbell and William Kent. It had already inspired the first house of the neo-Palladian movement and Inigo Jones Revival, William Benson's Wilbury, and Campbell and Kent no doubt recognized its significance as a precursor. They both exercised the censor's pen in altering

[76] Serlio, *Opere*, vii, fo. 149; P. P. Rubens, *Palazzi di Genova* (1622), Palazzo del Babilano Pallavicino. In both cases, such adaptation would have represented a degree of lateral thinking on Webb's part whilst scanning engravings, since neither Serlio nor Rubens provides a direct precedent. Serlio shows a central well, for water, and Rubens shows steps down to a cellar.

[77] J. Harris, *Sir William Chambers* (1970), 245.

[78] J. Paine, *Plans, Elevations & Sections of Noblemen & Gentlemen's Houses* (1767), pls. 33–4.

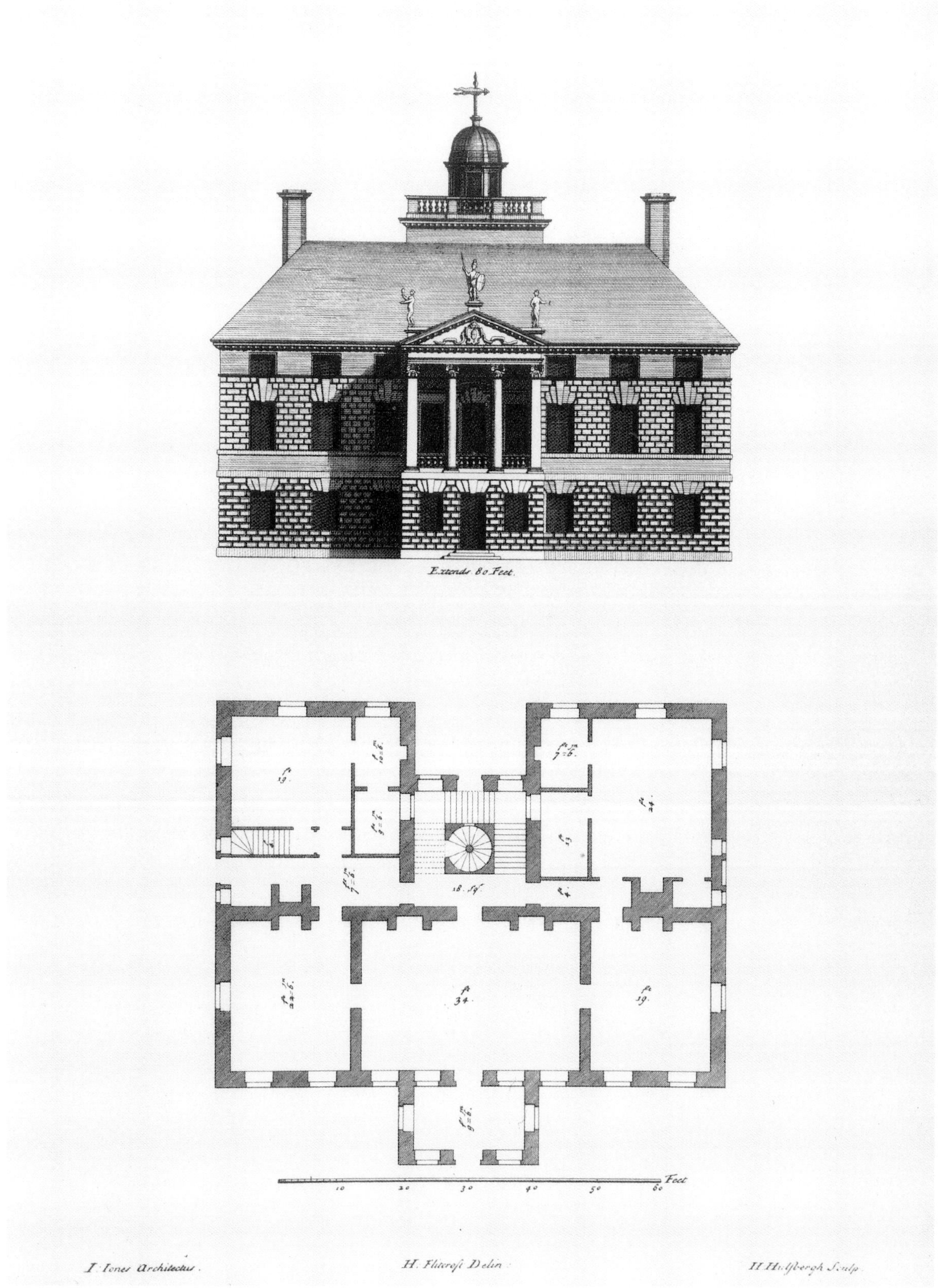

63. Amesbury Abbey: elevation of the south front and ground-floor plan, published by William Kent. The central staircase in the newel was oval, not round as shown here

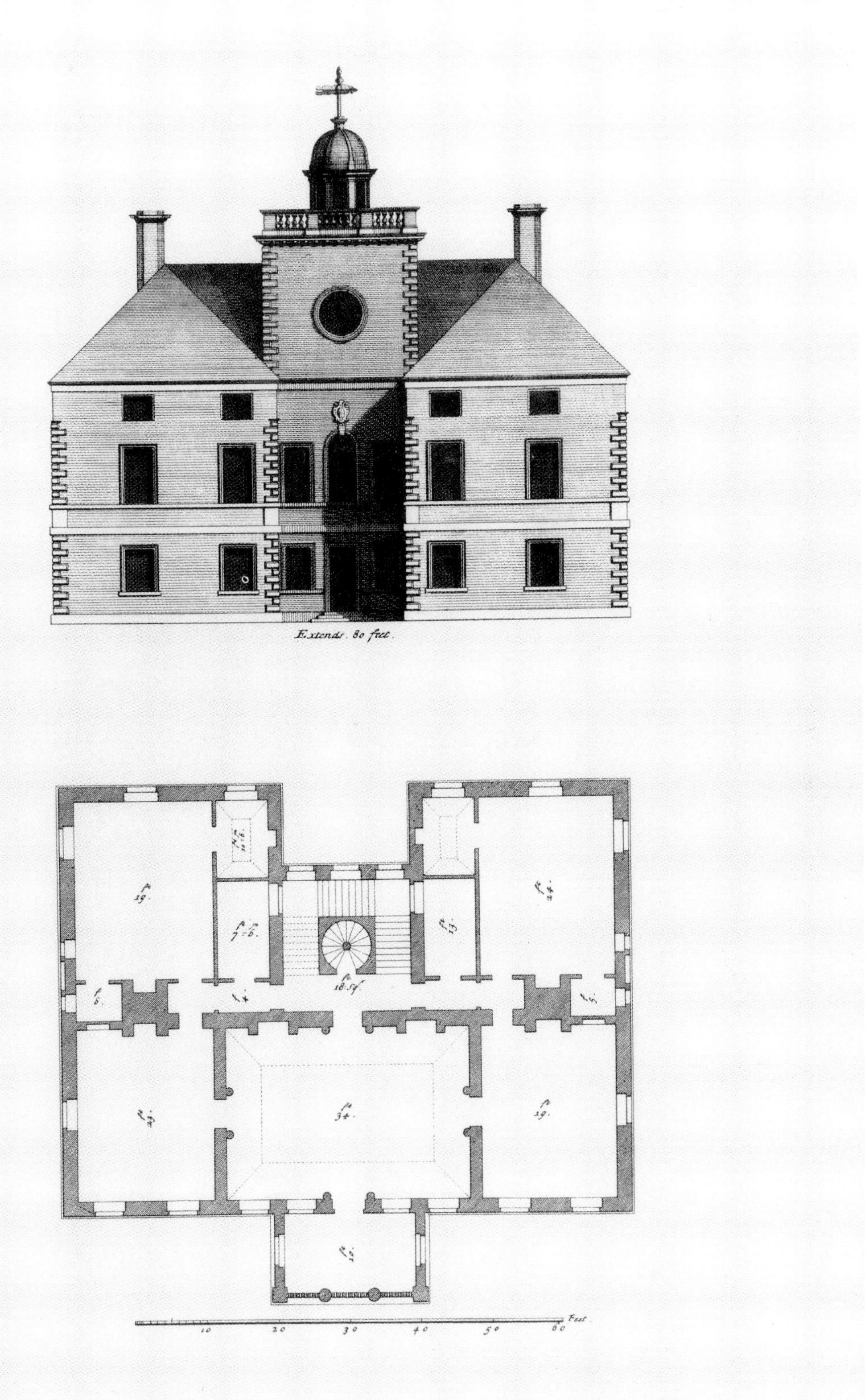

64. Amesbury Abbey: elevation of the north front and first-floor plan, published by William Kent. The north door was not placed centrally, as depicted here, but to the right of centre, to allow access into the house beneath the staircase landing

65 (*right*). The Villa Godi: plan and elevation; designed and built by Palladio in two campaigns, *c.*1537–42 and 1549–52

66 (*below*). Amesbury Abbey: cross-section of the principal south-side rooms, first floor, drawn by Wyatt Papworth in 1840–1, based on sketches made by C. J. Richardson in 1817 and 1829

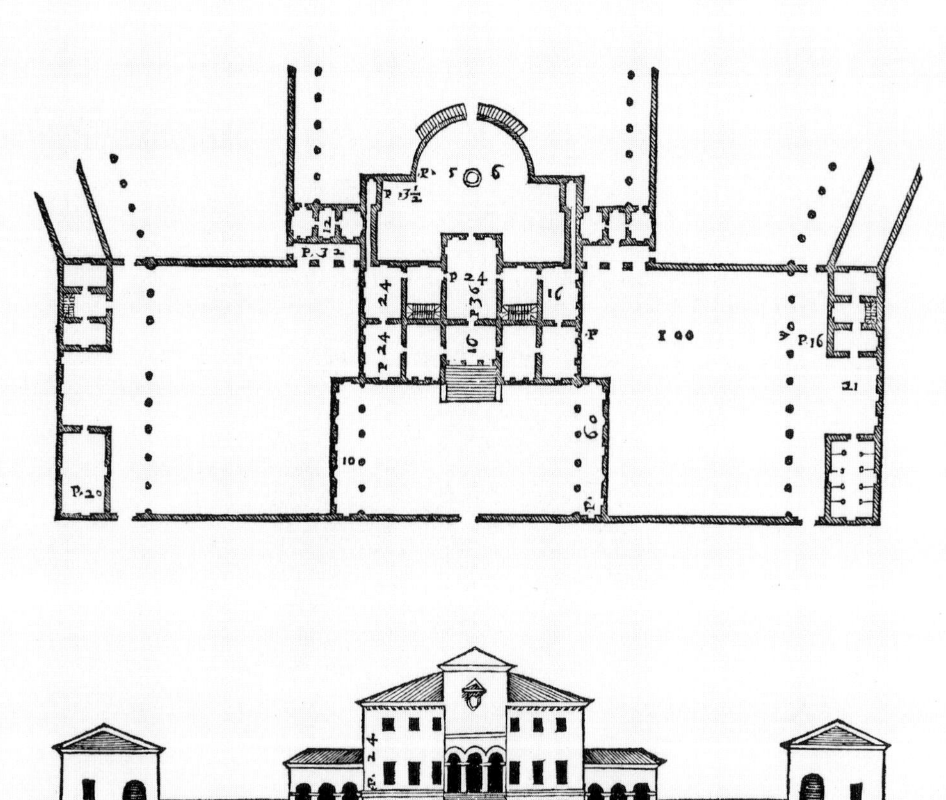

· SECTION · OF · THE · PRINCIPAL · APARTMENTS · OF · AMESBURY · HOUSE · WILTS ·

67 (*left*). Amesbury Abbey: design for a composite capital, incorporating the phoenix in flames, emblematic of the Seymour family. The inscription 'Ambresbury for Marquisse Hertford' shows that Webb's design was made before Hertford's restoration to the Dukedom of Somerset in September 1660

68 (*below*). Amesbury Abbey: the south front today, after Thomas Hopper's grandiose rebuilding of the 1830s

some of the details and in omitting Webb's emblematic, composite capitals which they perceived, probably, as being too eccentric for a canonical, Palladian design (pl. 67).

Later in the eighteenth century, when Amesbury was owned by the Duke and Duchess of Queensberry, its accommodation was increased by the addition of wings designed by Henry Flitcroft. These were swept away in the 1830s when the house was substantially rebuilt in a rhetorical late-Palladian style by the fashionable and eclectic country-house designer, Thomas Hopper (pl. 68). He retained some of Webb's walls and one of the original chimneypieces, but it is essentially Hopper's house, rather than Webb's, which we see at Amesbury today.[79]

John Webb's country-house practice, from the late 1640s until the Restoration, was considerable. In addition to the major works discussed above, he produced a Palladian design for the rebuilding of Cobham Hall in which we find the familiar coved saloon over an eight-columned entrance hall; designs for chimneypieces for Coleshill, Drayton House, and Northumberland House, and estimates for various works, including a portico, at Syon House. At Chevening he was responsible for two panelled rooms, the ground-floor saloon, which survives, and the first-floor High Room, which does not. At The Vyne, as well as building the projecting portico, he was responsibe for regularizing the garden front of the Elizabethan house and designing several chimneypieces.

In his theoretical drawings in which he redrew the reconstructions of the houses of the ancients made by Palladio and Scamozzi, and in his drawings of the Orders for a projected treatise, Webb was always methodical and always critical. He was a system-builder at heart, yet in his commissioned buildings he was always concerned to develop his systems according to the requirements of function, and he was always pragmatically prepared to trim them according to their cost. He was skilled in the synthesizing of designs, drawing repeatedly on a small number of sources, compulsively annotating and comparing 'authorities' as he worked his way towards the solution of the problem.

From a study of Webb's commissioned domestic designs, certain broad concerns and methods can be identified. He favoured grand, impressive spaces, particularly the antique sequence of columned halls and cube rooms, varying their disposition and their relationship with the stairs as the design developed. He favoured porticoes and first-floor loggias, despite the vicissitudes of the English climate, again recognizing them as significant features of classicism. Notwithstanding the preoccupation with grand effects, Webb also endeavoured to provide the separate suites of rooms which were beginning to be seen as necessary for domestic convenience.[80] This is especially apparent in his innovative designs for villas which, in effecting a balance between public and private, were justly celebrated by a later generation, even when their author was not.

The architect, wrote Roger North, following Vitruvius, 'must truckle to his master of expenditor who will truckle to ye mode of his time'.[81] The mode of the time was changing, and the architect increasingly was required to provide spaces which were geared to social

[79] With some further alterations by Detmar Blow.

[80] Cf. R. Evans, 'Figures, Doors and Passages', *Architectural Design*, 48/4 (1978), 267–78.

[81] R. North, 'Of Building', BL Add. MS 32540, fo. 46.

fastidiousness, great stress being laid in the later seventeenth and eighteenth centuries upon personal privacy.[82] At the beginning of the seventeenth century, according to North, 'the humor then being much after jollity, and dauncing, the gentry affected to have one great room', without the 'subservient accomodations, and back staires' which by the century's end had come to be regarded as essential.[83] The main stair 'must not be annoyed with disagreeable objects, but be releived of them by a back-inferior stairecase',[84] for, although 'it is no unseemly object to an English gentleman ... to see his servants and buissness passing at ordinary times',[85] 'if wee consult convenience, wee must have severall avenews, and bolting holes ... to decline passing by company posted about by accident. ... For it is unpleasant to be forc't to cross people, when one has not a mind to it, either for avoiding ceremony or any other reason.'[86] Here we see architecture being recommended as part of a defensive strategy against unwelcome and unpredictable territorial encroachments—the beginning of a trend which was to achieve its barren climax in the remorseless separation of functions and determined spatial and social prescriptions of the Victorian house, one of the main concerns of which appeared to be, to its most acute observer, 'that the paths of the servants and of the family and visitors shall never cross'.[87]

To gain an impression of the very different expectations of privacy and convenience in the mid-seventeenth and nineteenth centuries, we need look no further than the contrasting attitudes of Samuel Pepys and William Cobbett towards staying in inns. Pepys's matter-of-fact approach towards sharing rooms is demonstrated on several occasions in his *Diary*. On his tour of the West Country, for example, he and his wife came 'to a little inn, where we were fain to go into a room where a pedlar was in bed, and made him rise; and there wife and I lay, and in a truckle-bed Betty Turner and Willett'. The beds proved to be good but lousy, 'which made us merry'.[88] Cobbett, in the course of one of his 'Rural Rides', was lodged in 1826 in a room in Lyndhurst, 'the access to which was only through another sleeping room, which was also occupied'. The following morning found him hungry but 'imprisoned by ... *modesty*', 'not liking ... to go through a chamber, where, by possibility, there might be "a lady" actually *in bed*'. Hunger eventually overcame social squeamishness and the lesson was learned: 'I advise those, who are likely to be hungry in the morning, not to sleep in *inner rooms*; or, if they do, to take some bread and cheese in their pockets.'[89]

A full history of the development of the concept of privacy and its influence upon architectural requirements has yet to be written, but the realization of the importance of architecture as a civilizing force and the implicit identification of the private space as 'the locus of morality' is not new.[90] Sir William Chambers stated the case most eloquently:

The advantages arising to Society from Houses, are alone very considerable; as they have an

[82] L. Stone, *The Family, Sex and Marriage in England 1500–1800* (1979), 169–172.
[83] Colvin and Newman, *Of Building*, p. 127.
[84] Ibid. 123.
[85] Ibid. 129.
[86] Ibid. 137.
[87] H. Muthesius, *The English House* (1904–5); ed. D. Sharp (1979) 94.
[88] S. Pepys, *The Diary of Samuel Pepys*, ed. J. Warrington, iii (1955), 244, 11/12 June 1668.
[89] W. Cobbett, *Rural Rides*, ed. G. Woodcock (1967), 447.
[90] See R. Evans, *The Fabrication of Virtue* (1982), 406.

influence both on the body and mind: ... in places where the inhabitants are provided with commodious dwellings, in which they may breathe a temperate air amidst the summer's heat and winter's cold; sleep when nature calls, at ease and in security; study unmolested, and taste the sweets of every social enjoyment, we find them active, inventive and enterprising, with bodies fit for labour, and minds turned to contemplation: Agriculture and Arts flourish among them, and they are plentifully provided with all the necessaries and conveniences of Life.[91]

Chambers was writing in the 1750s, by which time the need for 'necessaries and conveniencies' was firmly established. But as early as the late-sixteenth century writers had begun to remark upon the improvements in lodgings and furnishings in houses and the increasing provision of separate service accommodation.[92] Despite Balthasar Gerbier's timely warning note, 'Too many Staires and back-Doores makes Thieves and Whores,[93] the new requirements of convenience, comfort, and privacy were increasingly satisfied by the architects of the seventeenth century by the introduction of these features and by the provision of closets and corridors. Corridors were of particular value in the new ordinance, eliminating the use of private chambers as through-rooms, speeding progress through the house, and reducing the risk of accidental contact, with all the perils which that entailed.

These requirements had arisen independently of the classical style with which they became associated.[94] It was the particular and most significant achievement of the architects of the time, especially John Webb, to harness native planning requirements to a sophisticated, European architectural style. In his design for Maiden Bradley, Webb placed rather too much reliance upon Palladian precedent and produced a plan which, although elegant, was unsuited to English requirements in that it did not achieve an appropriate separation of public and private space. In his later houses, on the grand scale at Durham House and in his prototypical villas at Gunnersbury and Amesbury, this deficiency was overcome: public and private spaces were grouped separately. At Amesbury, the provision of a central corridor, together with the Palladian nexus of groups of symmetrically disposed, interconnecting rooms, made this, in planning terms, the most remarkable and sophisticated house of the century.

[91] W. Chambers, *A Treatise on Civil Architecture* (1759), p. i.

[92] See W. Harrison, *Description of England* (1577–87); published together with J. Norden, *Surveyor's Dialogue*, 1608; ed. F.J. Furnivall (1877–8).

[93] B. Gerbier, *A Brief Discourse Concerning the Three Chief Principles of Magnificent Building* (1662), 14.

[94] The traditional English house plan, which comprised a range, one room deep, with cross wings, was beginning to be superseded in some parts of the country by the two-rooms-deep house, the double pile, as early as the mid-sixteenth century, long before it was recognized by architects that the symmetrical, rectangular house, with a central entrance, provided an ideal field for a symmetrical display of classical decoration.

5

ROYAL WORKS

As Surveyor of the Royal Works, Inigo Jones held sway over Court architecture for twenty years and Webb, quite reasonably, expected that, after the hiatus of the Civil War and Commonwealth, he would take over the official, controlling position at the Restoration. The circumstances of his frustration have been discussed above. Webb never had an official Office of Works position, yet he worked at Somerset House three times in his career, in the early and later 1630s under Inigo Jones, and again after the Restoration.[1] He was also, over a period of twenty-five years, engaged in producing abortive designs for a new Whitehall Palace and, after the Restoration, employed on the designing of a new royal palace at Greenwich. These two major palace projects drew from him his grandest performances.

SOMERSET HOUSE

Old Somerset House was demolished between 1776 and 1790 to make way for government offices: 'the largest building operation carried out at public expense during the Georgian era'.[2] The appearance of the old, decaying building was poignantly recollected in 1802 by Joseph Moser, who with others had accompanied the architect of the new buildings, Sir William Chambers, on a last tour of the old, before demolition: 'The general state of this building . . . presented to the mind in strong, though gloomy, colours a correct picture of those dilapidated castles, the haunts of spectres and residence of magicians and murderers, that have . . . made such a figure of romance.'[3]

It was at Somerset House in the 1630s that Inigo Jones, at the behest of the French-born Queen Henrietta Maria, had first employed those French decorative themes which were to be so triumphantly deployed by Webb at Wilton. Work on Somerset House was almost continuous from the late 1620s to the late 1630s (pl. 69), culminating in two grand, unbuilt designs for a new Strand frontage to the palace in 1638.[4] These, in Webb's hand, are meticulously realized drawings of Jones's ideas, which clearly are similar in mood and disposition of parts to the Whitehall drawings of the same period.

The first design, inscribed by Webb 'Not taken', shows a front of three main storeys with extensive mezzanine accommodation, with a central section of thirteen bays, linked by eleven-bay astylar blocks to three-bay end pavilions, all under a continuous roofline.

[1] His drawings for the water stairs represent his earliest surviving works for Jones: *RIBA Cat.* 46–9.

[2] *King's Works*, v. 363.

[3] Ibid. 262–3.

[4] *Worcs. Coll. Cat.* 17–19; *RIBA Cat.* 50.

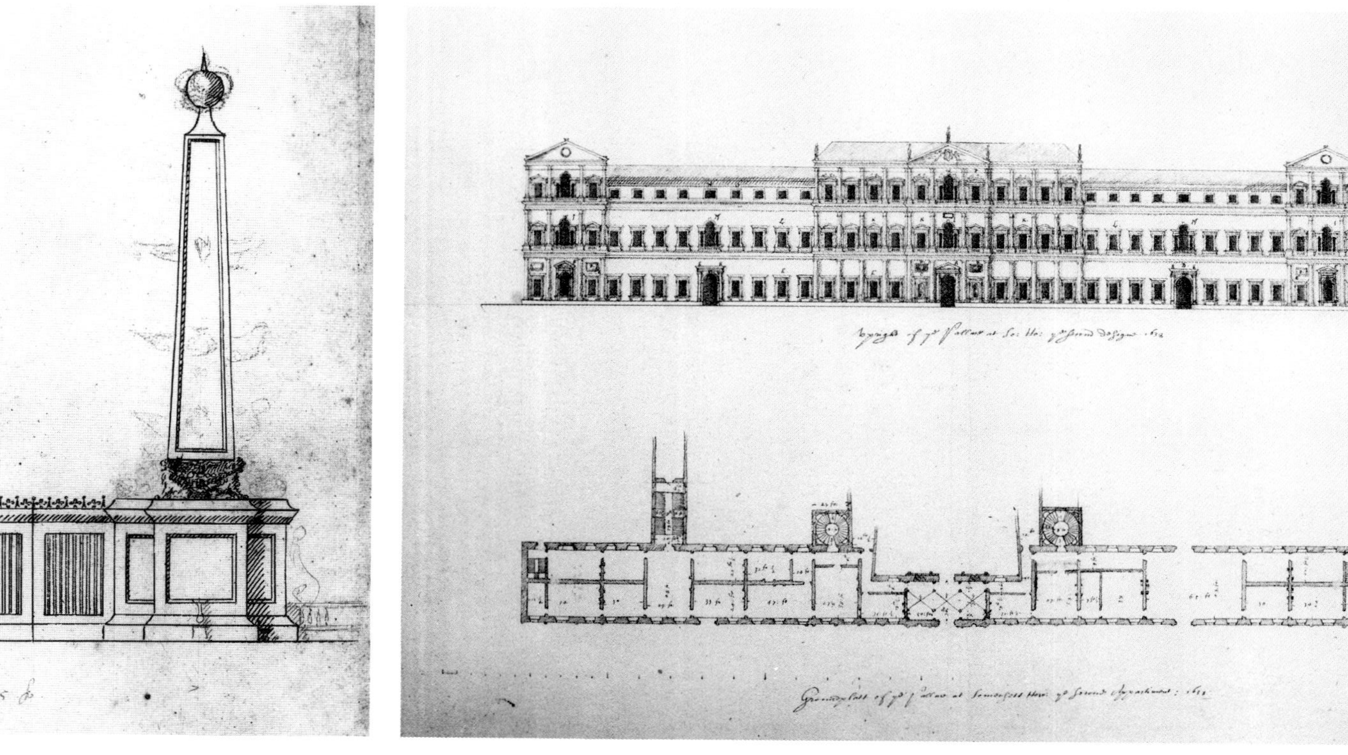

69. Somerset House: design for the obelisk gate at the head of the water stairs. This is one of a group of drawings by Webb made in the early 1630s for his earliest recorded project under the direction of Inigo Jones. The gates as built are shown in pl. 71

70. Somerset House: plan and elevation of Inigo Jones's second, unbuilt, grand design for the rebuilding of the Strand front, drawn by Webb, 1638

71. Somerset House: Webb's new range on the river front, built in 1661–4. S. Wale's view, published in 1761, shows the steeple of Gibbs's St Mary le Strand (1714–17) to the north, aligned with the water stairs

It borrows much from Scamozzi in its use of Venetian windows at the centre as an upward accent, and from Palladio's proposal for recasing the Ducal Palace in Venice.[5] In the second design, the roofline is broken as the sections between the centre and the pavilions reach only two and a half storeys (pl. 70). The overall width of the building was also reduced by six bays. The design is authentically Jonesian, relying for its effect on the accumulation of refined details rather than on the juxtaposition of large masses which Webb himself later was to favour. The designs contrast strikingly with the proto-Baroque grand design for Wilton by Isaac de Caus which dates approximately from the same time. The second Somerset House design has a clarity which is denied to the comparable Whitehall P and K schemes, because, although using the same vocabulary, it does not exhaust itself in the same ennervating pursuit of length, even though the design was longer than the available site. The plan on the same sheet as this second elevation shows that it was intended to tie in the new range with the existing sixteenth-century courtyard plan. It is, however, unlikely that the building was ever seriously contemplated.

At the Restoration, Somerset House became once more the home of Henrietta Maria, now the queen mother. She was absent in France for the whole of 1661, and when she returned in July 1662 she stayed at Greenwich because Somerset House was undergoing extensive alterations (pl. 71). These included work on 'her Mats. new stone building in the Garden ... the Stables Coachhouses and Mr. Gamon's house in Somersett Yard And the new brick building at the end of the Crosse Gallery in the Back Court of Somersett house'.[6] The 'new stone building' was the one which Colen Campbell inaccurately illustrated and which John Northouck described in 1773: 'The most beautiful front ... is towards the garden, situated upon an elevation, part of which was new building by Inigo Jones with a fine piazza and lofty apartments over it ... His design being left unfinished, the building towards the garden is very irregular.'[7] The reference to the 'piazza' brings Jones's Covent Garden to mind and, indeed, there is an apparent similarity between this arcade, with one and a half storeys over, and the arrangement of the houses on the earlier square. Campbell attributed the design to Jones, 'conducted by another hand'.[8] This hand was surely that of Webb, producing a design which recalled not only the work of Jones, but also such arcaded palazzi of the cinquecento as Palazzo Magnani in Bologna and Palazzo Guastaverza in Verona.

Work on the Gallery continued during 1663,[9] to be completed in the following year when Pepys, in October, 'saw the Queene's new rooms, which are most stately and nobly furnished'.[10] An eighteenth-century survey plan shows that, to the west of the main, five-bay elevation, there was another slightly shorter section containing a staircase which led up to the Presence Chamber, and a Privy Chamber, after which were the private apartments built for Anne of Denmark.[11] Two bays of the Presence Chamber were within the main building, whilst the first quarter of the room was in what in elevational terms

[5] D. Lewis, *The Drawings of Andrea Palladio* (1981), 204–5.
[6] *King's Works*, v. 255.
[7] J. Northouck, *History of London* (1773).
[8] Campbell, i.
[9] Cf. *Journal des Voyages de M. de Monconys*, ii (1666), 9: Somerset House 'où loge la Reyne mere, qu'elle fait rebastir à present pour la rendre un peu plus agréable' (May 1663).
[10] S. Pepys, *The Diary of Samuel Pepys*, ed. J. Warrington, ii, (1953), 59, 18 Oct. 1664.
[11] *King's Works*, v, fig. 22.

was the subsidiary building. Webb appears to have been forced to fit his new work into a rather constricted site, whilst giving emphasis to a central section which was not large enough for the spaces which it had to enclose. His design is necessarily a compromise, but none the less successful. The new addition was an elegant adornment of the river front and Chambers paid the tribute of echoing it in his Strand front entrance block.

WHITEHALL PALACE

Whitehall Palace was the main London residence of the sovereign between the reigns of Henry VIII and William III, but, being the subject of constant, piecemeal alterations, was, in relation to Louis XIV's Louvre and Philip II's Escorial, a palace in little more than name. Inigo Jones's Banqueting House was, wrote Chamberlain in 1621, 'too faire and nothing suitable to the rest of the house',[12] and in 1665 Sorbière referred disparagingly to the complex as 'a heap of Houses, erected at divers times, and of different Models'.[13] Building was carried on throughout the 1660s, Pepys being conducted round 'the King's new buildings at White Hall, very fine' by Hugh May in 1668,[14] but the making of a very detailed survey plan in 1669–70 was perhaps indicative of a desire on the part of the King to rationalize and make do.[15]

An attempt had been made to put the palace up for sale in 1658, following the death of Cromwell,[16] but nothing came of this and it stood empty until the Restoration, when Webb, styled 'surveyor of the King's houses', was granted £2,000 by the Lords and Commons and the Council of State to prepare Whitehall for the return of the King.[17] By his own account, he made it ready in a fortnight at a cost of £8,140 5*s*. 2*d*., of which he had received at the time of his petition only £500.[18] It is probably that, with his petition and the attached 'Breife', detailing his faithful service rendered to Charles I, he submitted certain of his plans for a new Whitehall Palace. These were in 1662 presumed by his son-in-law Dr John Westley to be fairly commonly known in Court circles, for in a letter to the Duke of Ormond he refers to Webb as 'a person well knowne to his Majtie and had not the place been disposed of at Bredagh, hee had beene surveyor generall of England. I presume yor Grace hath seene the Draught hee prepared for his Majtie the rebuilding of Whitehall.'[19] Webb himself refers to this project in the brief:

> he was Mr Jones Deputy and in actual possession of the Office upon his leaving London and attended his Matie in that capacity at Hampton Courte and at ye Isle of Wight where he received his Maties comand to designe a Pallace for Whitehall which he did untill his Maties unfortunate calamity caus'd him to desist.[20]

[12] In a letter to Sir Dudley Carleton, 23 April. (N. E. McClure (ed.), *The Letters of John Chamberlain* (1939)).

[13] Sorbière, *A Voyage to England* (1665), 16; see *Survey of London*, xiii, pt. ii (1930), 41.

[14] Pepys, *Diary*, iii (1953), 253, 29 June 1668.

[15] *King's Works*, v, pl. 36.

[16] Ibid. 265.

[17] *CSPD 1659–60*, p. 600, 16 May 1660.

[18] PRO SP 29/5 74 (see App. II).

[19] Bod. Carte MS 31, fos. 440–1; letter dated 19 Mar. 1661 (OS); for Westley, see R. Loeber, *A Biographical Dictionary of Architects in Ireland 1600–1720* (1981), 112–13.

[20] PRO SP 29/5, 74. 1 (see App. II).

Charles I was at Hampton Court from June to November 1647, and from then until December 1648 at Carisbrooke Castle on the Isle of Wight.

Charles II's interest in reviving the scheme is evidenced not only by Webb's drawings, one of which is dated 'Oct 17 1661', but also by a meeting recorded by John Evelyn in October 1664:

> his Majestie ... asked me if I had any paper about me un-written, and a Crayon; I presented him with both, and then laying it on the Window stoole, he with his owne hands, designed to me the plot for the future building of Whitehall, together with the Roomes of State, and other particulars, which royal draft, though not so accurately don, I reserve as a rarity by me.[21]

It is not, of course, clear from this whether the King was sketching his own design, one by Webb, or the one by the tiro Wren which was inspired by Webb and has been dated to 1664.[22] Whichever design it was, the passage indicates that here, as at Greenwich, the King was making Evelyn party to his fantasies of architectural grandeur, perhaps with the very practical end in view of sounding general opinion about the project: Evelyn was not a secretive man. The news certainly reached the Venetian ambassador, who dispatched the information: 'The King has decided to have Whitehall rebuilt in the style of the banqueting hall.'[23]

Plans therefore were afoot to rebuild the Palace in 1647–8, and again in the early 1660s, but the seeds of the idea probably were sown long before in the mind of Charles I during his visit to the Court of Philip IV. When, as Prince of Wales, he visited Madrid in 1623 with the Duke of Buckingham, in the unsuccessful pursuit of a Spanish bride, the Infanta María, sister to the King, he was accommodated in the old palace, the Alcázar.[24] This was a rectangular fortress built around two, large arcaded courtyards which were separated by a spinal range which contained the monumental, ceremonial staircase, and divided the King's and Queen's sides of the palace. It was in this building that the dual functions of royal residence and centre of government were served in a strictly hierarchical fashion which greatly impressed the visiting Prince. He endeavoured later, to his ultimate cost, to emulate the intense formality of the Court of Philip IV on less conducive English soil, after he had himself become King. The Alcázar was refaced and partially remodelled by Gómez de Mora three years after Charles's visit. Prior to this, although it contained several stately rooms, it was no match for the Escorial as a coherent piece of absolutist architecture. Admired throughout Europe as 'an Entire and glorious Fabrick',[25] the Escorial (pl. 72) was visited by Charles and Buckingham on their way home and

[21] J. Evelyn, *The Diary of John Evelyn*, ed. E. S. de Beer (1959), 466, 28 Oct. 1664.

[22] K. Downes, 'Wren and Whitehall in 1664', *Burlington Magazine*, 113 (1971), 89–92.

[23] *Calendar of State Papers, Venetian, 1664–6*, p. 55.

[24] P. Gregg, *King Charles I* (1981), 82–3; J. Elliott, 'Philip IV of Spain' in A. G. Dickens (ed.), *The Courts of Europe* (1977), 172–3.

[25] R. Bargrave, 'A Relation of Sundry Voyages and Journeys' (*c*.1646), Bod. Rawlinson C. 799, fo. 129. Plans of the Escorial were published in 1587 by Pedro Peret (see O. Schubert, *Geschichte d Barock in Spanien* (1908), 37–8). It was referred to as 'the most magnificent pallace of all Europe ... the fairest building that I ever saw in my life ... a hundred times more magnificent than ... any in Italy' (J. Eliot, *Ortho-epia Gallica* (1593), 44–5). Francisco de los Santos's *Descripcion del Real Monasterio de S. Lorenzo del Escorial* appeared in 1657, with further editions in 1667, 1681, 1698, and 1764. An abridged, English version appeared in 1671. See also G. Kubler, *Building the Escorial* (1982).

72. The Escorial: view from the west, published in 1809. This vast monument (680′ by 530′), part monastery, part palace, built by King Philip II in the sixteenth century, was visited by Charles, Prince of Wales, and his companion, the Duke of Buckingham, in 1623 on their way home from Madrid. Reminiscences of it recur in the abortive schemes for Whitehall Palace

73. Whitehall Palace: reconstruction of the design for the palace, published in 1749, based on the Webb drawings published by William Kent. The view here is from the Charing Cross side

reminiscences of it recur in the abortive schemes for Whitehall which were produced for the King by Jones and Webb (pl. 73).

The first documented evidence for Charles's encouragement of these schemes dates from the 1630s. A letter written by one Richard Daye in 1638 states that 'they say His Majesty hath a desire to build [Whitehall] new again in a more uniform sort',[26] and, *a fortiori*, Sir William Sanderson, in his 1658 *Compleat History of the Life and Raigne of King Charles*, refers to the imposition of levies for a palace attendant upon the Londonderry Charter, datable approximately to 1637–9. This was an instance of the King's endeavours through the office of Star Chamber to raise money without reference to Parliament. On this occasion, those concerned were to have

> contributed a very ample Sum of Money by way of Composition towards the erecting of a Royal Palace for his Majesties Court in Saint James's Park, according to a Model drawn by Inigo Jones his excellent Architectour, and to have taken down White-hall towards the Thames, carrying the common way in the room thereof, directly from Charing-cross straight through Cannons- row to Westminster hall leaving the River-side an open Wharf quite along[27]

There was, therefore, to be a new palace stretching from Whitehall into the park, with the road being moved closer to the riverside. Although the scheme then and later never reached the stage of being referred to in Works Accounts, its paper reality is attested by a large body of drawings (about seventy) which are now mainly at Chatsworth and Worcester College.

These drawings (not, by far, a complete set) were in the late seventeenth and eighteenth centuries presumed to be from the hand of Inigo Jones, but in 1912 J. A. Gotch suggested that they were in fact by Webb,[28] and later, in a magisterial study, Margaret Whinney confirmed the draughtsmanship (though not in all cases the ideas expressed) as being in almost all instances that of Webb and classified the drawings into seven groups from three periods.[29] Forty years later, Whinney's categories still obtain and provide the necessary basis for any rehearsal of the evidence. The seven groups are as follows: P ('Preliminary'); K (the basis of the engravings published by William Kent,[30] which provided a rich crop of Jonesian details for the neo-Palladians in the early eighteenth century); C (used by Campbell for *Vitruvius Britannicus*);[31] E (a series of 'Elaborate' drawings); T ('Taken' to Charles I); D (a 'Dated' drawing), and S (the 'Small' scheme). There are two further drawings in an unknown hand (Z).[32]

The drawings demonstrate how, over a period of twenty-five years, Webb learned from and then adapted the work of Jones, before evolving a style which was very much his own.

The drawings in group C were allegedly made in 1639 by Jones and, though they are

[26] E. S. de Beer, 'Whitehall Palace: Inigo Jones and Wren', *Notes & Queries* (30 Dec. 1939), 471–3.

[27] Ibid. According to Sanderson, the City of London's 'usurpation of more liberty than their Patent would impower' in 'their Plantation of London Derry in Ireland' was questioned in Star Chamber and appropriate fines 'imposed upon the Undertakers'.

[28] J. A. Gotch, 'The Original Drawings for the Palace at Whitehall', *Architectural Review* (June 1912).

[29] M. Whinney, 'John Webb's Drawings for Whitehall Palace', *Walpole Society*, 31 (1946), 45–107. The drawings referred to in the present account follow Dr Whinney's numeration.

[30] Kent, i. pls. 1–50.

[31] Campbell, ii. pls. 2–19.

[32] John Harris has added a second Z drawing to the one identified by Dr Whinney: *Worcs. Coll. Cat.* 56.

loosely relatable to the P scheme in the disposition of courts, their general handling, the inaccuracy in the rendering of the Banqueting House, and the indiscipline of the proportions rule out the attribution if not the date. They were made available to Campbell by William Emmett, the son of Maurice Emmett, Master Bricklayer in the Royal Works. The Works connection could be a guide to the accuracy of Emmett's statement that 'The incomparable architect Inigo Jones ... in ye year 1639 presented these designes for ye building of Whitehall to King Charles ye First: which through ye iniquity of ye Times could not be put into execution,'[33] but it does not guarantee it. The looseness of handling of the drawings distinguishes them from others in the Whitehall group and it is not impossible that Emmett was wholly mistaken and that these drawings emanate from the office of Wren rather than from that of Jones. This becomes more likely when Wren's small post-fire scheme of 1698 is considered: it combines Webb's S scheme with aspects of the C plan.[34] The C drawings certainly have no connection with Webb, so, for the purposes of the present study, can be deemed to be irrelevant. All the other schemes (except Z) are in Webb's hand and many have inscriptions written by him.

Sir John Summerson has argued that, of these other schemes, only P can be said to reflect the ideas of Inigo Jones.[35] It is for a palace of eleven courts, in St James's Park (thus leaving space for a new riverside road), twice the size of the Escorial. The Idea behind the Escorial was probably the Temple of Solomon, a building which exerted considerable fascination from the sixteenth to the eighteenth century.[36] Reconstructions of it, following the dimensions given in the Bible, were seen as test cases to prove the compatibility of Christian revelation and the culture of classical antiquity, a correspondence in which John Webb the sinologist would have rejoiced.[37]

The building of the Escorial had been completed under the direction of Juan de Herrera,[38] and it was one of his pupils, the Jesuit Juan Bautista Villalpando, who was responsible for the most renowned published reconstruction of the Temple of Solomon.[39] The reconstruction certainly would have been known to Jones, as would the Escorial itself, through engravings. That it was of significance for Webb as well need not be doubted (cf. Greenwich Palace), and even Sir Roger Pratt, who tends to be considered a less archaeologically inclined architect than either Jones or Webb, nevertheless subscribed to the prevailing seventeenth-century view of the continuity of history: 'It is conceived that the example of all good Architecture was originally taken from the Temple of Solomon, and from the Jews communicated to the Grecians, from thence to the Romans, and from them to their Provincials.'[40]

Jones's designing of a New Jerusalem in St James's Park would have underlined the

[33] Whinney, 'Drawings', p. 48.

[34] M. Whinney, *Wren* (1971), pl. 153.

[35] J. Summerson, *Inigo Jones* (1966), 127–34.

[36] R. Taylor, 'Architecture and Magic: Considerations on the Idea of the Escorial', in D. Fraser, H. Hibbard, and M. Lewine (eds.), *Essays in the History of Architecture Presented to Rudolf Wittkower* (1967), 81–109.

[37] Cf. W. W. Appleton, *A Cycle of Cathay* (1951) 19–20, for those prodigious leaps of the imagination by which Jesuits in China were able to link Catholicism with the teachings of Confucius.

[38] J. B. Bury, 'Juan de Herrera and the Escorial', *Art History*, 9/4 (1986), 428–49.

[39] J. Prado and J. B. Villalpando, *In Ezechielem explanationes*, ii (1604). The plates of the temple were re-engraved by Hollar for Bishop Brian Walton's *Biblia polyglotta*, i (1657), for which Webb drew the title-page.

[40] R. T. Gunther, *The Architecture of Sir Roger Pratt* (1928), 286.

Solomonic connotations of Stuart kingship which had been reinforced by Bishop Williams in his sermon *Great Britain's Salomon* (*sic*), preached at the funeral of James I.[41] The building of the palace would have provided 'an indestructible guarantee of the sovereign values which the house of Stuart embodied' and, moreover, supplied 'a grave and fitting backcloth for the bloodier revolution which it would most certainly have helped to precipitate'.[42]

Both the Escorial and Villalpando's reconstruction of the Temple gain their effects by massive extent, their rooflines broken by towers, but the buildings generally being accumulations of small units, without Baroque emphasis. This is precisely the nature of Jones's palace: it is a collection of small statements, given emphasis at appropriate points by pavilions, in the manner of Philibert de l'Orme's unexecuted design for the Tuileries (pl. 74).[43]

One of the most striking features of Jones's design (pl. 75) was the large round court, inspired perhaps by the circular atrium in Scamozzi's reconstruction of Pliny's villa at Laurentium: most of Jones's detailing is Scamozzian.[44] The use of the circular court at Whitehall intrigued Walpole, who found it 'without meaning or utility', but Whinney suggests that it might have had a theatrical function.[45] This brings to mind Jones's reconstruction of Stonehenge as a Roman temple, which Webb on his behalf supported by reference to Vitruvius' description of the classical theatre. It might be that the introduction of a circular court at Whitehall was a parallel no less archaeological than that between the Escorial and the Temple of Solomon.[46]

The King's and Queen's courts on the park side of the P-scheme palace, behind the royal apartments, were distinguished by caryatid porticoes, reminiscent of Lescot's figures at the Louvre. Between these courts, with its entrance on the great, central, colonnaded court, was the chapel, in precisely the same relative position as that of the Escorial (P4), replacing the staircase, which in earlier drawings occupied this space. Jones's two main staircases are of especial interest (P1, 2, 3). They do not follow the Escorial in being of the Imperial open type, which Webb was to favour later in domestic works, but they are of three flights. Two vaulted flights lead to a mezzanine, after which one open return flight in each case leads to the upper floor. Such a scheme occurs in the Scuola di San Rocco in Venice, of *c.*1550, and Jones must have been aware of it. His stair employs the illusionistic device of varying the width of the space: the upward flights to the mezzanine grow narrower, and would have appeared therefore to be longer, whilst the return widens and would have appeared, when ascending, to be shorter.

The P scheme does not include the Banqueting House, a building which was to cause a great deal of trouble in many of the later schemes because of its scale and its unusual disposition, raised on a half-storey basement. It is surprising that Jones would have been prepared to sacrifice his masterpiece, but it demonstrates perhaps that he had not

[41] G. Parry, *The Golden Age Restor'd* (1981), 31–2.

[42] Summerson, *Inigo Jones*, pp. 127–34.

[43] A. Blunt, *Philibert de l'Orme* (1958), pls. 56–7.

[44] J. Harris, S. Orgel, and R. Strong, *The King's Arcadia* (1973), 146–7.

[45] Whinney, 'Drawings', pp. 62–3.

[46] Cf. A. A. Tait, 'Inigo Jones's "Stone-Heng"', *Burlington Magazine*, 120 (1978), 155–8.

74. Whitehall Palace: elevations of river and park fronts (P8)

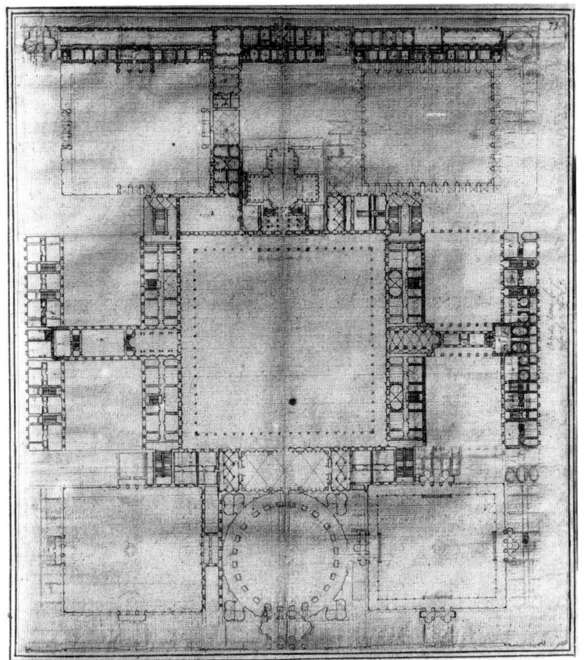

75. Whitehall Palace: sketch plan (P4). The round court is at the Thames side of the palace, with the royal apartments facing the park

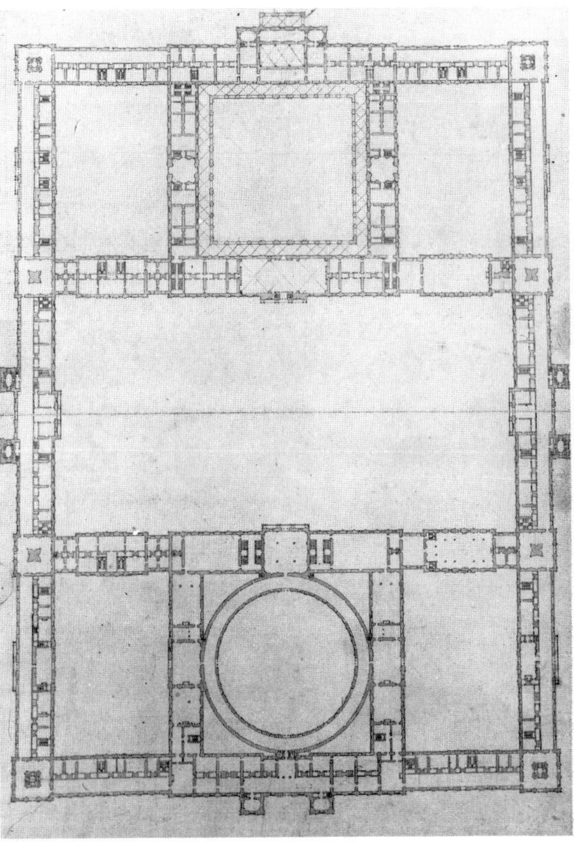

76. Whitehall Palace: first-floor plan (K2), cf. pl. 73. The round court is now on the park side, together with the state rooms. The Banqueting House is at the south-east corner of the great central court, lower left on the plan

77. Whitehall Palace: elevations of river and park fronts (K6)

envisaged the Banqueting House as being from the first a stage in the building of a new palace.[47] It is inconveniently aligned in relation to the river, and none of the later plans which include it is wholly satisfactory.

The K scheme is datable to the same time as P (1637–9) and represents an alternative plan which includes the Banqueting House.[48] It is for a deeper palace than P, stretching into the park and also projecting a not impossible 40 feet into the river. The state rooms remain on the park side and the circular court has been moved there as well (pl. 76). The great distance which visiting ambassadors would have had to travel through the palace to reach the King, having arrived by water, would have emphasized the monumental nature of their undertaking and engendered an appropriate sense of awe.[49] The scheme as a whole has greater clarity than P, being more conveniently planned and having ranges of two and three storeys without the blurring intervention of two-and-a-half storey sections which gave P an unrelieved aspect (K6, 7) (pl. 77). With this scheme we find 'an ambition to generalise loftily', which for Summerson results in the loss of what matters so much in Jones, 'precision of contrast and delicacy of articulation'.[50] The inference to be drawn is that, if K is not by Jones, then it must be by Webb, but it is rather an accomplished design for the Webb of the later 1630s, even allowing for the fact that he was working on Wilton at that time. Even if we suggest a later dating, the directness of the scheme's development from P in its use of entrance towers, wall arches, and the variety of room sizes suggests the influence of the older man. K is perhaps a work of collaboration between Jones and Webb, with the pupil drawing out and embellishing a series of given ideas, rather than working it all out for himself, just as he was at Somerset House in 1638 and, indeed, at Wilton.

Whilst P is to be regarded as Jonesian, and K as by Jones and Webb together, the E scheme can only be by Webb alone. It is a development of the earlier designs, but in the ideas expressed and in the style of draughtsmanship it compares with certain of the theoretical drawings[51] and with the designs for Durham House, and is datable therefore to the mid-1640s. The design draws on both P and K in two different, related sets of drawings, both highly finished sets of elevations without plans. They were possibly intended to be presentation drawings with which Webb could underline his claim to Jones's position as Surveyor in more propitious times.

Behind the three-storey park front (E9) (pl. 78) is a single great court, with pedimented blocks on all four sides. On the other side, in the same position as in K, are the Banqueting House and its pendant (E1). The river front is of two storeys, with three-storey end pavilions, with a dome over the entrance surmounted by the figure of Neptune. The change from the two storeys at the river to the three at the park is effected half-way along

[47] Cf. Webb's note on the Corinthian Hall in his copy of Palladio's *Quattro libri* (ii. 39), at Worcester College: 'But where this hall is made to stand by itselfe as ye Banquetting house at Whitehall doth, or where the work is very great, then it may be made vaulted . . .'

[48] The drawing technique of the K-scheme elevation and sections is very similar to the technique of the Somerset House wash drawing of 1638 (*Worcs. Coll. Cat.* 17).

[49] Cf. H. Murray Baillie, 'Etiquette and Planning of State Apartments in Baroque Palaces', *Archaeologia*, 101 (1967), 169–99.

[50] Summerson, *Inigo Jones*, p. 128.

[51] Cf. *RIBA Cat.* 194–204.

78. Whitehall Palace: elevation of park front (E9)

79. Whitehall Palace: cross-section behind the river front, showing central, circular courtyard (E12)

80. Whitehall Palace: detail of courtyard elevation (E16)

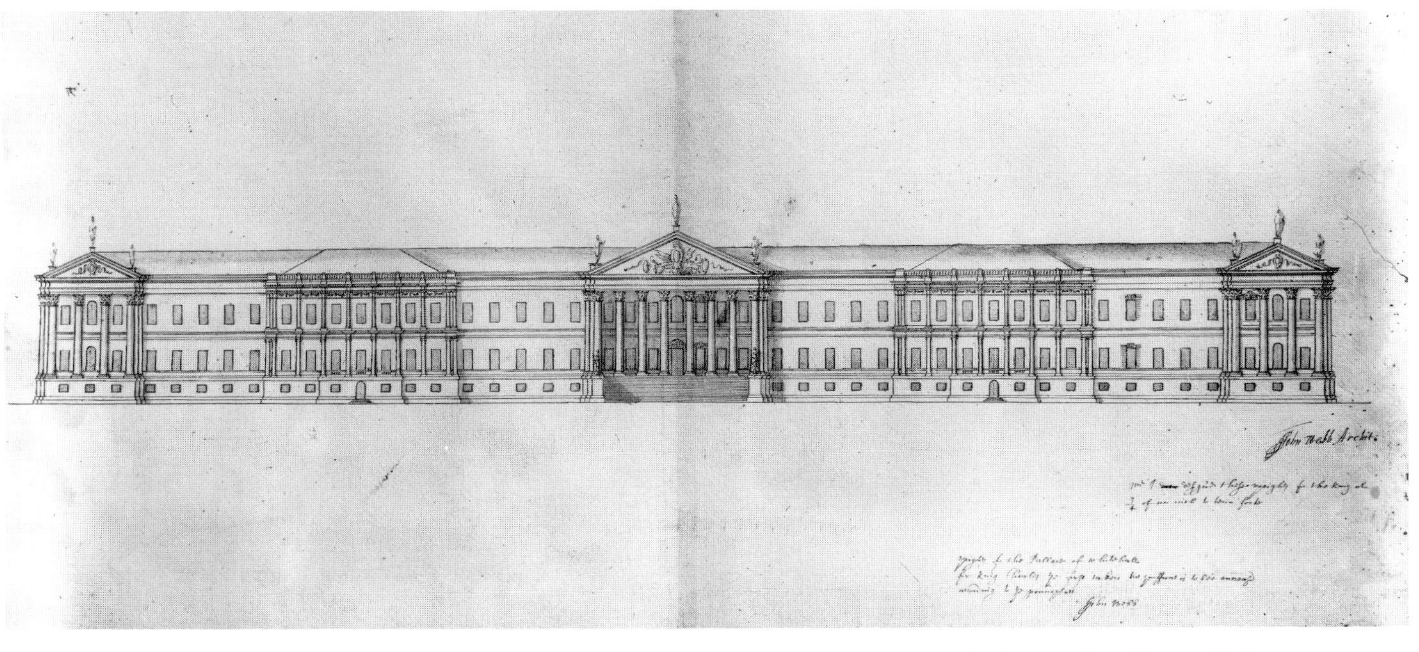

81. Whitehall Palace: the 'Taken' elevation of the river front, including the Banqueting House (T3)

the long, side ranges (E4). In the centre of the three-storey section is a side entrance, marked by cupolas which recall the K scheme. This asymmetrical arrangement makes it difficult without the benefit of a plan to see how the central courts were to be organized. A cross-section of the courts directly behind the river front shows that there were to be five small ones there (E12), some containing caryatids (pl. 79). The central court was to be circular, with a giant order of columns carrying statuary. As with the earlier designs, there is much use in the E scheme of surface decoration and, despite the use of the courtyard giant order (more Palladian here than Baroque), Webb's own identifiable mature style has not evolved, even though there are intimations of it in the heavy voussoirs within pediments which were to appear in their most emphatic form at Greenwich. His handling of details in the E scheme is more idiosyncratic than the overall disposition of the elevations. The manner in which the voussoirs are allowed to cut into the frieze, for instance (E15, 16) (pl. 80), is indicative of a trained mind which knows precisely when and how to break the rules.

In comparison with the schemes which have gone before, T shows a markedly different emphasis and is in keeping with what is known of the Webb style of the later 1640s. Like the Durham House elevation of 1649, it is concerned with large accents, employing the giant order, rather than treating the elevation as an accumulation of small units. The single surviving elevation for the scheme (pl. 81) does look barer on paper than it would have done if built, because the details have not been drawn: from the decorative point of view, the development from E to T would not have been such a leap as might appear. The plans develop ideas adumbrated in P and K and, despite additions and variations, the scheme is comprehensible as part of the whole sequence of designs. It does not so much embody new ideas, apart from the introduction of the giant order in Baroque fashion at points of emphasis, as refine and adapt elements which were present already in the earlier projects. It does this with great skill, and it is with the T scheme that Webb can be seen to have emerged from Jones's shadow as an independent architect of high standing.

The elevation is inscribed by Webb: 'Upright for the Pallace of Whitehall for King Charles the first taken' (T3). This note implies the existence of Charles II, so it was perhaps inscribed and submitted by Webb at the Restoration with his petition for the Surveyorship, as proof of his having designed a building acceptable to the King's father after he had attended him at Hampton Court and Carisbrooke and 'received his ... command to design a Pallace' (1647–8). The elevation is of the river front and it includes the Banqueting House and its pendant, with a giant-order portico of eight columns and giant-order, three-bay end pavilions. It is 800 feet in extent and fits one of the two plans (T2), but it is 'to bee encreased according to ye groundplatt', and therefore would fit the 'Taken' ground plan which is 900 feet wide and 1,100 feet deep (T1) (pl. 82), very slightly smaller than K.

The design provides enough space for a road next to the river, and extends deep into the park behind. The Banqueting House is now part of the entrance front and, with the benefit of hindsight, it is surprising that what appears to be the obvious solution to the problem of its inclusion took so long to achieve. The elevation, however, is not successful,

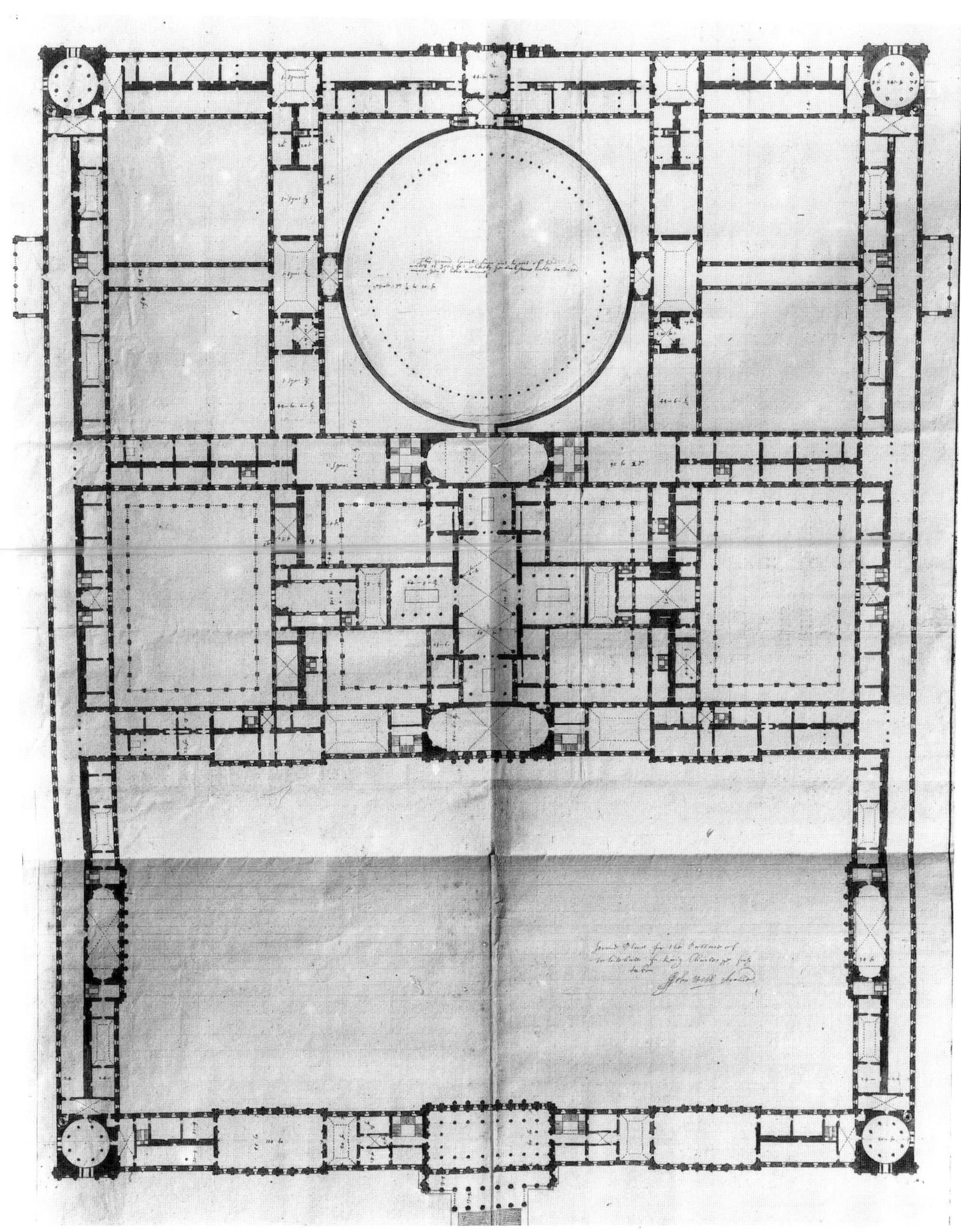

82. Whitehall palace: the second ground plan of the 'Taken' scheme (T1). The round court is on the park side of the palace

because the superimposed orders of the Banqueting House are not in the same scale as Webb's giant order. Also, because the half basement of the older building sets the height of the main floor, Webb's columns are not able to rest as emphatically on the ground as they were to do at the King Charles Building. There is a very noticeable hesitancy in the handling of Webb's order at the angles, where he sets a half column and a pilaster behind his main column, perhaps in an attempt to shade the transition to the Banqueting House system. At the corners of the elevation, the columns of the return fronts are visible: a shimmering effect which gives an unnerving impression of instability. Such a hesitancy in dealing with angles occurs elsewhere in Webb's work, at both the contemporary Durham House and in the later schemes for Whitehall. Between the giant order and the Banqueting House sections there are short, astylar ranges, a variation in articulation which would have been more successful if, as well as being set back, they had been set lower. According to the plans, the side elevations would have been extremely long and unrelieved.

In plan, the T design retains the tripartite division into three groups of courts of the earlier schemes. The circular court is back at the park end, and the single great court, having been in the middle at K, and at the park end in E, is now behind the river front. The central range is much narrower than in either P or K. The central section of it is filled by a very impressive cruciform group of grand spaces, disposed around a rectangular, vaulted hall. This is approached on the long axis through apsed vestibules and square rooms with corner columns, ending in two-column screens. To each side of the hall are further columned rooms, after which are rooms with coved ceilings, set on a transverse axis and, finally, at one end of the arm of the cross, a chapel and, at the other, possibly, a council chamber. The arrangement is much more harmonious in the final plan than in the earlier, where the central great room was differently aligned and the clarity of the cross vitiated. A sequence of state rooms of this planning quality had not been designed before in England, and it is not until the work of Robert Adam that a comparable antique splendour is essayed again. Webb is here, once again, revealing his indebtedness to the reconstructions of the ancient house made by Palladio and Scamozzi, just as he was in his designs for Durham House. The occurrence here of the apsed vestibule, which occurs frequently in Webb's designs, built, unbuilt, and theoretical, suggests the further influence of the Roman Palazzo Farnese, a source which might have contributed also to the wall arches and arcaded courts of the Whitehall schemes.[52]

As in the K scheme, the private apartments in the T plan are at the park side, with state rooms around the circular court. With a diameter of 300 feet, this court is 80 feet wider than the one in the earlier scheme. In the K plan, all the apartments are inward-looking, with galleries around the outside to house the picture collection. In the first of the T plans, this arrangement is transposed and the apartments are placed on the outside, but, with some exceptions on the park front, the K plan is preferred for the finalized T scheme.

[52] The plan of the Palazzo Farnese was bound in at the back of Webb's copy of Serlio (RIBA).

At the main entrance towards the river is a large, columned hall, with staircases to each side and a way through to the Banqueting House and its pendant. In the first plan, this sequence is much more consummately handled than in the final one: after the stairs comes a transverse, apsed room with the through-route delimited by columns. Such an arrangement, with its sense of grandeur and element of surprise, would have provided a worthy foretaste in the final plan for the delights of the cruciform group in the centre of the complex.

The few surviving interior drawings for the P scheme (P12–14) show that, if further proof were needed after the Banqueting House, Inigo Jones could design magnificently Roman interiors. This skill was passed on to Webb, who added to it something which, as far as the P scheme can tell us, Jones lacked, the ability to weld these units into a sequence of spaces which flow with ease into one another. It is reasonable to note that, apart from his apsed rooms, Webb did not employ the curved surface in the manner of the contemporary masters of the Roman Baroque,[53] but according to his rectilinear lights he produced for Charles I a design for a palace which Louis XIV would have found hard to emulate. Charles, of course, was in no position to build it and, when his son was restored to the throne, its grandiose manner and massive extent were clearly more than he could contemplate. Webb, therefore, in 1661, on the only dated drawing in the Whitehall group, suggested a contracted scheme.

The D drawing, a sketch (pl. 83), is related to T, having a tripartite division of courts with a single large one at one end, but it is of a much more feasible size: 832 feet by 634 feet 6 inches. The main axis is no longer from the river to the park but from Charing Cross to Westminster, with the Privy Garden to the south as in the old palace, an open space to the north, the park to the west, and gardens running down to the river. There is no sign of a road. There are porticoes on the east and west fronts and the Banqueting House is visible on the east river-front range. A sketch of the gateway for the Charing Cross entrance suggests that the palace was to retain the floor disposition of the Banqueting House and there was to be a return to the towers used at points of emphasis in K. This design represents a caesura in Webb's Whitehall designs: no other drawings are connected with it.

It was probably about the same time as D that the Z drawings were made. Z1 shows some affinity with earlier schemes, being a cross-section through a range, with the Banqueting House just making an appearance to one side. It is evidently a drawing for a large scheme, but, with its *mélange* of French and Palladian elements and an incorrectly drawn Banqueting House, it cannot be directly linked with any of the other projects. Certainly, it is not by Webb, but other hands might well have been working on Whitehall on behalf of Charles II before the introduction of Wren in 1664. Whinney tentatively ascribed the drawing to Hugh May, but the mason–architect's style brings Willem de Keyser to mind. There are no known drawings by him with which to compare the present examples, but he was paid for work at both Whitehall and Greenwich in 1661.[54]

[53] Despite his recognition of the fact that 'it was always accounted one of the Elegancies of Architecture, to make commixtures of Forms in one and the same Structure' (*A Vindication of Stone-Heng Restored* (1665), 110). [54] *King's Works*, v. 140, 266.

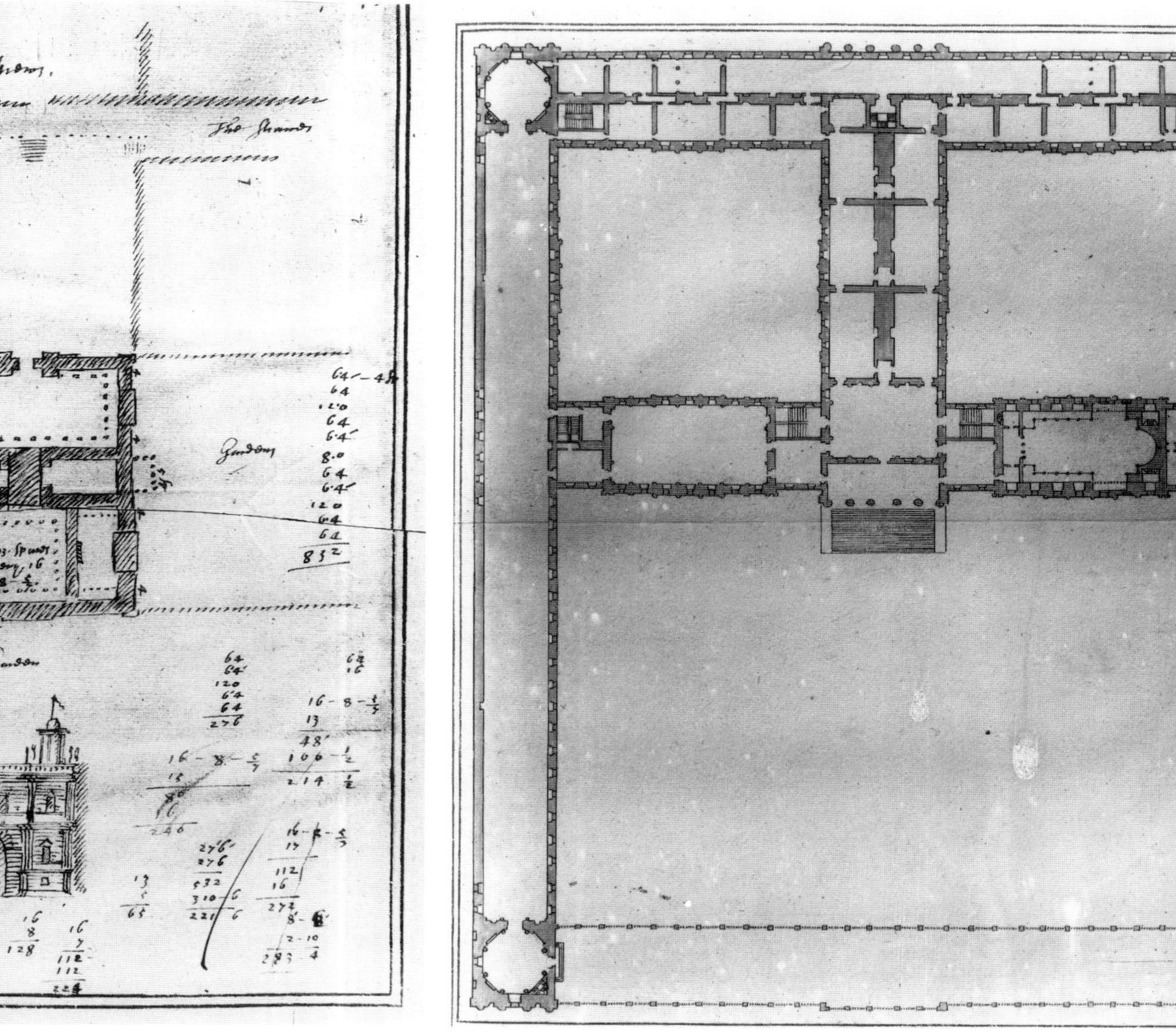

83. Whitehall Palace: block plan and elevation of the gateway of the scheme dated 1661. Here the palace is axially aligned from Charing Cross (at the top of the drawing) to Westminster, rather than from the river to the park (D1)

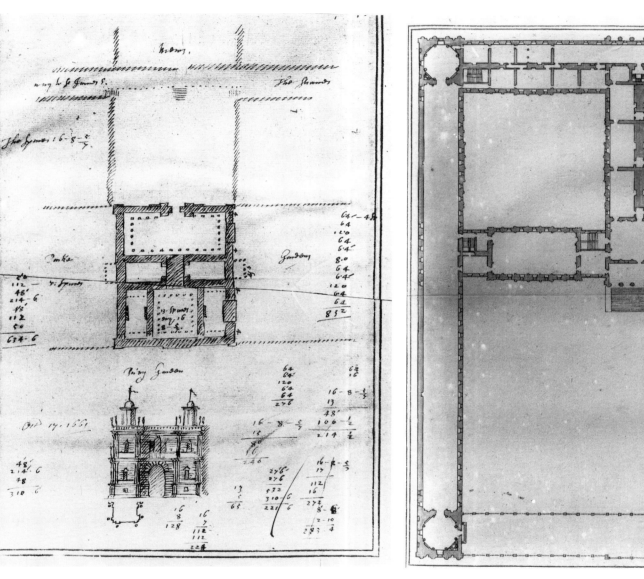

84. Whitehall Palace: the S-scheme plan, for a palace with an open courtyard towards the river (S3); cf. the plans for Greenwich Palace, pls. 88 and 89

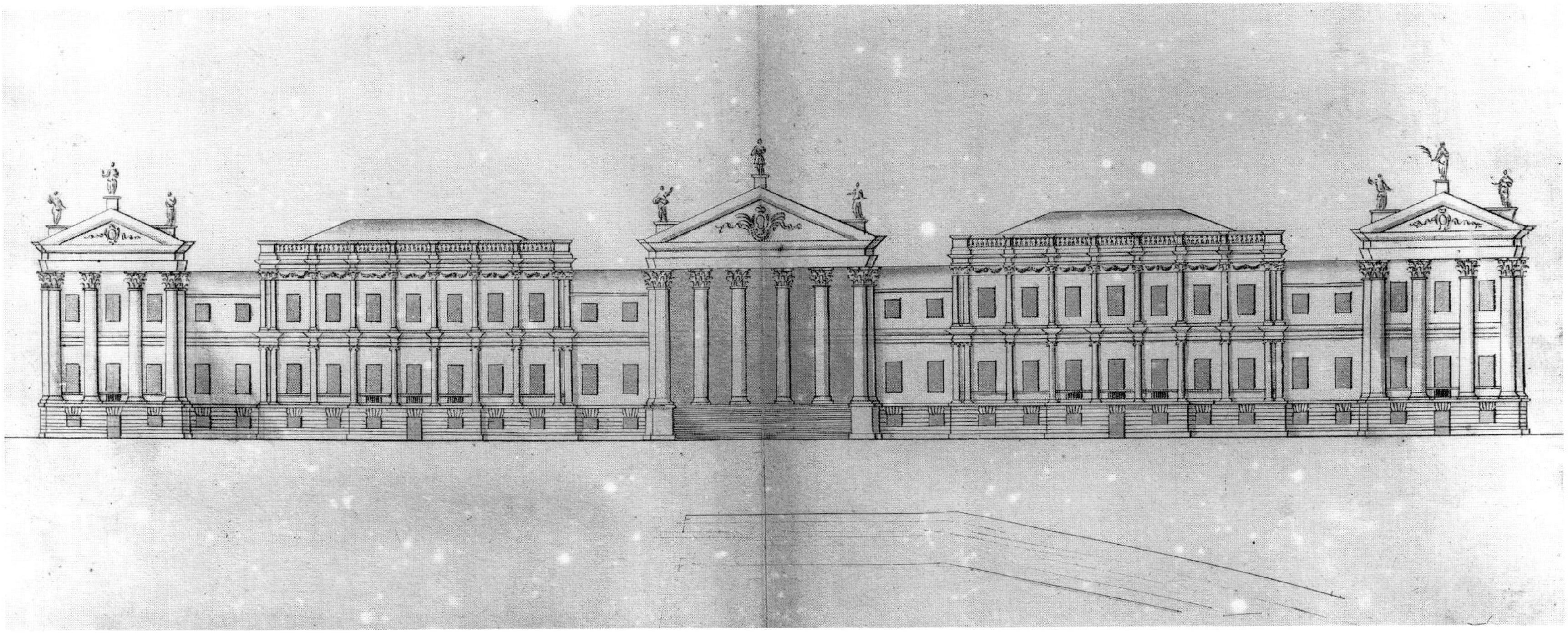

85. Whitehall Palace: design for the river front of the S scheme, showing the pavilions at the ends of the courtyard wings (S11)

86. Whitehall Palace: one of the alternative designs for the river front of the S scheme (S8)

The S scheme might be contemporary with D, demonstrating a desire on the part of the architect to provide a more manageable design for Charles II, but, as it is even smaller than D (694 ft. by 564 ft.), and as it appears to be the product of an entire rethinking of the problem, resulting in a solution comparable with Greenwich, a 1663–4 dating is perhaps more likely. It is interesting that Webb does not mention these Whitehall drawings in his petition of 1669: it underlines the unofficial nature of the project and the degree of wishful thinking involved in the minds of both architect and patron.

The scheme is recorded in two plans and eight elevations, as well as a block plan, which demonstrate again the problems posed by the Banqueting House. Whereas the demolition of Jones's building could be contemplated by its creator in 1637–9, within ten years sentimental reasons would have perished the thought, and at the Restoration, as Vertue records, 'King Charles 2d was unwilling to comply with some designs for rebuilding Whitehall; because they proposed to pull this [the Banqueting House] down'.[55] Webb's designs, therefore, although not as distinguished as Greenwich, were trying to make the best of an impossible job. To try to design something to go with the Banqueting House was a pursuit essentially at odds with his mature style, but even so he succeeded rather more than Wren did when he was faced with the same, intractable problem at the end of the century. It is ironic that Jones's two extant masterpieces, the Banqueting House and the Queen's House, should not only have set new standards for architectural design in England, but also have prevented the next two generations from acting upon the findings as they would have wished. Thus stress was laid, all too physically, upon the hermetic nature of Jones's architectural achievement.

Webb's first plan for the 'Small' scheme (S2) is for a palace of one large and two small courts, with the Banqueting House and its pendant, a chapel, separated by an entrance hall. There are flaps attached to the drawing over the river and park fronts, which show alternative arrangements of the latter's staircases and the whole of the river-front range. The alternatives for this show a wide flight of stairs leading up to a portico, on each side of which are covered walks, with piers supporting the upper storey or, with the flap down, sequences of service-rooms: pastries, kitchens, butteries, livery-rooms, etc. In the second plan (S3) (pl. 84), these alternatives are abandoned in favour of a terrace, so the closed rectangle of the great court has become an open court, flanked by the long side wings, giving a new, Baroque emphasis to the main, central range of buildings. The similarity with the Greenwich plan is clear. The private apartments are again on the park front, with the state rooms at right angles in the central block, disposed to each side of a spine wall. Further suites of rooms are provided in the wing towards Charing Cross, but the opposite long wing appears to be given over wholly to a gallery. On the park front there is another gallery (215 ft. by 24 ft.) and, above it, a library.

All the surviving elevations represent proposed alternative treatments of the main front. As far as can be gathered from the plans, the long fronts are as unrelieved as those of the T scheme. The park front receives the emphasis of an applied order at centre and ends, but again, as in the T scheme, the entrance here appears to have been relegated to the

[55] Vertue, I. 149.

basement, a consequence of the difficulty of harmonizing the new design with the storey system of the Banqueting House.

For the main front, the drawings suggest eight alternatives for the central feature between the Banqueting House and the chapel. Six of the eight have a giant order and the one elevation to show the complete front, plus the end pavilions at the river side (S11) (pl. 85), shows that a giant order was to be employed there too: a contraction of the T scheme.

Webb here handles the order well, but on two of the drawings (S5, 10) he exhibits again a tendency towards hesitancy at the angles of the portico. Of the other three giant-order designs, two have porticoes flanked by turrets, one with the frontispiece set on a concave curve (S8) (pl. 86). Such a curve also occurs in one of the two drawings which repeat the superimposed orders of the Banqueting House (S7). It has been noted that the curved wall is rare in the work of Webb, but it does occur occasionally in his theoretical villa and country-house façades.[56] Here, its use recalls the work of Le Pautre and suggests that Webb's knowledge of French engravings was not confined to those illustrating ceilings and chimneypieces. The other drawing to repeat the Banqueting House orders (S4) shows a frontispiece with three-bay, superimposed arcades, taken with minor alterations from the loggia around the round court of the P scheme (P10)—further evidence of the continuity within the Whitehall projects.

Five of the elevations follow the floor levels of the Banqueting House, with steps up to the portico, but four of these also have additional basement entrances to each side, with openings which break into the main floor level above. It is not clear in these how entry to the Banqueting House and the chapel would have been effected. The remaining three elevations ignore the Banqueting House floor level and have only one main entrance with high openings taking up the half basement and most of the main floor.

In all the S elevations, Webb has improved on the T scheme by breaking up the roofline and making his astylar, linking sections lower as well as recessed.

The crucial problem in the designing of any very large, architecturally ambitious structure is one of making a large number of small units cohere into a satisfying whole, or, alternatively, relating simple masses to each other without engendering monotony. Jones's P scheme failed in the pursuit of the first ideal and Webb's T in the second. The S scheme comes nearer than its predecessors to a satisfactory solution, in terms of size and style, but even the most successful of the ideas required considerable compromise on the part of the architect. It might be that the difficulty of finding an adequate answer to the problem was as much a contributory factor in the designs' remaining on paper as the King's lack of money and the delicate political situation. That they were regarded, however, as being the most acceptable of the designs offered is demonstrated by the manner in which they were utilized by Wren in 1664–5 and again after the fire of 1698. This conflagration effectively closed the history of Whitehall as a royal palace.

[56] Cf. *RIBA Cat.* 192–3.

GREENWICH PALACE

By his own account, in his petition of 1669 for the Surveyorship, Webb, 'After having prepared Whitehall for yr Majesties happy restauration ... withdrew into the country, from whence afterwards in 1663 by yor Royall appointment being sent for, to react for yor Majestie at Greenwich, hee readily obeyed.'[57] This recall was confirmed officially in November 1666, when Webb was enjoined to work on the building of 'Our palace at Greenwich ... according to your best skill and judgment in Architecture, as our Surveyor Assistant unto Sir John Denham, Knight of the Bath, Surveyor General of our Works',[58] at a fee of £200 per year, plus travelling charges. This was payable from January 1664, the very month in which work began on the King Charles Building, the first and only block of a projected three-range palace. Webb appears in the Works Accounts for 1664 as the recipient of 'riding charges' from Greenwich to London and back.[59] His plans for the new building are dated 1663,[60] and his scheme to enlarge the Queen's House by the addition of pavilions is datable to the same year.

Some works were carried out at Greenwich before the summoning of Webb.[61] In June 1661 Arthur Haughton, Purveyor to the King's Works, was paid for 'taking the plott of Greenwich house'. In July Willem de Keyser was paid for 'the draughts with the upwrights for the intended Building at Greenwich',[62] and in August a warrant was issued to Hugh May, Paymaster of the Works, recorded in the Treasury Books in October as being '£1000 ... for repairs at his Majesty's house at Greenwich and for making an additional building thereto'.[63]

The making of a plan was an action consistent with the need to survey the property before making good the depredations of the Interregnum. De Keyser's drawings, and the payment issued to May, were further steps in the process of putting Inigo Jones's Queen's House in readiness for the return of the queen mother, Henrietta Maria, from France. The existing building was extended in 1661–2 by the addition of the two, first-floor Bridge Rooms, which have elaborate plaster ceilings by John Grove, and further accommodation was provided by the partitioning of the two south-side corner rooms.[64] Repair work elsewhere in the house remedied two decades of neglect.

Some discussion certainly was taking place at this time concerning the building of a new palace. In October 1661 John Evelyn consulted the new Surveyor of the Works, Sir John Denham,

> about the placing of his Palace at Greenewich which I would have had built betweene the River & the Queene's House, so as a large Square Cutt, should have let in the Thames like a Baye etc: but Sir Jo: was for seting it on Piles at the very brink of the water, which I did not assent to, & so came away, knowing Sir John to be a better poet than Architect, though he had Mr. Webb (Inigo Jone's Man) to assist him.[65]

[57] PRO SP 29/251 120, pub. in *Wren Society* 18 (1941), 156 (see App.II).

[58] *Audit Office Enrolments*, vi. 129; *CSPD 1666–7*, p. 286, 24 Nov. 1666.

[59] PRO Works 5/5.

[60] *RIBA Cat.* 122–4.

[61] *King's Works*, v. 140 ff.

[62] PRO Works 5/2.

[63] *Calendar of Treasury Books*, i (1660–7), 291, 3 Oct. 1661.

[64] G. H. Chettle, *The Queen's House* (1937), 39–40.

[65] Evelyn, *Diary*, p. 430, 19 Oct. 1661. Webb was referred to as Denham's Deputy in May 1664 (PRO Works 5/5).

And in January 1662 'His Majestie entertaind me with his intentions of building his Palace of Greenewich & quite demolishing the old; on which occasion I declard him my thoughts.'[66] But, bearing in mind that Evelyn discussed the proposed new Whitehall Palace with Charles II in 1664, it is presuming too much to suppose that the Greenwich discussions, at this stage, were any more than the King's habitual palatial musings. Evelyn's mentioning of Webb at this early date is of no consequence in the present context because, as the holder of the Reversion of the Surveyorship, he would have been linked automatically in observers' minds with the Surveyor himself and, as he was the practised architect, Evelyn could find comfort in the thought that any mistake by Denham would not be irreversible. It is rather ironic, in the light of Evelyn's criticism of Denham, that, when Webb's building was begun in 1664, piles were needed to carry it in the wet ground.

During 1662 the pulling down of the decayed old buildings at Greenwich began, but at this stage there was still no firm plan to build anew. Demolition was still going on in 1664. A warrant of February 1662 prohibited the transport of stone from Portland without the permission of Denham, because it was needed for the repair of the King's houses and St Paul's.[67] All the effort at Greenwich, therefore, before Webb's recall in 1663, went into the demolition of some older buildings and the addition of new rooms at the Queen's House. In neither of these activities did he play any part. Following his arrival, however, further extensions were put in progress.

In May 1663 work began on the digging of foundations at the south-east and south-west corners of the Queen's House for the addition of pavilions, but progress was desultory and, beyond a marking out of the ground and the underpinning of the quoins, nothing was achieved.[68] Of the four drawings by Webb,[69] detailing his proposals for the addition of these pavilions at all four corners of the building, one includes a tentative proposal for further lateral wings. This can be associated with the comments of M. de Monconys, who saw the house in June 1663: 'il ne reste qu'un bastiment a l'Italienne, au bout d'une fort grande basse-cour, qu'on peut plustost nommer un champ ... l'on fera deux ailes qui accompagneront ce corps de logis'.[70] In August 1666 work recommenced on the foundations 'next the Park', and in May 1667 the ground was set out for all four pavilions.[71] A model 'for the addition to the Queen's buildings' was made by William Cleere.[72] In the plan with wings the pavilions had staircases within, but in the variant schemes, although the basic idea remained the same, the stairs were to adjoin the pavilions, which therefore could have more accommodation space with self-contained lodgings on each floor. The plan foundered and three years later the foundations were filled in.[73]

Webb's proposed additions would have altered entirely the character of the Queen's House, increasing not only its accommodation, but its scale as well. It would appear from the sequence of events that, after the addition of the Bridge Rooms, Charles II, whilst toying with the idea of a new palace, at first merely was party to the aggrandisement of

[66] Evelyn, *Diary*, p. 435, 24 Jan. 1662.
[67] *CSPD 1661–2*, p. 279, 20 Feb. 1662.
[68] PRO Works 5/3.
[69] *RIBA Cat.* 166–9.
[70] *Voyages de M. de Monconys*, ii, (1666), 83.
[71] PRO Works 5/9.
[72] PRO Works 5/10.
[73] PRO Works 5/15.

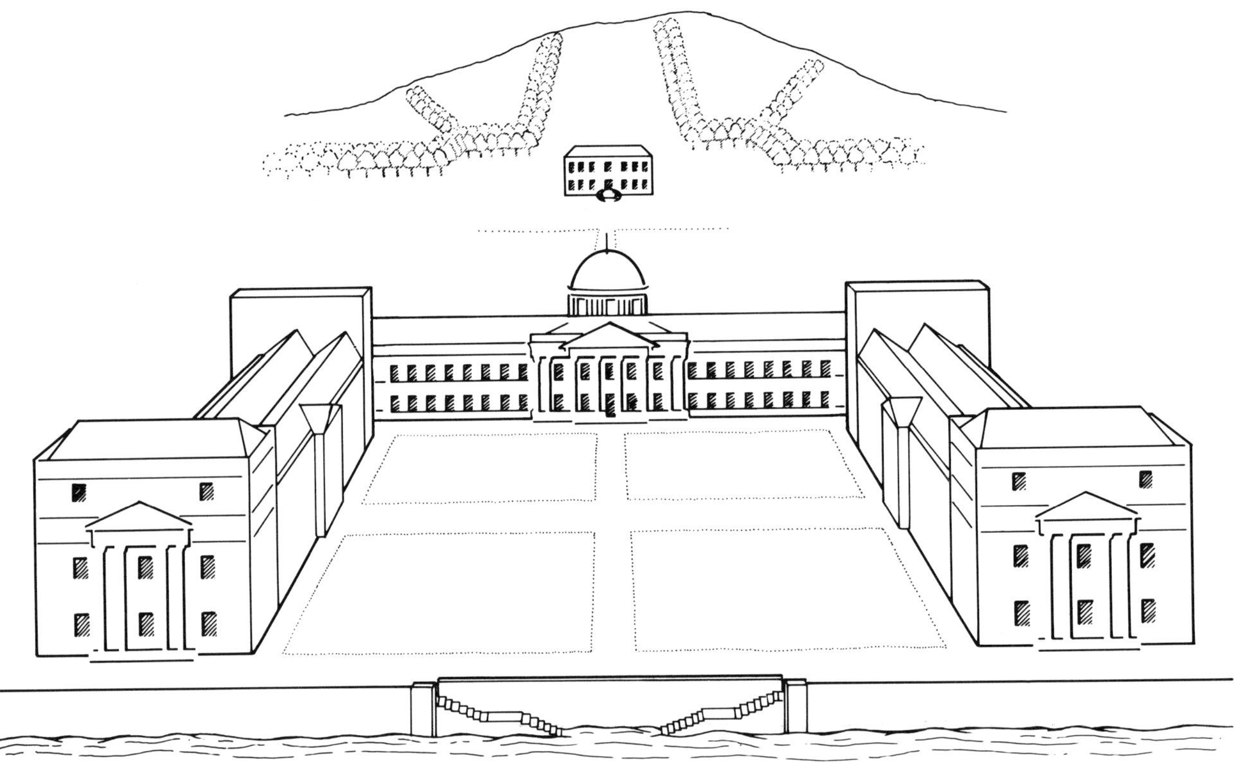

FIG. 6. INITIAL PROPOSAL FOR GREENWICH PALACE: reconstruction looking south, showing a three-range palace with the Queen's House beyond (the King Charles Building is on the right).

the Queen's House by the addition of pavilions and wings. This plan was shelved and Webb proposed instead a separate, three-range palace to the north, between the Queen's House and the river (fig. 6). Only the west wing of this, the present King Charles Building, was built. The ground for it was staked out in January 1664 and work continued throughout the remainder of the decade. It must have become apparent to Webb at an early stage that his full scheme would never be completed, and that the most he could hope for would be the erecting of two long ranges, facing one another across a court, with the Queen's House, rather than the third range, providing a more distant, central accent (fig. 7). The Jones building was too small to perform the task satisfactorily, so the addition of a dome was considered and the proposals to build pavilions at each corner resurrected.

The scheme by this time had become linked in Webb's mind with the idea of closing the vista from the river by building a 'Grott & ascent' on the hill in the park to the south of the Queen's House (fig. 8).[74] The design for this was dated 1665 by Hawksmoor on a

[74] J. Bold, 'Greenwich: "The Grott & ascent by mr. Webb"', *Burlington Magazine*, 129 (1982), 149–50.

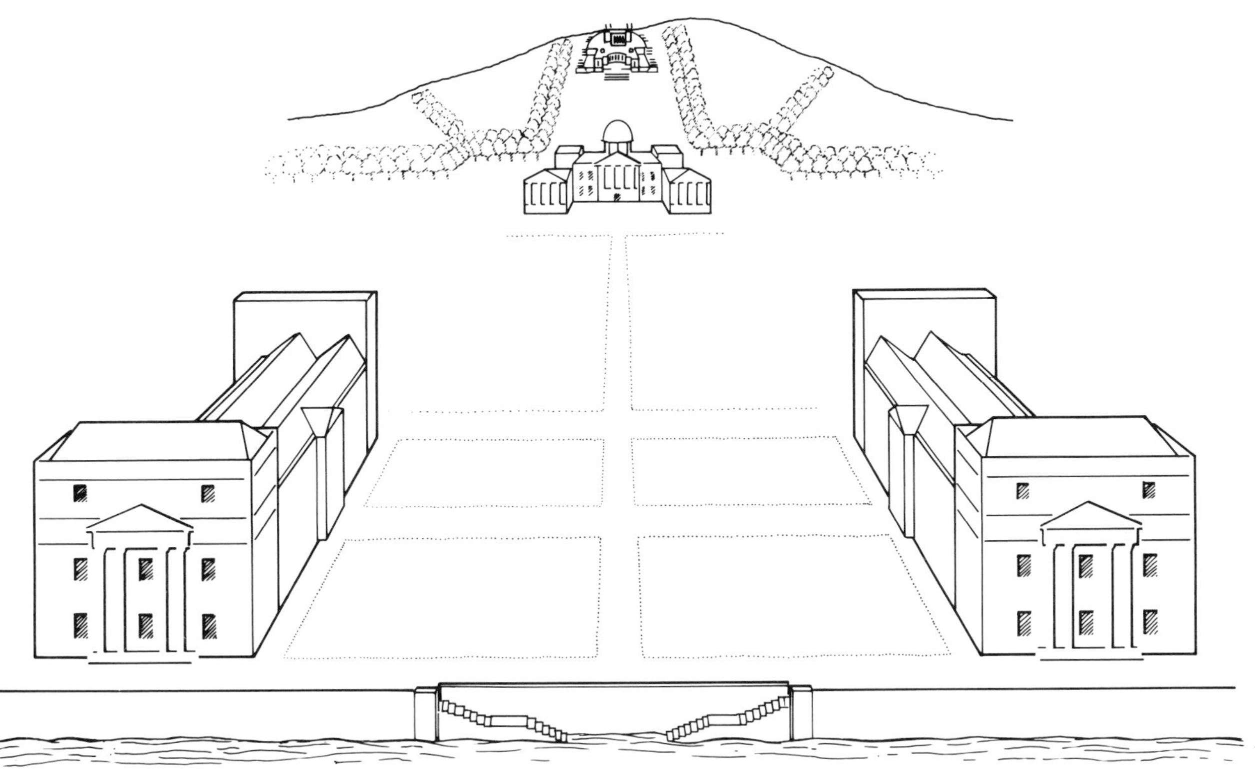

FIG. 7. REVISED PROPOSAL FOR GREENWICH PALACE: reconstruction looking south, showing a two-range palace with the enlarged Queen's House and the 'grotto and ascent' beyond

plan of Greenwich which he made in 1723, on which he also noted, 'The Grand Esplanade by monsr Le Notre'.[75] Charles II, with Versailles in mind, had, in a letter written in 1664, enjoined his sister Henriette to 'Pray lett le Nostre goe on with the modell ... he may add much to the beauty of the desente by a cascade of watter'. Possibly in this connection, payment was made in 1665 to carpenters for 'the making of a modell for ye Fountaine in the Parke'.[76] Le Nôtre's design for formal gardens survives, but, apart from the planting of trees, there is no evidence to suggest that it was carried out.[77] Webb's scheme appears to have been similarly stillborn. His drawings show a complex of garden buildings and steps; a multi-terraced scheme, spread over four different levels, contrived to regularize the ascent of the hill.[78] The main building, a single-storeyed, concave arcade with pavilions, owed much to Bramante's scheme for the exedra of the Cortile del Belvedere in the Vatican, and, by extension, the first century BC Temple of Fortune at

[75] K. Downes, *Hawksmoor* (1979), no. 358, pp. 94–7. Hawksmoor's plan is at Wilton House.

[76] Chettle, *Queen's House*, pp. 42–4.

[77] E. de Ganay, *André le Nostre* (1962), pl. 156.

[78] RIBA, Boy. Coll. 18, 1 & 2.

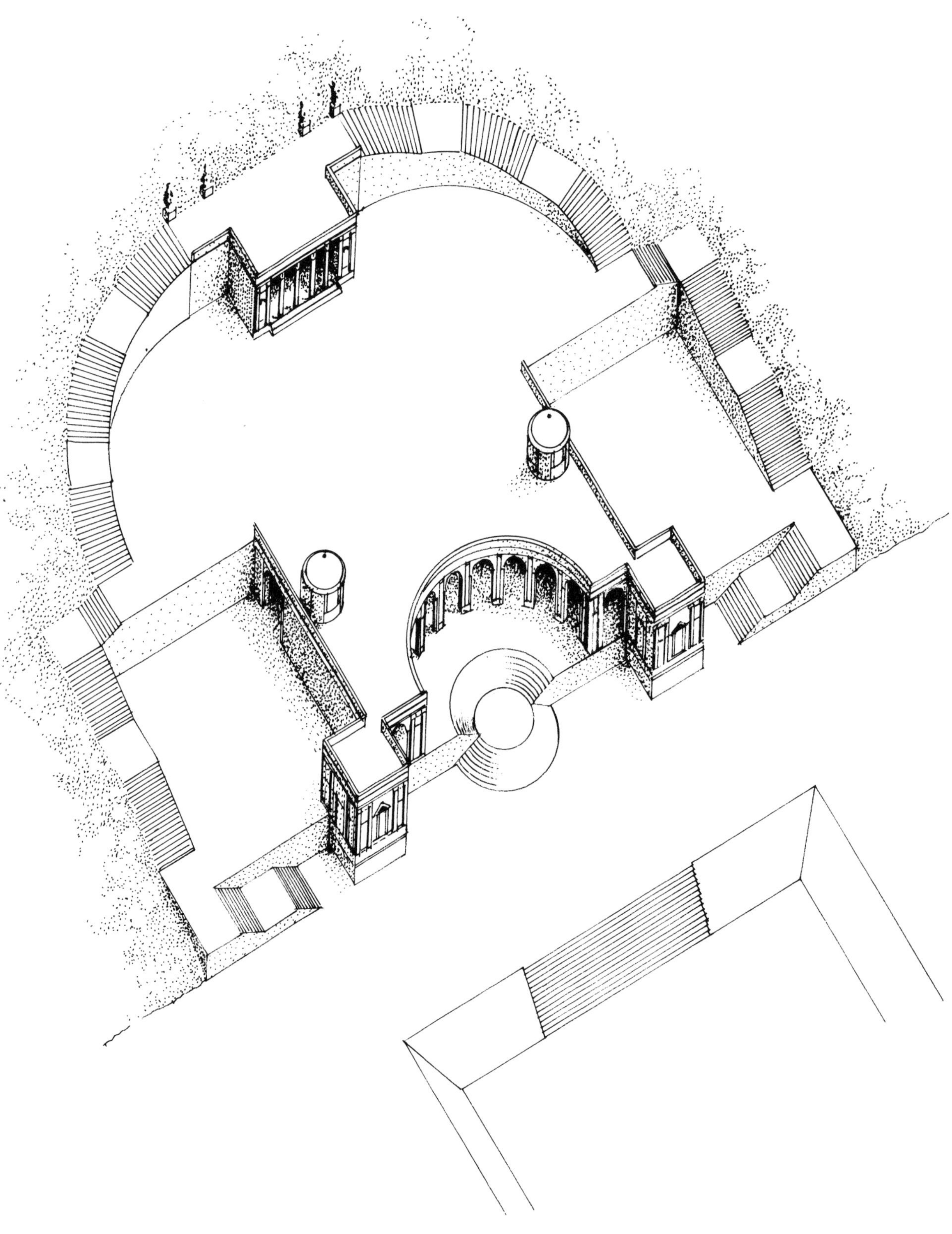

Fig. 8. greenwich palace: reconstruction of the proposed 'grotto and ascent' on the hill to the south

Palestrina, which probably inspired it. Bramante's design was known to Webb through its publication by Serlio, and he perhaps was familiar also with Suarez's reconstructions of the antique Temple, published in 1655.[79] At the higher level, on top of the hill, Webb closed the view with a rectangular pavilion surmounted by statues. Inside, he placed one of his favourite, recurring, apsed spaces, an echo of the vestibule of the King Charles Building which he was erecting at the bottom of the hill.

Even though work on the King Charles Building petered out towards the end of the decade, with no trace of Webb's grand interiors having even been begun, he clearly still had hopes that the matching range opposite would be built and, as late as 1673, after his death, there was a warrant for £10,000 'to be employed for finishing the part of the palace at Greenwich lately erected and for laying the foundation of another part of the said palace'.[80] No money was paid, but, if work had gone on, then the additions to the Queen's House probably would have been recommenced as well. The building's unsuitability as a grand, central accent, and the undesirability of closing the view from it to the river by the addition of a new cross range, was to prove a thorn in the sides of both Wren and Hawksmoor when they came to build at Greenwich. The unobstructed view, and access to the river, came to be regarded as sacrosanct. Indeed, when the site was granted for the building of the Naval Hospital in 1694, the central avenue was specifically excluded (pl. 87).[81] Hawksmoor, writing in 1728, referred to the late Queen Mary's desire to keep the Queen's House approach from the Thames open, 'and she retained a desire to add the Four Pavilions to that Palace, according to Inigo Jones's Design [*sic*], that she might make that little Palace compleat as a Royal Villa for her own Retirement, or from whence Embassadors, or publick Ministers might make their Entry into London'.[82]

Leaving aside the Whitehall Palace schemes, the drawings for Greenwich represent the largest single group of drawings by Webb for a specific building. According to his sale catalogue, Hawksmoor owned ninety-seven of them,[83] and it is likely, given the presence of a Greenwich plan in the Clarke collection at Worcester College,[84] that there were more besides. Approximately fifty survive, nearly all in the RIBA.[85]

Webb's plans for the King Charles Building are dated 1663. The associated three-range plans are undated, but they must be from the same year. They propose a palace disposed around three sides of a courtyard, with the fourth side open to the river. The connecting range in the Worcester College drawing is a single pile (with an alternative double-pile suggestion on a flap), with a central hall with grand staircases to each side. A drawing

[79] S. Serlio, *Tutte l'opere d'architettura et prospetiva*, iii (1619), fos. 119v–120; J. M. Suarez, *Praenestes Antiquae libri duo* (1655). Three engravings from Suarez are published by R. Wittkower in 'Pietro da Cortona's Project for Reconstructing the Temple of Palestrina' in *Studies in the Italian Baroque* (1975), 119. Bramante's Belvedere scheme also lay behind an early design by Palladio for the Villa Pisani which was in Webb's possession (RIBA XVI/7): cf. H. Burns, *Andrea Palladio 1508–1580* (Arts Council, 1975), no. 329. Palladio's own reconstructions of the Temple of Fortune postdate the Pisani design: cf. Burns, *Palladio*, nos. 447–52; Lewis, *Drawings*, pp. 143–7. These would not have been known to Webb, as they remained in Italy until purchased by Lord Burlington in 1719.

[80] *Calendar of Treasury Books*, iv (1672–5), 160, 13 June 1673.

[81] *Wren Society*, 18 (1941), 111.

[82] N. Hawksmoor, 'Remarks on the Founding and Carrying on the Buildings of the Royal Hospital at Greenwich' (1728); published in *Wren Society*, 6, (1929), 17–27.

[83] K. Downes, 'Hawksmoor's Sale Catalogue', *Burlington Magazine*, 95 (1953), 332–5.

[84] *Worcs. Coll. Cat.* 89.

[85] *RIBA Cat.* 120–63.

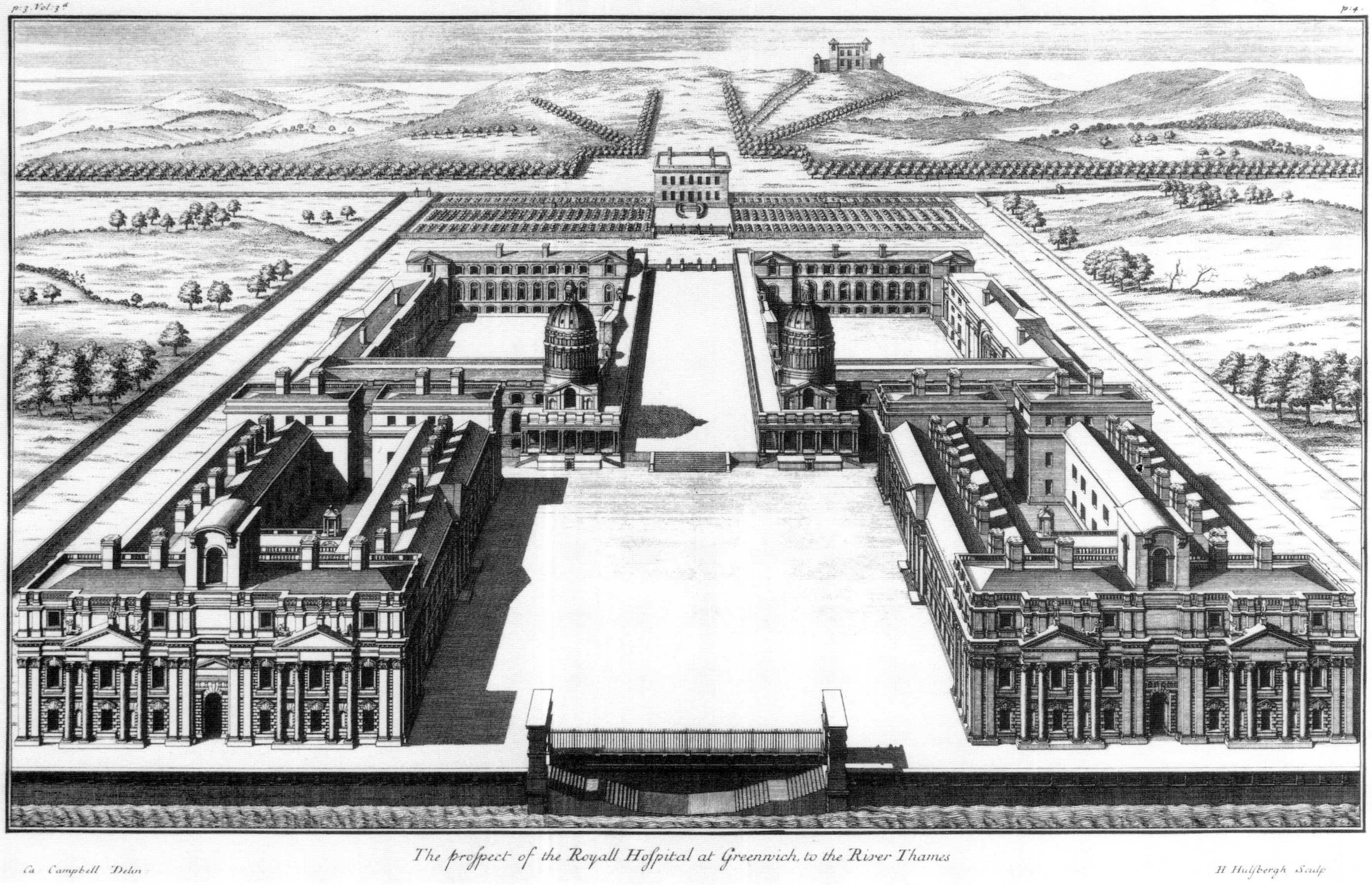

87. Royal Naval Hospital, Greenwich: view from the north. Webb's King Charles Building is on the right-hand (west) side, facing the main court; Inigo Jones's Queen's House is in the middle distance and, on top of the hill, to the west of the main axis, is Wren's Royal Observatory, built in 1675–6

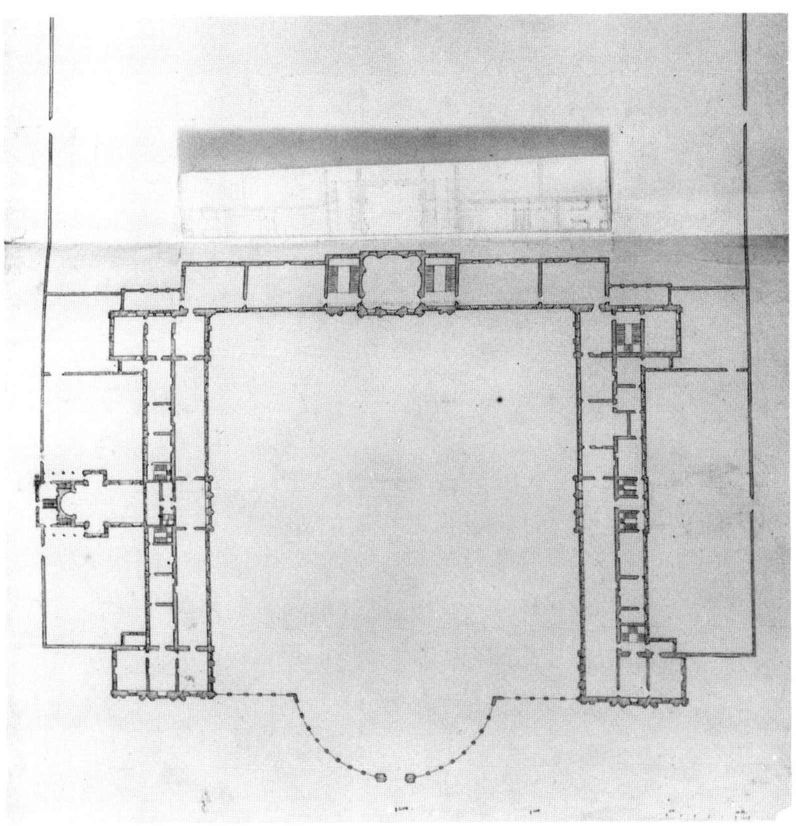

88. Greenwich Palace: first-floor plan for three-range palace with an open court towards the river

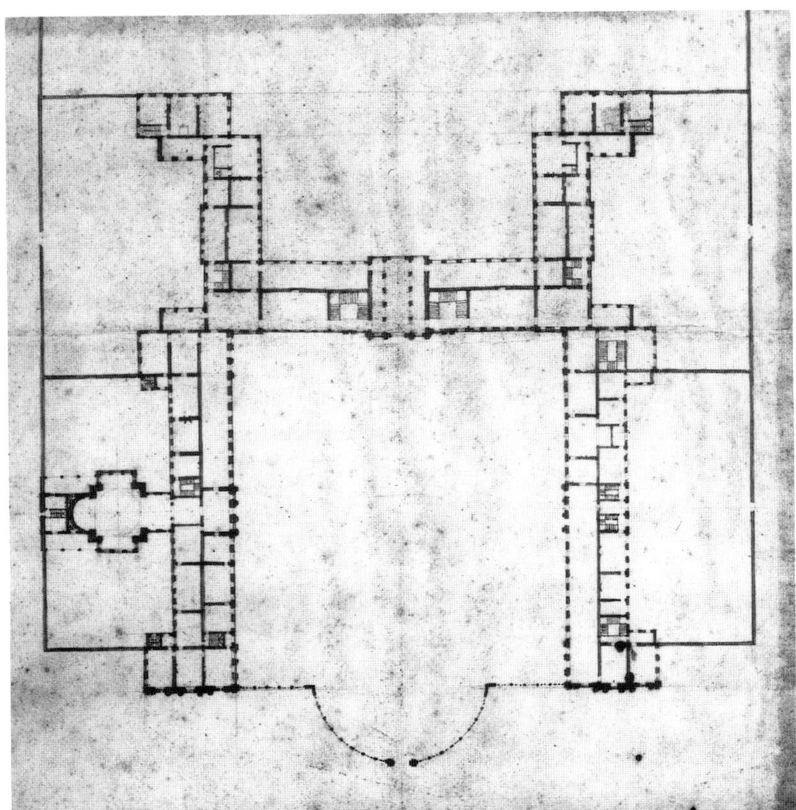

89. Greenwich Palace: alternative first-floor plan for three-range palace with further wings to the south

at All Souls College from the Webb office shows that this central feature was to be domed.[86] The open disposition of the plan, and the hesitancy at the angles of the portico, link the scheme with Whitehall, particularly the contemporary S scheme. There is a debt also to the earlier K scheme, where a similar hall was flanked by staircases. There, it had four columns; in the alternative Greenwich plan (RIBA) it has eight. There is no surviving elevation for this variant: an attic rather than a dome must have been intended. The continuity in Webb's use of antique motifs is here underlined: the hall of eight columns, taken from the ancient house, had occurred in the designs for Whitehall, in the K and T schemes, in the designs for Belvoir and Durham, and, again, in the executed design for Gunnersbury.

The Worcester College plan shows a Latin Cross chapel projecting east of the palace's east wing (pl. 88). This is similar in plan to the chapel proposed for Whitehall[87] and it appears in greater detail in a drawing of 1670,[88] which confirms that, even at this late stage, Webb was hoping that the east wing would be constructed. In the RIBA plan the chapel is in the same position, but there it conforms more to the Greek Cross type, with a dome (pl. 89). This plan differs also from that at Worcester College in proposing two further ranges, enclosing a smaller court, on the south side of the central range of the palace. These contain bedchambers and other state rooms and it has been suggested that they might have provided suites for the Duke and Duchess of York, in addition to those for the King and Queen in the main wings.[89]

Both the Worcester and RIBA plans show the central range connected to and overlapping the southern ends of the long, lateral wings. At an early stage this idea was superseded by the designing of a vestibule link. This is shown on the west-range plans, giving access to the grand staircase in the south pavilion. The change must have been prompted by the realization that progress might be slow and that the King Charles Building should be self-contained. The vestibule does not survive, but it was certainly built according to Webb's plan: it is clearly visible in paintings by Danckerts and Vorsterman.[90]

The executed King Charles Building represents the King's side of the palace (pl. 90). The main part is of two storeys, two rooms deep. The end pavilions have an extra floor, and further rooms to the west, which in block form further underlines the similarity with Belvoir. The main state rooms were to be on the first floor, with access from the vestibule and the south, pavilion, staircase to, firstly, the Presence Chamber and then, *en suite*, the Privy Chamber, King's Bedchamber (distinguishable by its alcove), Cabinet Room, and Long Gallery (150 ft. long). Downstairs, with access gained through the central, east-front, apsed vestibule, was a further suite of private rooms disposed along the north end of the east front. These included a Waiting Room, Dining Room, and Withdrawing Room (figs. 9 and 10). Work on the interior was restricted to a minimum of decoration,

[86] All Souls College, v. 25; reproduced in *Wren Society*, 8 (1931), pl. XX. This drawing is by an unknown draughtsman, presumed to be working under Webb's direction. It is in the same hand as one of the theoretical house designs (*RIBA Cat.* 175). The reddish-brown wash and the draughting style are not paralleled elsewhere in the Webb drawings.

[87] Whitehall drawings, S3.

[88] *RIBA Cat.* 121.

[89] *King's Works*, v. 141–4.

[90] G. Callender, *The Queen's House, Greenwich, a Short History 1617–1937* (1971), has clear reproductions of these.

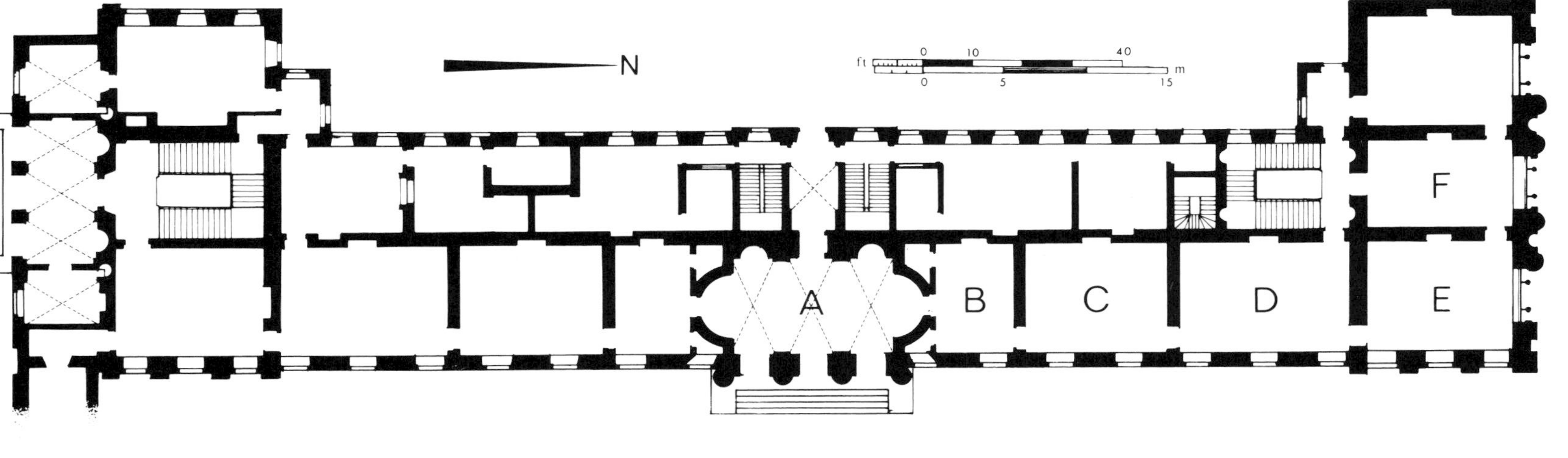

Fig. 9. King Charles Building, Greenwich: Ground-Floor Plan

A Entrance Vestibule
B Waiting Room
C Ante Room
D Dining Room
E Withdrawing Room
F Cabinet Room

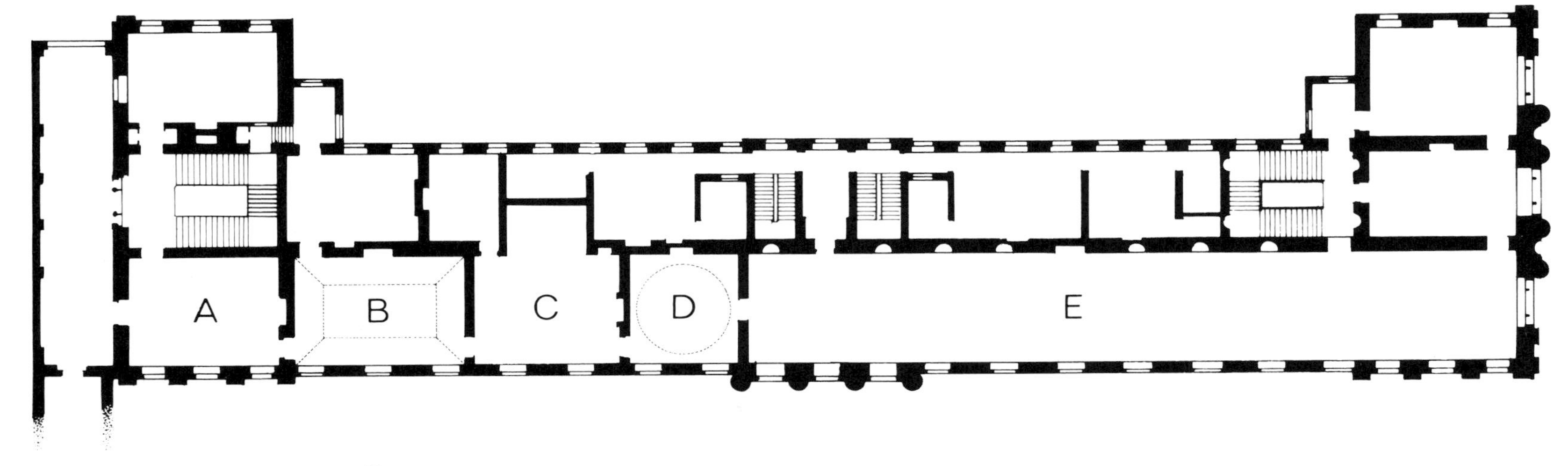

Fig. 10. King Charles Building, Greenwich: First-Floor Plan

A Presence Chamber
B Privy Chamber
C King's Bedchamber
D Cabinet Room
E Long Gallery

90. King Charles Building, Greenwich: view looking north along the east front

91. King Charles Building, Greenwich: the ground-floor entrance vestibule at the centre of the east front, looking north

and all that survive now of Webb's work are the east-front vestibule, the main north staircase, with its associated stone doorways, a bolection moulded, stone fireplace, and the doorcases in the ground- and first-floor central, east–west passages.[91]

The south pavilion staircase, which rises to the first floor only, was built according to Webb's plan, but was remodelled in the early eighteenth century, probably to the design of Hawksmoor, to provide space for a back stair from ground to attics. This was separated from the main stair by an inserted wall, arcaded so as to allow for a borrowed light. The three tiers of openings originally contained sash windows; they are now blocked.[92] The bearer from under the landing of Webb's stair, carved in 1666 by Henry Phillips and Richard Cleare,[93] was reused in the remodelling, but the original balustrade was removed to be replaced by an ironwork balustrade for which an agreement was made with Tijou in 1707.[94] The north staircase rises around an open well to the first and attic floors, thus providing access to the top floor of the adjoining pavilion. The stair is of stone, with turned, wooden balusters. The associated doorcases, also of stone, have broken pediments carried on brackets.

The east-front vestibule (pl. 91), a development from the entrance designed for the earliest Whitehall scheme, is without doubt one of Webb's finest rooms.[95] It is very austere, in contrast with the extreme richness of the proposed state rooms: Republican rather than Imperial in mood, but, in its command of space, equally masterful. It is an exciting room because it succeeds in its effects by architectural rather than decorative means, by controlling and manipulating the space in which the spectator acts. The eloquence of its stonework is worthy of Hawksmoor, and it stresses, along with the east front of the building, how far Webb was the father of the English Baroque style. The room is faced with ashlar. It has semi-circular recesses at each end and two similar but smaller recesses on the west wall, all ceiled with semi-domes. The ceiling cove springs from pilasters, with groins cutting back over each bay of the side walls. The soffits of the three, arched openings in the east wall were richly carved by Joshua Marshall and John Young in 1666.[96] These openings are now glazed.

The exterior of the building largely follows Webb's drawings (pls. 92 and 93). One of the plans shows only a single pilaster at the angles of the north, river front, but this is changed to coupled pilasters, as executed, in further plans. These also show tripartite windows on both floors of the front, intended to mirror the window in the centre of the south front, but, as built, the windows became single openings, following the elevational drawing. This front was rebuilt to the original design after bomb damage in the Second World War. The only major divergences to be seen now from Webb's elevations are at the centre of the east front, where the statues were omitted from the roofline, and on the south front, where the ground floor had to be made good after the removal of the original three-arched entrance vestibule.

[91] RCHME, *London*, v, (1930), 21–7.

[92] RCHME inventory notes, 1928 (held in National Monuments Record): the wall next to the secondary stairs has borrowed lights, six with round heads and the three topmost square, all with moulded sashes. Cf. *Wren Society*, 6, (1929), 55.

[93] PRO E 351/3438.

[94] *Wren Society*, 6 (1929), 55.

[95] It was restored after bomb damage in the Second World War (DOE Works' Drawings).

[96] PRO Works 5/9.

92. King Charles Building, Greenwich: the centrepiece of the east front; in the tympanum of the pediment the reclining figures of Fortitude and Dominion of the Sea support the cartouche of the royal Stuart arms

93. King Charles Building, Greenwich: drawing for the south front, showing the projecting ground-floor vestibule which would have linked this building with the cross range of the palace. The vestibule was built but was subsequently demolished after the abandonment of the three-range palace scheme

94. King Charles Building, Greenwich: design for the ceiling of the Presence Chamber

The King Charles Building, Webb's masterpiece, has come to be regarded, properly, as the first Baroque building in England, relying, as it does, on large statements, emphatically made. The giant order is employed, with no sign of hesitancy, at the centre and ends of the façade, where the upward accent is reinforced by the pediment and attics. The pronounced horizontality of the firmly emphasized string course, and the precisely cut rustication, is ruptured by both the order and the emphatic keystones in the window pediments. It is this evident tension which is maintained between horizontal and vertical elements which commands the attention of the viewer. Webb here is using the classical language, inherited from Inigo Jones, Palladio, and antiquity, to new and more dramatic ends. It is, none the less, a language with which the educated observer would have been familiar. Sources for the elements of the King Charles Building façade may be found in the work of Palladio and Scamozzi: Palladio's Palazzo Valmarana may be suggested as a source for the order, and his Palazzo Thiene for the exaggerated keystones. The overall disposition of the block, with its central portico and end pavilions, may be read as a development of the scheme by Scamozzi which also influenced the design of Wilton.[97] There is a continuity in Webb's use of his sources and in his architectural evolution: the King Charles Building's motifs were adumbrated in earlier designs, for Whitehall Palace, Belvoir Castle, and Durham House. In overall form, and in elements of plan and elevation, Greenwich represents the concluding stage of Webb's prolonged meditation on the problem of adapting antique precedent, as interpreted by Palladio and Scamozzi, to the requirements of seventeenth-century England.

It is in the very nature of historical investigation that interpretations of the past evolve and mutate according to circumstance and fashion. So, to stress that the King Charles Building was a conclusion, is not to deny that it also represented a beginning. It was not Baroque in the manner of contemporary seventeenth-century works in Italy, to which Jones had been blind and with which Webb was unlikely to have been familiar,[98] but, by the welding of a long front into a single, dramatic unit, sitting firmly on the ground, it constituted the first statement of its type by an English architect—one that was to be of great importance as a precedent for the next generation. It is a tribute to its compositional balance that it survives without the cross range, whose central dome would have provided, in the true manner of the Baroque climax, the concluding upward accent.

As it is a piece of undeniably great architecture, it is particularly surprising to find that, when it was decided to proceed with the building of the Naval Hospital at Greenwich, demolition of the King Charles Building was contemplated. Sundry workmen, in the disparaging words of Hawksmoor,

> indifferent to . . . whether they get Money by destroying or erecting Fabricks, gave their Opinion that it was nothing but a Heap of Stones, and that it might lawfully and reasonably be destroyed,

[97] V. Scamozzi, *L'idea della architettura universale* (1615), I. iii. 284.

[98] Webb appears to endorse the view of Lord Arundel, expressed in a letter to Jones, shortly before his death in 1646, that 'Italy *was no more* Italy', there being 'such decay of Architecture, Sculpture, Painting and all that was good and vertuous from what not 40 Years before he had seen therein' (*A Vindication of Stone-Heng Restored* (1655), 182). Webb might have seen a copy of Falda's *Chiese di Roma* (1655), but a more likely source for his Baroque, considering his interest in French interior design, was the *Desseins de plusieurs palais* of Antoine le Pautre (1652).

and turn'd into Ornaments for slighter Buildings . . . But her Majesty . . . order'd it should remain, and the other Side of the Royal Court made answerable to it, in a proper Time.[99]

Progress of the work

The incomplete, first range of Greenwich Palace cost Charles II £36,000.[100] The ground was staked out in January 1664 and in February the labourers began the digging of three foundation ditches, 250 feet long and 6 feet wide and deep.[101] A dam, filled with marsh earth, 80 feet long, 7 feet deep, and 4 feet wide was constructed, and in May piles were driven and pumping was going on day and night: the foundations were extending into the bed of the river. In March Pepys 'did observe the foundation of a very great house for the King, which will cost a great deale of money'.[102] In July, the masons were putting Portland stones between the piles, and in August the foundations were complete, the labourers filling up the ends with marsh earth.[103] Kentish and 'Scottish' stone was also used in the foundations, but, above, Portland stone facings were used exclusively. Scaffolding was set up immediately for the masons and bricklayers. Work went on all around the building at once, scaffold being erected at the north end in October, for the setting of the first and second pillars, and all along the east side for the range of 'Mr Marshall's work' and 'Mr Young's work'. In December the carpenters set up a frame for the setting of the four pilasters on the east side of the south end of the building.[104] The masonry work throughout was divided between Joshua Marshall and John Young, who shared the east front, and Stephen Switzer and Thomas Wise, who built the south pavilion.[105] Marshall alone was responsible for the north pavilion and the sculpture of the east and north front pediments, comprising, respectively, the royal Stuart arms supported by the reclining figures of Fortitude and Dominion of the Sea, and the arms supported by Mars and Fame. John Young was responsible for the stonework of the west, back front, including the pediment and its cartouche of the Stuart arms flanked by military trophies. Almost 2,400 tons of Portland stone were employed,[106] sawn to size on the site by the masons, Marshall, for example, being paid £5 4*s*. 2*d*. in September 1664 for sawing 2,500 feet of blocks '@ ½d/foot at 1″ deep'.[107] The master bricklayers throughout were Maurice Emmett and Thomas Pattison.

In May 1664 Webb was paid for an eleven-day visit to Portland and Lyndhurst,[108] but, later, such tasks were delegated, Switzer being paid for attending the ordering of stones in July 1665,[109] and Webb's 'servant', Robert Somerton, who figures in the Accounts as the recipient of 'riding charges' along with Webb, in 1667 making a journey to Portland

[99] N. Hawksmoor, 'Remarks', p. 20.

[100] R. Dodsley, *London and its Environs Described*, iii, (1761), 70. According to the computation of John Newman (*King's Works*, v), expenditure overall at Greenwich to 1672 was £42,000, and, from 1665 to 1672, £27,755.

[101] PRO Works 5/4.

[102] Pepys, *Diary*, i (1953), 494, 4 Mar. 1664.

[103] PRO Works 5/5.

[104] Ibid.

[105] PRO Works 5/8.

[106] *King's Works*, v. 148.

[107] PRO Works 5/6.

[108] PRO Works 5/5.

[109] PRO Works 5/8.

to settle quarry business and make an agreement with the quarrymen.[110] In January 1665 Richard Gammon was reimbursed for 'money by him laid out for the carriage of trunks out of Somersetshire from John Webb Esq Deputy Surveyor with draughts, booke prints and papers in them for his Majesty's service'.[111] Gammon was a Clerk of Works who, like Webb, had married a 'kinswoman' of Inigo Jones. His bringing of the papers from Webb's place of retirement is an indication that work on the exterior was progressing steadily, and inspiration now was needed for the designing of the interior fittings: Webb's earliest interior drawings are dated 1665.

By July 1665 the ground-storey walls had risen to the 'upper side of the fascia against the first floore',[112] and in November the scaffold was moved from the portico to the Thames-side pavilion for the setting of quoins and capitals.[113] Meanwhile, there were several scaffolds within and around the walls of the building for the bricklayers.

In January 1666 foundations were dug for the great stairs at the south end of the building.[114] These are shown on one of Webb's plans, leading up to the entrance vestibule. In February scaffolding was moved round to the back front for the masons to enrich the architrave, frieze, and cornice. By April 'up to the under parte of the architrave' was complete all round the building, and the entablature and pediments finished by November.[115] The rate of progress now began to slacken.

Scaffolding was in place in March 1667 for the vaulting of the 'alcove room' (the King's Bedchamber) and for roofing work.[116] In April the scaffold next to the Thames was repaired for the masons to 'make good what has layed all winter'. Robert Streeter, the Sergeant Painter, was paid £4 'for painting stone collor in distemper the figures and Compartments for the 2 frontispieces being farr bigger than the life',[117] but the masons continued to be employed on the portico and pavilions throughout 1668 and 1669, Marshall 'twice taking down and setting up the pieces adjoining the pillars entering into the portico and ... making severall alterations about the said new building'. Switzer and Wise in 1668 were making alterations to the south pavilion, and in 1669–70 Marshall was setting up the upper rail and balusters on the Thames pavilion. He did not present a bill for the carvings which Streeter painted until May 1668, when he claimed £200 'for carving 2 compartments with the Kings armes engraven in them, and 4 figures lying on the sides in the 2 frontispieces towards the Thames and Garden'.[118]

In February 1668 new joists had to be laid in the Gallery floor, which had been damaged in the works. In February 1669 the roof was finished, and in November and December 1669 flaws in the bases of the east front and Thames pavilion columns were repaired.[119] At the beginning of the following year, boards were nailed up at the Thames pavilion, which completed the boarding up of all the lower windows, begun in July

[110] PRO E/351/3438.
[111] PRO E/351/3278.
[112] PRO Works 5/7.
[113] PRO Works 5/8.
[114] Ibid.
[115] PRO Works 5/9.
[116] Ibid.
[117] PRO Works 5/10.
[118] PRO Works 5/12.
[119] PRO Works 5/13.

1669.[120] Work, by this time, had almost ceased, Pepys observing that the King's house 'goes on slow, but is very pretty'.[121] Webb was paid his last month's salary in July 1670, when the Extraordinary Account was theoretically closed.[122] Work continued slowly after this, miscellaneous maintenance still going on in 1673,[123] but it is with the payments to Marshall for completing the balustrade; to Streeter for painting doorcases, windows, rails, and balusters; to Edward Martin, for plastering several ceilings, and to John Grove for three, fretwork ceilings, that the Greenwich account truly can be said to have closed. This took place on 31 October 1672, which, too neatly to be fictional, was the day after Webb died.[124]

Of Webb's interior designs, one set certainly was put in progress, that for twelve marble chimneypieces: five of best and five of ordinary white marble, and two of mixed marble. Webb recorded 'Particulars of the Chimneys sent for to Lygorne',[125] drawing sections of the mouldings for the pieces for the Grand (presumably, Presence) Chamber, Cabinet Room, Withdrawing Room, and the room below it. These were first considered in 1665,[126] and designs were dispatched to Leghorn in 1667,[127] the marbles arriving at Greenwich in March 1669.[128] As well as the chimneypieces, there were five blocks of best white and two blocks of black and yellow marble, and 4,496 white marble, angle paving stones. The work had by this time slowed down to such an extent that there was no possibility of doing anything but put the marbles into store: they were taken into the cellar of the Queen's House, not to be removed until 1693, when they went to Hampton Court.[129] There are no chimneypieces now at Hampton Court in Webb's grand style, but many of the bolection moulded examples might be surrounds which originally were intended for Greenwich.

If Webb's complete, decorative scheme had been executed at Greenwich, it would have provided a fitting comparison for the suite of rooms at Wilton, which now stands as the sole, surviving example of the Caroline grand style. Webb's drawings of 1665–6 give us some idea of what might have been, providing details of the decoration of all the main floor state rooms.[130] The coved ceilings, with inset, rectangular panels surrounded by foliage and figures, are comparable with certain of the Wilton designs, although more freely drawn and densely textured (pl. 94). The degree of naturalism in the foliage is

[120] The building remained boarded up and fenced around, used as a storehouse, until it passed out of royal hands in 1694 for conversion to use as part of the Naval Hospital. In his drawings for the King Charles Building, Webb followed his customary practice of showing the window openings blank, but the intended form of the windows is worth considering since this was a period of innovation in window design. Sliding windows had been used, apparently for the first time in England, in the works of 1661–4 at Somerset House, and it might be presumed that Webb intended to fenestrate the King Charles Building in the same way. However, by the early 1670s, counterbalanced, vertically sliding sash windows were being introduced and it is possible that Webb would have incorporated these at Greenwich if the block had been completed during his lifetime. By the time of the building of the Naval Hospital, the use of sash windows was a matter of course and the King Charles Building was completed accordingly (see H. J. Louw,' 'The Origin of the Sash-Window', *Architectural History*, 26 (1983), 61–2).

[121] Pepys, *Diary*, iii. 374, 16 Mar. 1669.

[122] PRO E 351/3438.

[123] PRO Works 5/19, 5/20.

[124] PRO E 351/3438.

[125] *RIBA Cat.* 163.

[126] *CSPD 1665–6*, p. 171 (?1665).

[127] PRO Works 5/9, 5/10.

[128] PRO Works 5/14, 5/18. In Barlow's *Journal* ('of his life at sea . . . from 1659 to 1703'), reference is made to a visit to Leghorn in 1668: 'So we staying there some days, the other fireship that was with us was ordered to go into the Mould and fit herself for the loading of white and blue marble stone for to carry to England, which was to be laid in the King's house, which was building at Greenwich' (*Barlow's Journal*, i, transcribed by B. Lubbock (1934); the original MS is in the National Maritime Museum; I owe this reference to Erica Davies, of the Museum).

[129] PRO Works 5/46.

[130] *RIBA Cat.* 129–62.

particularly advanced for its date. For the ceiling of the Cabinet Room, a small dome was intended, in the spandrels of which were to be cartouches of the four continents, over which eagles spread their wings. In the surviving, 'not taken' design, Webb illustrates part of the area devoted to Europe, noting in the margin: 'The allusion, ys his Mats Eagles—with/his shipping, spread their wings/over the whole world.' Such an allusion was an appropriate piece of propaganda during the period of the Second Anglo-Dutch War (1665–7), although the attack on the Thames and the Medway in 1667 showed it to be rather hollow.

Among the chimneypieces we find Webb's familiar Francophile swags, garlands, and broken pediments, with the addition in the Bedchamber of putti. The pediment of the overmantel of this piece is very like the surviving example at Drayton, whilst that for the Gallery is similar to the one at Lamport. Two, alternative designs are offered for the Cabinet Room, one with superimposed orders and one without.

Foliage and putti also decorate the friezes, and in the King's Bedchamber a direct source for the ornament can be cited (pl. 95). Following his adaptations from Barbet and Cotelle, Webb has turned for his frieze of putti and foliage to Le Pautre's *Frises et ornements à la moderne*, which was published in 1661. A connection with Wilton is also indicated by the drawing for the doorcase between the Cabinet Room and the Long Gallery (pl. 96). Like the door in the Double Cube Room, this has a composite order (with lion and unicorn capitals) (pl. 97), carrying a broken pediment which supports the reclining figures of Liberality and Magnanimity. The pediment here is elegantly curving—in this respect, an improvement on the angularity of the Wilton piece.

The most striking and unusual decoration was reserved for the alcove in the King's Bedchamber (pl. 98), which is a unique example of the use of the palm-tree motif in the decoration of the period. Webb had used palm fronds before, on chimneypieces and overmantels at The Vyne and Wilton, and Jones had employed the theme in masques—palm-tree decoration featuring in the 1635 *Temple of Love*. In *Neptune's Triumph*, which was scheduled for 1624 but not performed (because of a diplomatic impasse regarding the French and Spanish ambassadors), the tree represented was intended to be the banyan, a mystical Tree of Harmony, symbolizing the harmonious strength of the Court, but Jones's drawing is of palm trees, the choice of which, given its Solomonic connotations, cannot have been accidental. The representation of James I as Solomon, ruling judiciously over his Holy City, was part of Jacobean, official imagery.[131] This concept is something which Webb, in his alcove design, appears to have been anxious to revive. His main source for the decoration would have been Villalpando's engraving of the Sanctuary of Solomon's Temple, which shows it decorated with palm trees, in the *In Ezechielem explanationes* of 1604. Webb's palms grow out of Corinthian columns, in a manner underlining the compatibility of classical antiquity and Christian revelation.

The building of large palaces, in the seventeeth century, was the prerogative of absolute monarchs: Solomons in fact as well as image. Charles II was not such a man and, being more pragmatic than his father, despite ambitions, he could not, at this time, comfortably appear to harbour absolutist thoughts. It is for this reason, as much as the financial one

[131] Parry, *Golden Age*, pp. 21, 26–9; S. Orgel, *The Illusion of Power* (1975), 70–7.

95 (*above*). King Charles Building, Greenwich: design for the entablature of the King's Bedchamber

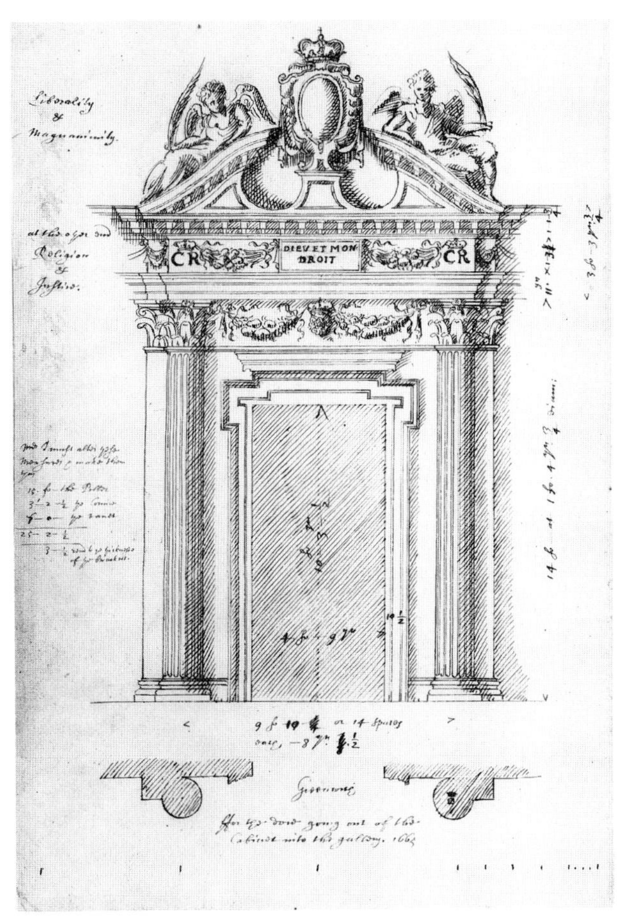

96 (*right*). King Charles Building, Greenwich: design for the doorcase for the door between the Cabinet Room and the Long Gallery. The reclining figures of Liberality and Magnanimity frame the cartouche

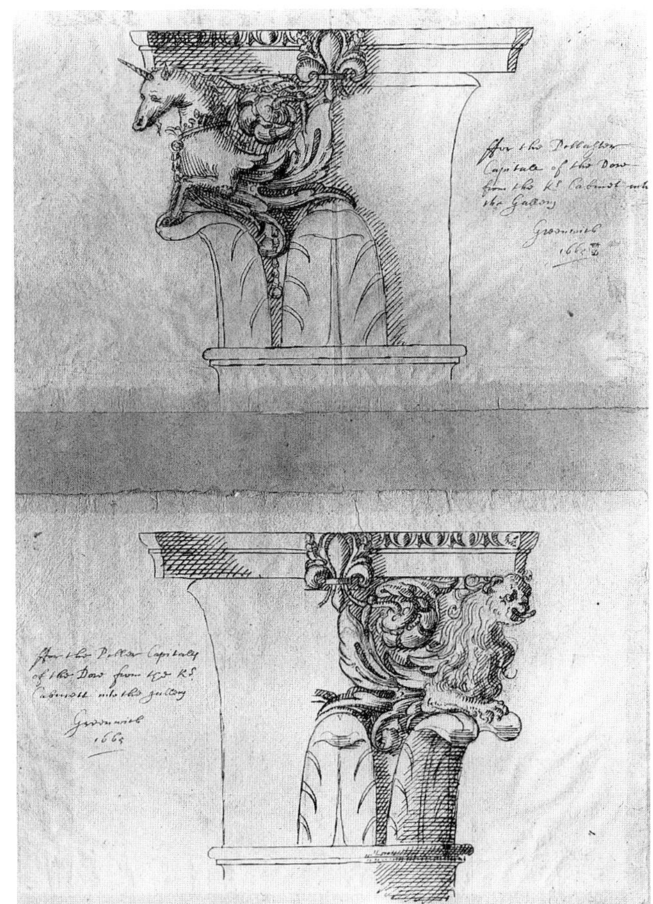

98 (*above*). King Charles Building, Greenwich: design for the alcove of the King's Bedchamber; engraving after Webb's drawing

97 (*left*). King Charles Building, Greenwich: design for composite capitals for the door between the Cabinet Room and the Long Gallery; the unicorn and lion are from the royal arms

(although the two were linked), that the Greenwich work was curtailed, leaving its architect to retire 'at leasure, until his Majesty shall bee gratiously pleased to proceed towards the perfecting of his new Royall Palace at Greenwich'.[132] Charles did not proceed either here or at Whitehall, although in 1682 some effort seems to have been made to commence fitting up the King Charles Building.[133] Little was done and the following year found the King turning to another site, suitably positioned in relation to the coast in case of crisis, Winchester.

Nevertheless, King Charles's financial position did have a damaging effect on the progress of the works. Webb claimed in 1669 that 'yor Majestie was gratiously pleased to grant yor Petitioner a Salary of £200 p Ann for Greenwich; but Dread Sir it hath been so slowly paid that yor Petitioner hath spent out of his own estate little lesse than £1,000 in ordering that worke, besides the neglect of his owne houshold affaires'.[134] In April 1667 a report to the King by Denham and two other Officers of the Works (probably Webb and Francis Wethered, the Comptroller) stated that 'the charge of building Greenwich Palace from February 1664 to February 1667 was £26,433 7*s*. 11$\frac{1}{4}$*d*., whereof £17,696 13*s*. 4*d*. has been paid; and request that £10,000 may be assigned for work this year, since out of £10,000 granted last year at £1,000 per month, only £4,600 has been received'.[135]

The following March the same petitioners, and Edward Marshall, claimed that moneys remaining unaccounted for in the hands of Sir Robert Palmer, cofferer to the late King, should, after the discharge of debts, be directed towards the building at Greenwich.[136] Webb is said to have discovered Palmer's concealment, incurring expenses of 9*s*. 6*d*. in the process, and as a reward he requested that he be paid, in his capacity as Inigo Jones's executor, £500 which Charles I had borrowed from Jones.[137] The King promised that the recovered money should be used only at Greenwich, but said that he had already allowed a sufficient reward for the discovery.

In December 1668 it was ordered that all the fines from the King's Bench should be employed for the Greenwich works.[138] The previous year a warrant had been issued to the Commissioners of Prizes to sell the 'Deborah' of Amsterdam, the proceeds to go to Greenwich.[139] Finances thus came in a rather piecemeal fashion, from special grants which rapidly fell into arrears, and from unexpected prizes. It was not a sound basis upon which to build a palace, and, although it is an architectural tragedy that Charles was not able to utilize fully the talents at his disposal, it remains a wonder that anything was built at all.

[132] Introduction to Webb's expanded MS 'Essay' on China; Wells Cathedral.

[133] PRO Works 5/33, 5/35.

[134] PRO SP 29/251 120, pub. in *Wren Society*, 18 (1941), 156 (see App. II).

[135] *CSPD 1667*, p. 60, Apr. 1667.

[136] *CSPD 1667–8*, p. 297, 18 Mar. 1668.

[137] PRO Works 5/12; cf. *CSPD 1641–3*, p. 362, 28 July 1642: 'Receipt by the King for £500 lent by Inigo Jones, Surveyor of Works, which he promises to satisfy again'—this had been taken to the King at Beverley by Webb.

[138] *Calendar of Treasury Books*, ii, (1667–8), 433, 502, 7 Sept. and 7 Dec. 1668.

[139] *CSPD 1666–7*, p. 452, 14 Jan. 1667.

6

CONCLUSION

THE career of John Webb as architect, author, connoisseur, and stage-designer may be accounted a success, notwithstanding his failure to achieve the high office for which, by training, experience, and inclination, he was fully equipped. In the course of a working life of over forty years he firmly established himself, firstly as a worthy heir to Inigo Jones and, secondly, as a great and innovative architect in his own right. In so doing, he played a significant part in establishing the intellectual and social position of the architect in England, during a turbulent period which was characterized by uncertainty, experiment, and realignment in all areas of speculative thought and its practical application.

Webb himself was far from sanguine about the upheavals of his times—'innovations in Religion', he wrote, being 'alwaies attended with dreadfull iudgments'[1]—and, as we have seen, sought solace and explanation in the investigation of the remote. In so doing, he underlined his own place in history, as part of the architectural continuum which extended from the Pyramids to the Banqueting House and beyond.[2] The line often appeared to waver and frequently was seen to decline, particularly when contemporary endeavours were measured against the unsurpassable achievements of the ancients of the Golden Age. Nevertheless, the line remained unbroken and continued to be so until late in the eighteenth century, when a more sophisticated view of the historical process supplied the intellectual backdrop to a new age of confident experimentation. Even Colen Campbell, writing in 1715 in his polemical and partial introduction to *Vitruvius Britannicus*, whilst equating the Jonesian achievement with that of Palladio, had not had the temerity to suggest that contemporary architecture could equal, let alone surpass, that of ancient Rome.

John Webb saw himself as heir to a great tradition. He analysed and interpreted the historical reconstructions of Palladio and Scamozzi; he borrowed selectively from the drawings and treatises of these and other masters of the Italian and French Renaissance; he learned directly from the instruction and example of Inigo Jones. By mid-career he had succeeded in evolving an architecture with its roots in tradition but, the criticism of Sir Roger Pratt notwithstanding, wholly applicable to contemporary requirements. This was no mean achievement, since the upheavals of the seventeenth century were manifested as much in the social requirements of domestic architecture as they were in the better known, public fields of politics and religion.

Thanks to Colen Campbell's *Vitruvius Britannicus*, and to Lord Burlington's sponsorship of publications by William Kent, Isaac Ware, and John Vardy, the architecture of Inigo

[1] J. Webb, *Historical Essay* (1669), 130. [2] Cf. J. Rykwert, *The First Moderns* (1980), 465.

Jones and John Webb was brought to a wide audience in the early eighteenth century. Neo-Palladianism, based as much upon the work of Jones and Webb as upon that of Palladio and Scamozzi, was a triumph of Burlingtonian patronage and propaganda. Thanks in large measure to his efforts, it had by the 1730s become established as the national style.[3] The work of Webb, generally attributed at the time to Inigo Jones, was, along with the undisputed work of the master, crucial to its development. Webb's houses, through engravings, were well known to many who would not have had the opportunity of visiting them. Even those who did see the originals, however, appear to have looked at them through eyes which were conditioned by engravings, seeing them as they saw the illustrations of the work of Palladio in the *Quattro libri*, as two-dimensional objects, divorced from context, flat upon the page. This raises questions about the way in which architecture is perceived and the extent to which perceptions, and therefore interpretations, change according to the preconceptions of the viewer and the mode of presentation.

The homogeneity and planar precision which was imparted by the engraving technique is analogous to the uniformity which is imposed nowadays by photography—a uniformity which tends to mask details, flatten profiles, and simplify relationships. In photography, these disadvantages may be considered to be among the expected drawbacks of the medium and, because we are so familiar with the technique, we make the necessary allowances. In the Campbell/Kent engravings, the divorcing of the object from its context, framed by plain, white paper rather than by its landscape, imparted an iconic quality which was translated, perhaps unconsciously, into neo-Palladian architecture itself, which, unlike the work of Jones and Webb, is essentially two dimensional and static. In this, it contrasts most strikingly with the fully modelled architecture of the English Baroque, the style which neo-Palladianism displaced in fashionable and influential circles. Webb's example, particularly at Greenwich, had been as crucial to the development of this earlier style as it was to become to the later, and we might speculate how much more Palladian the architecture of the Naval Hospital might have been if Wren and Hawksmoor had looked at the King Charles Building through eyes attuned as much by engravings as by the building itself.

It may be considered remarkable that Webb's work could have been taken up by two very different architectural factions. In fact, it is a tribute to his architectural integrity that this was possible. Such integrity demands respect. He drew consistently and selectively upon tradition with the intention of producing a formulation in touch with the past but appropriate to the developing requirements of his changing times. The internal consistency of that formulation, as it evolved over forty years, was, despite misattribution, to provide an inspiration and a model for generations to come. It is to John Webb that we owe the establishment of the Jonesian stylistic synthesis which held sway in English architecture for over a century.

But it is in the less visible although no less important field of house planning that Webb achieved what is arguably his more important legacy, the elegant and delicate balance

[3] See RCHME, *Wilton House and English Palladianism* (1988).

of family and service, and public and private accommodation. This achievement, again arrived at through a close and rigorous consideration of past examples and present requirements, is the most provocatively relevant for the architecture of our own time.[4] Certainly, if the architecture of the past is to teach us anything today, it is to this inner content that we should be looking, rather than to those outer, stylistic manifestations, which in the hands of the majority of practitioners of the complex art are mere vulgar notations, devoid of meaning. Architecture, as a later, greater architect observed, 'has nothing to do with the various "styles" . . . [it] has graver ends; capable of the sublime, it impresses the most brutal instincts by its objectivity; it calls into play the highest faculties by its very abstraction'.[5] This was as true in the seventeenth century as it was when it was written in 1923. It remains true today.

[4] For the distillation of past principles and their transformation to new purposes, see W. Curtis, 'Principle and Pastiche' and 'Modern Transformations of Classicism', *Architectural Review*, 176 (Aug. 1984), 11–21, 39–45.

[5] Le Corbusier, *Vers une architecture* (1923): trans. F. Etchells, *Towards a New Architecture* (1927), 25–6.

CATALOGUE OF ARCHITECTURAL WORKS

THIS catalogue lists all of John Webb's known architectural works and projects. It excludes those houses for which a previous attribution has not been sustainable on stylistic or documentary grounds: Kirby Hall, Sherborne Lodge, Stapleford Park, St Giles's House, and Tythrop.

The catalogue is arranged in alphabetical order by place, and lists the patron, the date of the work, the location of drawings, publication by Colen Campbell or others, and important references. Where the work is discussed fully in the text a cross reference is given and the catalogue entry is of a summary nature.

Webb's theatre designs, for auditoria and for scenes, have been analysed fully elsewhere: S. Orgel and R. Strong, *Inigo Jones, The Theatre of the Stuart Court* (1973); J. Orrell, *The Theatres of Inigo Jones and John Webb* (1985). For a brief discussion, see Appendix I.

AMESBURY ABBEY, WILTSHIRE

(see also pp. 94–100; pls. 63–8)

Marquess of Hertford (restored to Dukedom of Somerset, Sept. 1660; d. Oct. 1660)

*c.*1659–64

New house built on the site of an older priory. Wings were added, to the designs of Henry Flitcroft, for the Duke and Duchess of Queensberry, *c.*1750–61. The house was rebuilt by Thomas Hopper for Sir Edmund William Antrobus from 1834, incorporating some original walls and one of Webb's bolection moulded chimneypieces (see RCHME, *Wilton House and English Palladianism* (1988)). The coat-of-arms cartouches from the north and south fronts of Webb's house survive in the present *porte-cochère*. Webb's gatepiers, which originally formed the entrance to the forecourt, were resited at the entrance to the grounds between 1773 and 1805, at the time of the creation of the south drive.

Composite capital (Chatsworth Album 26, no. 127), inscribed 'Ambresbury for Marquisse Hertford'. This depicts the phoenix in flames, emblematic of the Seymours, set in acanthus leaves. Survey drawings of Webb's house by Wyatt Papworth (plan, elevation, section, gatepiers), 1840–1 (RIBA, W13/16, 2–5), based on sketches made by C. J. Richardson in 1817 and 1829 (Metropolitan Museum of Art, New York, no. 26.85, fos. 167r, 167v, 236r–241r). House illustrated and described by C. R. Cockerell, 1823 (Diary, RIBA MS Collection; edited version published by J. Harris, 'C. R. Cockerell's "Ichnographica Domestica"', *Architectural History*, 14 (1971)). Campbell, iii, pl. 7. Kent, ii, pls. 8–9. Engravings showing the house after the addition of wings published 1787 (Harrison & Co., *Picturesque Views of the Principal Seats of the Nobility and Gentry in England and Wales*) and 1826 (R. Colt Hoare, *History of Modern Wiltshire*, ii, iii, after a drawing by Buckler, made in 1805, now in the Mellon Collection).

ASHBURNHAM HOUSE, LONDON

(pl. 99)

William Ashburnham, Cofferer of the King's Household

*c.*1662–5

Remodelling, attributed to Webb; extant.

Plan and section of staircase, attributed to

Inigo Jones, published by Isaac Ware (*Designs of Inigo Jones*, pls. 6–7). Complete survey drawings (H. Sirr, 'Ashburnham House and the Precincts of Westminster Abbey', *Journal of the RIBA*, 3rd ser. 17 (1910)).

The lease of Ashburnham House in Little Dean's Yard was granted at the Restoration to William Ashburnham by the Dean and Chapter of Westminster. This small, fourteenth-century rubble building was then remodelled to provide monumental spaces within a small compass; particularly a grand staircase (pl. 99) and a first-floor drawing-room whose disposition was conditioned in part by the existing thick walls. The attribution of this work to Webb rests on Batty Langley's remarks in *Ancient Masonry* (i (1736), 391): 'This staircase ... the Earl of Ashburnham ... did inform me was built by Mr. Webb, a Disciple of Inigo Jones, not by Inigo Jones himself, though perhaps the design might have been made by Inigo Jones, and executed by Mr. Webb.'

The stairwell is domed, with an upper gallery, and its panelled walls are articulated by Ionic pilasters. It achieves monumentality on a small scale, all its members being subtly scaled down to fit a space of only 23′ by 14′6″. Outside this basic rectangle, there is a smaller space which contains the short flight from the entrance hall and, above, the landing which gives on to the ante-room (to the drawing-room) and the dining-room. Both of these spaces, in being outside the domed area, enable the viewer to comprehend the whole ingenious structure, in all its doll's house unreality, from outside its focal point.

Webb's interest in spatially innovative staircases was demonstrated at Gunnersbury and Amesbury, but both of these had to be moved through to be understood; at Ashburnham House the viewer acts around rather than within the space, the overall effect owing more to French than to Italian precedent. The spatial inventiveness of Ashburnham is such that the attribution to Webb may be questioned, although his illusionist design for the Cabinet Room at Wilton, dated 1649 (*RIBA Cat.* 172), does offer a parallel for the treatment of the upper gallery and dome. A further, stylistic parallel may be drawn, between the carving of the foliage in the tympanum of the arch over the ante-room doorway and that of the carving of the balustrade of the staircase at Lamport.

In 1707–8 Lord Ashburnham made arrangements to transfer all the marble chimneypieces from Ashburnham House, Westminster, to Ampthill Park, Bedfordshire, which he had bought in 1690. He told his London agent, Macburnye, to replace them all with plain deal chimneypieces, since 'I am resolved to let or sell my house as soon as maybe' (Sussex CRO, Lewes; Letter Books of 1st Baron Ashburnham, Ashburnham MS 4448). There is no sign of these chimneypieces at Ampthill today.

As well as the staircase, the drawing-room also at Ashburnham House was domed, but this enrichment was lost when a third storey was added to the house in 1821.

BELVOIR CASTLE, LEICESTERSHIRE

(see also pp. 75–9; pls. 47–8; figs. 4–5)

The Countess of Rutland

1654–68

Proposals for a new house to replace the one which had been 'slighted' by the Parliamentary forces in 1649: plans, elevations and design for a capital (*RIBA Cat.* 104–12); finalized scheme published by Kent (ii, pls. 22–4). Not executed.

Rebuilding of old castle, following the existing plan, 1655–68. Building accounts (Belvoir Archives, Misc. MS 67) show high points of expenditure in 1656–7, 1664, and 1667. Drawing for 'Architrave Freeze & Cornice' 1667 (Belvoir Archives, Map 127).

The Countess died in 1671, and her husband, the 8th Earl, in 1679. With the death of the Countess, the impetus for the new work at Belvoir was removed, since the Earl preferred to live at his family home, Haddon Hall. Work

99 (*left*). Ashburnham House, Westminster: the galleried staircase, viewed from the first-floor landing

100 (*below*). Butleigh Court: Grace Webb's early eighteenth-century view of Webb's house in Somerset

on the decoration of Belvoir did not resume until the 1680s, on the chapel in 1682 (Belvoir Archives, Misc. MS 67), and on the staircase and the new Countess's rooms in 1686 (HMC, 12th Report, Appendix, Pt. V, Rutland MS Vol. II (1889), 108, 110). The castle was remodelled by James Wyatt 1801–13, damaged by fire 1816, and reinstated by *c.*1820.

Survey plans of Webb's rebuilt castle, made by John Spyers in 1779 for Capability Brown, together with Brown's proposals for alterations, dated 1780 (Belvoir Archives, Map 131); unexecuted. Model of the house made in 1799, displayed at Belvoir.

Views published by J. Badeslade and J. Rocque (*Vitruvius Britannicus*, iv (1739), pls. 47–8). View of castle in the background of *Portrait of a Grey Arab and his Groom*, catalogued as a painting by James Ross but subsequently attributed to J. B. Closterman (*c.*1660–1711) in *Sporting Paintings* (catalogue of an exhibition, Lane Fine Art, London, 1982), pl. 31.

BUTLEIGH COURT, SOMERSET

(pl. 100)

John Webb

*c.*1670(?)

Additions to an older house?

In 1653, John Webb agreed a payment of £8,420 to Thomas Symcocks Esq., for 'lands in fee simple in the manor Butley, the hundred of Whitley and the capital messauge or farm of Butley' (PRO C8/115/183). Butleigh was Webb's principal home from 1654 until his death, although he continued to have rooms in Scotland Yard during the 1650s (*King's Works*, iii. 157–8).

There is no mention of a new house in the litigation which followed his death, but he possibly made additions to the existing building. However, the evidence is by no means clear. An eighteenth-century topographical drawing of a nine-bay house with Italianate, tripartite loggias, set *in antis* at each end of the front, has been published by John Harris as Webb's house (*The Palladians* (1981), 52; RIBA Drawings Collection, K4/4(21)). The drawing is untitled, but the association with Butleigh was suggested by its being one of a group which included late-eighteenth-century drawings by William Paty for additions and alterations to Butleigh Court (J. Lever (ed.), *Catalogue of the Drawings Collection of the RIBA: O–R* (1976), 32; and Harris, *The Palladians*, p. 104). Although this is suggestive, it is not conclusive since the drawing does not correspond with either the depictions by John Buckler (1830s; Pigott Album, Somerset Archaeological & Natural History Society, Taunton; preparatory drawings BL Add. MS 36380, fos. 87, 89) or with the early eighteenth-century topographical view signed by Grace Webb (RIBA Drawings Collection, K4/4(1)) (pl. 100), although it has some elements in common with them. The Buckler and Webb views show a classical, south-facing range of seven bays, possibly of the late seventeenth century, situated to the west of the original sixteenth-century house. It is parapeted, of two storeys, with circular or *œil-de-bœuf* windows lighting the basement. All of these features occur also in the anonymous drawing published by Harris. Since Buckler also illustrates the west side of the house, and the east side was occupied by the older buildings, the front with loggias could have been situated, possibly, to the north.

There is no trace now of the house lived in by Webb, its place having been taken in 1845 by the large Tudor-style mansion designed by John Chessell Buckler, the artist's son.

CHEVENING, KENT

(pl. 101)

The 14th Lord Dacre

1655

Works to the existing, possibly uncompleted house; executed but altered subsequently. Designs for composite capitals (Bk. of Caps., fos. 28–9). Campbell, ii, pl. 85 ('said to be designed by Inigo Jones'). For a family connection with another commission, see also below, The Vyne.

Chevening is said to have been built by the 13th Lord Dacre (W. H. Ireland, *History of the County of Kent*, iv (1830)), but it might have been unfinished at the time of his death in 1630. During the recent (*c.*1970) restoration it was noted that there was a change from Midlands oolite to local sandstone in the quoins a few stones above first-floor level. This is suggestive, perhaps, of a desire to complete and secure the fabric of the building rapidly and cheaply, possibly leaving the interior unfinished (J. Newman, *West Kent and the Weald* (1976), 210–13; Mr Newman has kindly made available to me the notes which he made at the time of his visit to the house in 1970).

Webb's work in 1655, mentioned in a letter to Sir Justinian Isham of Lamport, involved his designing 'ornaments of wainscott for a roome in Kent for my Lo:Dacres wch is 31 fo:long 22 broad and 24 fo:high . . . his roome is very noble and hee bestows much cost upon it, but I am confident yors wilbe more proportionable' (J. A. Gotch, 'Some Newly Found Drawings and Letters of John Webb', *Journal of the RIBA*, 3rd ser. 28 (1921), 574). This high room does not survive. It was situated at first-floor level at the centre of the garden front, above the panelled saloon. Webb's room was seen by Roger North in the later seventeenth century when it was, surprisingly, still unfinished: 'The cheif room above is not finished, and was intended to be done with lunetts and small lights *all'Italiana*' (H. M. Colvin and J. Newman (eds.), *Of Building—Roger North's Writings on Architecture* (1981), 71). Webb's work might have been stopped before getting properly under way since Francis, Lord Dacre, went abroad in 1655 'on some discontent between him and his lady' (*DNB* s.v. Francis Lennard). Webb possibly was responsible also for the panelled saloon on the ground floor, below the high room, which was, in the words of Roger North, 'sett off with pilaster & arcuated wanscote'. This room survives, but the panelling was reset in the early eighteenth century, to allow for the widening of the fireplace and the insertion of an extra door, and more recently much of it was renewed by the last Lord Stanhope, who died in 1967.

The Chevening estate was bought by James, the 1st Earl Stanhope, in 1716 (see A. Newman, *The Stanhopes of Chevening* (1969)). Between 1717 and 1721 he employed Thomas Fort on substantial additions and alterations to the house. In 1708 Stanhope had been presented with a set of rare tapestries by Frederick I of Prussia and these provided the occasion for the horizontal division of Webb's one-and-a-half storey room, in which they were to be displayed, the depth of the tapestries determining the new height. Fort's chimneypieces in the Tapestry Room and in the newly created attic-room above, appropriately for an Office of Works man, are massively Vanbrughian in manner (*Country Life*, 47 (1920), 548–56). Fort's attic-room was subdivided in the early nineteenth century. The 4th Earl, writing in 1848, noted that: 'The two rooms over the Tapestry Room were originally one, and were in 1727 the Library, in 1753 the Billiard Room, afterwards the Great Nursery, and were between 1801 and 1816 divided by my father who used the larger room for his sitting room and the smaller for his bedroom' (Kent CRO U 1590 699/4).

COBHAM HALL, KENT

(pl. 102)

The 4th Duke of Lennox and Richmond

1648

Design for rebuilding; unexecuted. Elevations towards courts and sections of cross wings (*Worcs. Coll. Cat.* 73).

This project for the Palladian rebuilding of the existing Elizabethan house upon its original plan was, like Durham House, stillborn, a victim of a time which was unpropitious for building. After the execution of Charles I, the Royalist Duke is said 'never to have had his health or his spirits again', but to have 'pined

101 (*right*). Chevening: elevation, ground, and first-floor plans of the house which Webb worked on in 1655. The ground-floor panelled saloon and the first-floor high room are at the centre of the garden side, uppermost on the plans

102 (*below*). Cobham Hall: designs for rebuilding, unexecuted; elevations towards the courts and sections of the cross wings

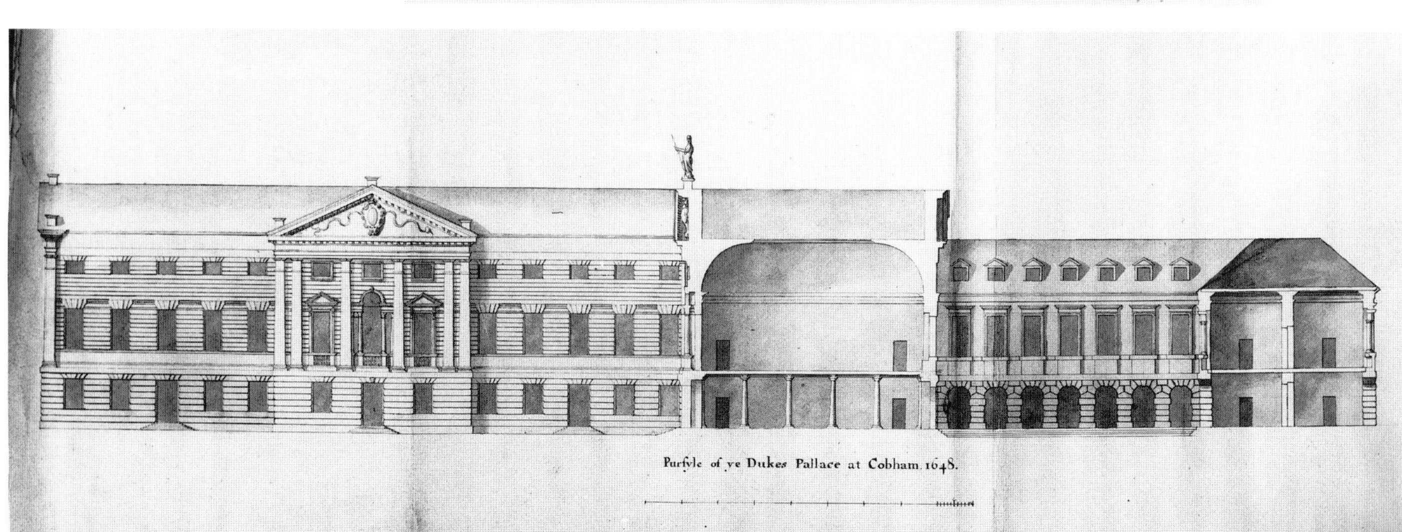

away in his house mourning for his Majesty's person'. It was left to the 6th Duke to make improvements to the house at the Restoration, and he employed Peter Mills rather than Webb on the designing of a new cross wing (H. M. Colvin, 'Peter Mills and Cobham Hall', in H. M. Colvin and J. Harris (eds.), *The Country Seat* (1970), 43–4).

Webb's grand design (pl. 102) has similarities with both the Durham House and Belvoir Castle schemes: the coved 35-foot high saloon over a columned entrance hall in the cross range relates it to the former, whilst the applied one-and-a-half storey portico, raised above the ground floor, anticipates the latter.

COLESHILL HOUSE, BERKSHIRE

(pl. 103)

Sir George Pratt

*c.*1647

Design for a chimneypiece and overmantel (*RIBA Cat.* 113); designs for composite capitals (Bk. of Caps., fos. 21–3, and Worcester College, 3 capitals pasted into J. Berain's *Desseins de cheminées* (Clarke collection)).

Sir Roger Pratt's Coleshill of *c.*1657/8–*c.*1662 was destroyed in 1952. The history of the building of the house and the nature of Webb's involvement are by no means clear (see N. Silcox-Crowe, 'Sir Roger Pratt', in R. Brown (ed.), *The Architectural Outsiders* (1985), 5–7; for a fuller discussion, see also Silcox-Crowe, 'The Life and Work of Sir Roger Pratt 1620–85' (University of Reading Ph.D. thesis, 1986)).

Between *c.*1645 and *c.*1662 there were possibly three, consecutive houses on adjacent sites at Coleshill. In 1645, in his will, Sir Henry Pratt enjoined his executors to collect any outstanding debts to finish 'my building in Colcell if I shall leave any part thereof unfinished at my decease' (PRO PROB 11/207,41). He died in 1647 and, according to Sir Mark Pleydell, the owner of the house from 1728, the house was burnt down 'soon after' the wedding of his son, Sir George Pratt, which also took place in 1647. Pleydell informs us, not necessarily reliably, that Sir George Pratt, for whom, according to the inscriptions on the drawings, Webb's designs were made, 'began a seat in ye prest Cucumber Garden and raised it one Story, when Pratt and Jones arriving causd it to be pulled down and rebuilt where it now stands. Pratt and Jones were frequently here and Jones was also consulted about ye Cielings' (H. Avray Tipping, *English Homes*, 4/1 (1920), 5). The presence of Inigo Jones in Pleydell's account is curious: Jones died in 1652 and there is no evidence in Sir Roger Pratt's notes to suggest that the two ever worked together. Furthermore, an aging Jones, unlike the more pragmatic Webb, would not have been working for a patron with republican sympathies: Sir George, unlike his Royalist father Sir Henry, was active in supporting the Commonwealth. It is equally unlikely that Webb would have been producing interior designs for a house whose walls had been raised only one storey, and it is implausible to suppose that he might have been collaborating with Sir Roger Pratt on the house which Pratt designed for his cousin Sir George in the later 1650s. Pratt certainly did not admire the work of Webb and, besides, Webb's designs were for a house articulated by the orders; Sir Roger Pratt's epoch-making Coleshill was astylar.

It is likely that Pleydell was conflating, mistakenly, several pieces of information and a more plausible sequence of events might be suggested:

(i) that Jones was consulted by the Royalist Sir Henry about a new house (or alterations to an old one) *c.*1645 or before;
(ii) that, after Sir Henry's death, Webb produced designs *c.*1647 for the fitting up of the interior of the uncompleted house for Sir George;
(iii) that this house was burned down and Sir George determined on the building of a new house in the cucumber garden;
(iv) that this house was begun but, upon the

advice of Sir Roger Pratt, was demolished before its shell had been completed, to be replaced by the new house which he designed for an adjacent site.

Webb's design for a chimneypiece and overmantel, framed by Corinthian pilasters, was engraved by Vardy as a design of Jones (*Some Designs of Mr Inigo Jones and Mr Wm Kent* (1744), pl. 8) (pl. 103). Vardy also published the magnificent chimneypiece after Vignola, which Pratt designed for the upper-floor saloon of Coleshill, as a design of Jones (Vardy, *Some Designs*, pl. 11). Thus the myth of Jones's involvement in Coleshill III was perpetuated. (Avray Tipping (*English Homes*) believed that this chimneypiece dated from the eighteenth century, but the arms and bust of Sir Mark Pleydell, dated 1755, together with the flanking urns, were later additions.)

Webb's designs for composite capitals, for 'ye Front', 'ye Atrium', and 'ye Great Chamber' were based on capitals by G. B. Montano (*Cinque libri di architettura: Architettura con diversi ornamenti* ... (1636); and drawings in the Larger Talman Album, Ashmolean Museum, which came from either Jones or Webb).

DRAYTON HOUSE, NORTHAMPTONSHIRE

(pl. 104)

The 2nd Earl of Peterborough

1653

Designs for chimneypieces; executed (*RIBA Cat.* 114–15).

The Earl of Peterborough fought for Charles I against the Parliamentary forces in 1643–4 and again in 1647. He was twice wounded and twice went into exile. He compounded for his estates in 1646 and 1649, spending his time until the Restoration in retirement at Drayton. During this period he employed Webb on work in the Elizabethan wing of the house (*Country Life*, 137 (1965), 1216–7, 1347–50; N. V. Stopford Sackville, *Drayton House* (1939); G. Jackson-Stops, *Drayton House* (1978)).

There is a possibility that Webb might have been involved in work throughout the wing, but no accounts survive. Three rooms are arranged *en suite*: the Green and Blue Drawing Rooms, originally a parlour and withdrawing-room, and the State Bedchamber. Webb's two drawings are for the chimneypieces and overmantels in the bedchamber and in the preceding withdrawing-room (the latter dated 1653). Only the overmantel in the bedchamber survives (pl. 104). This carries the Earl's elaborate coat of arms, flanked by bulbous garlands which hang from a scrolled, open pediment.

In addition to the chimneypieces, Webb probably was responsible for the doorcases of the bedchamber and withdrawing-room. On the floor above, the Dacca Room, reached by a stair from the bedchamber, has seventeenth-century mouldings which suggest that Webb's work at Drayton, despite the Earl's debts, might have been more extensive than the two surviving drawings suggest.

In the early eighteenth century William Talman was responsible for designing the new south front towards the entrance courtyard. His incorporation of emblematic composite capitals in the order which frames the doorway may be interpreted as a tribute to his predecessor.

DURHAM HOUSE, LONDON

(see also pp. 69–74; pl. 46; figs. 2–3)

The 4th Earl of Pembroke

*c.*1641(?)–*c.*1650(?)

Unexecuted designs for new house. 6 drawings (*Worcs. Coll. Cat.* 81–8). These comprise 4 plans (1 of which is dated 1649) and 1 elevation for a large new house, and 1 elevation for a smaller design.

During the reign of James I, the Strand and Ivy Lane frontages of Durham House were granted to Robert Cecil, Earl of Salisbury. He demolished the stables and erected the New

103 (*left*). Coleshill House: design by Webb for a chimneypiece and overmantel, engraved by John Vardy

104 (*below*). Drayton House: Webb's surviving overmantel in the State Bedchamber

Exchange in their place—this took up approximately half of the available frontage. The Exchange was opened in 1609 and survived until 1737. Webb's smaller design was intended, perhaps, to fit the remaining space. His larger design, for a house situated behind the Exchange, if executed would have been visible in its entirety only in an oblique view (*Survey of London*, 18 (1937); a detail from Morden and Lea's map of London (1682), is reproduced, p. 27).

GREENWICH PALACE, LONDON

(see also pp. 126–46; pls. 1, 87–98; figs. 6–10)

Royal Works

1637–72

1637: redrawing by Webb of a design by an anonymous French designer for a fountain (*Worcs. Coll. Cat.* 90–1).

1663–70: unexecuted proposals for adding pavilions, wings, and cupola to the Queen's House (*RIBA Cat.* 166–9).

1664–72: designs for a new palace of three ranges, of which only one, the King Charles Building, was executed, 1664–72: plans of three-range palace with flap showing variant arrangement for cross wing (*Worcs. Coll. Cat.* 89); plan and elevations of three-range palace by an unknown draughtsman (All Souls College, v. 21, 25–6); plan of three-range palace with further wings to south (*RIBA Cat.* 120); plan of chapel (*RIBA Cat.* 121); plans and elevations of King Charles Building (*RIBA Cat.* 122–8); designs for interiors of King Charles Building (*RIBA Cat.* 129–63). (*King's Works*, v. 140–52).

1665: unexecuted design for a pavilion on the hill to the south (RIBA, Boy. Coll. 18, 1–2; J. Bold, 'Greenwich: "The Grott & ascent by mr. Webb"', *Burlington Magazine*, 129 (1982), 149–50).

In 1694 the King Charles Building and adjoining lands, excluding the avenue leading from the Queen's House to the river, passed from royal ownership to trustees, for conversion to use as the Royal Hospital for Seamen. As Surveyor at Greenwich from 1696 until 1716, Sir Christopher Wren was responsible for the layout of the ranges which were built over the next fifty years (Campbell, i, pls. 82–9; iii, pls. 3–4). The Hospital continued in use until 1869; four years later the buildings became the home of the Royal Naval College.

GUNNERSBURY HOUSE, MIDDLESEX

(see also pp. 90–4; pls. 60–2)

Sir John Maynard, MP; Protector's Sergeant (1658), King's Sergeant (1660)

*c.*1658–63

New house on the site of an old manor house; demolished 1800–1. One surviving overmantel, now at Milton Manor House, near Abingdon, placed on an eighteenth-century chimneypiece (*Country Life*, 104 (1948), 1333).

Drawing of chimneypiece for 'The little Parlor' (*RIBA Cat.* 116); published by I. Ware, with embellishments (*Designs of Inigo Jones*, pl. 5). Composite capitals (Bk. of Caps., fos. 30–1, and Chatsworth Album 26, nos. 128, 134). A letter from Webb to Edward Marshall, 17 Oct. 1658, principally concerning a pedestal for the Earl of Northumberland, refers to measuring off the work at Gunnersbury (RIBA, Boy. Coll. 17); published by W. Grant Keith ('Six Houses in Search of an Architect', *Journal of the RIBA*, 3rd series, 40 (1933), 732–3). Webb refers to Gunnersbury in *A Vindication of Stone-Heng Restored* (1655), 88: '... Ballisters between the Intercolumns of the Portico, which serving for a leaning Height (as in the Loggia of Sir John Maynard's House at Gunnersbury)'; and in his copy of Palladio (Worcester College): 'Observe that in this Cornice Palladio differs wholy from the rule of all others ... see the cornice I made of this kind for Gunnersbury ... where ... I have brought it to follow ye constant rule' (Palladio, i, facing p. 50).

Campbell, i, pls. 17–18. Further engravings were published by S. Wale (in R. Dodsley, *London & its Environs Described* (1761)); Evans (1787); and W. Angus (*Seats of the Nobility & Gentry* (1797)). Wale's view of the south front shows a formal garden bounded by a scalloped wall, after the model of Palladio's Villa Badoer. This provided a well-judged counterpoint to the columns of the portico. The wall was removed and the grounds landscaped during the occupancy of the house by Princess Amelia, who owned it from 1762 until her death in 1786. According to Angus, the Princess was responsible for improving the gardens, to which 'many additions were made by Plantations, additional Grounds, and elegant Erections'.

5 watercolours, now in Gunnersbury Museum, by the fashionable, topographical painter, William Payne, were produced of the house and grounds for Walter Stirling, who had bought the property in 1792:

(i) House viewed across the park from the south, s. and d. W. Payne 1792; Museum No. 1760.
(ii) House from south east, s. and d. W. Payne 1793; 2008.
(iii) View looking east across south front, s. and d. W. Payne 1792; 2009.
(iv) House viewed from north, with stables and offices flanking forecourt, s. W. Payne; 2010.
(v) View of temple and lake, s. and d. W. Payne 1792; 2011 (all 29 cm. × 41.5 cm.).

HALE LODGE, HAMPSHIRE

(see also pp. 52–4; pl. 27)

John Penruddock

1638

Designs for 'a Lodge in a Parke': 3 elevations and plans (*RIBA Cat.* 117 (published Kent, ii, pl. 5), 118; *Worcs. Coll. Cat.* 74).

Webb's first important, independent design, based on Jonesian and Palladian prototypes. The patron, John Penruddock, succeeded to the estate upon the death of his father Thomas in 1637. It is not known whether this lodge was built: certainly, there is no trace of it at Hale today. The present Hale Park, built for himself by Thomas Archer, was altered extensively by Henry Holland in the later eighteenth century. An earlier connection between the Penruddocks and Inigo Jones might be inferred from the design of Hale Church, whose walls were 'newly laid and raised' in 1631. The new work represents an artisan version of Jones's contemporary St Paul's Covent Garden (*Country Life*, 155 (1974), 263–6).

HASSENBROOK HALL, ESSEX

(pl. 105)

Henry Fetherstone

1638

Design for stables 'for Mr Fetherstone 1638' (*RIBA Cat.* 119). An elevation and plan for a four-bay, dormered building, comprising stables and carriage house with, presumably, lodgings above (although in this schematic design, there are no stairs to the upper level).

Hassenbrook Hall itself, an early seventeenth-century house, has been altered at various dates. If built at all, the stables do not survive.

LAMPORT HALL, NORTHAMPTONSHIRE

(see also pp. 80–9; pls. 50–9)

Sir Justinian Isham

1654–7

New wing added to older house (extant). Webb's wing subsequently was extended by Francis Smith of Warwick and his son William (*c.*1732–40), who made additions to each side. The ceiling of Webb's entrance hall was altered in 1738, to the designs of William Smith, the plasterwork being executed by John Woolston of Northampton. His staircase was replaced during the nineteenth century. Further works were carried out elsewhere in the house during the nineteenth century by Henry Hakewill, Henry Goddard, and William Burn.

33 drawings: main elevation, walls, and ceiling of entrance hall, decorative details (including full-size drawings for the workmen to follow), designs for gateway and for the chapel or 'depository' (Northamptonshire CRO IL 3079 A1–30, A50). Ten letters from Webb to Isham (Northamptonshire CRO IL 3956 A51). Nine of the letters were published by J. A. Gotch, together with a listing of all the drawings (with the exception of A50, which was not known to him) in 'Some Newly Found Drawings and Letters of John Webb', *Journal of the RIBA*, 3rd ser. 28 (1921), 565–82. The further letter was published by J. Bold in 'John Webb and the Lamport Recinct', *Notes & Queries*, NS 28/1 (1981), 55–6. Engraving by B. Cole, 1761.

LUDLOW, SHROPSHIRE

(see also p. 56)

Colonel Edward Harley

1655

Correspondence concerning the building or alteration of a 'Country habitation'; apparently unexecuted (*Wren Society*, 18 (1941), 154–5).

MAIDEN BRADLEY, WILTSHIRE

(see also pp. 54–5; fig. 1)

Colonel Edmund Ludlow

*c.*1644–50

Design for house: ground and first floor plans (*Worcs. Coll. Cat.* 92).

Ludlow became a Colonel in 1644 and was promoted by Cromwell to Lieutenant General in 1650. He had been born at Maiden Bradley in a house described by Aubrey in 1671 as being 'handsome' and 'well built', but 'dilapidated since the late warres' (H. M. Colvin, *A Biographical Dictionary of British Architects 1600–1840* (1978), 872). The house was on a farm called South Court, later known as New Mead, which was rented from the Seymour family (R. Colt Hoare, *Modern History of South Wiltshire*, i (1822), 16). According to Colvin, a house on this site was demolished *c.*1881, but Aubrey's remarks suggest that Webb's house was not built. The main house at Maiden Bradley, the late seventeenth-century Seymour mansion (Campbell, ii, pl. 56) also was largely demolished in the nineteenth century.

It is worth noting in the context of Maiden Bradley that one of Webb's theoretical drawings (*RIBA Cat.* 174) shows a design for a farmhouse with offices and stables, grouped around a quadrangle. This is said to be the earliest surviving English design for a complete farmstead (J. M. Robinson, *Georgian Model Farms*, 1983, pp. 36–7).

NORTHUMBERLAND HOUSE, LONDON

(pl. 106)

The 10th Earl of Northumberland

*c.*1655–60

Work on the south front and in the state rooms. Designs for chimneypiece and overmantels 1657 and 1660; designs for their capitals (Bk. of Caps., fos. 32–3). The house was demolished in 1874.

Upon the marriage in 1642 of Lady Elizabeth Howard to the 10th Earl of Northumberland, the Strand palace then known as Suffolk House was transferred to the bridegroom upon his payment of £15,000 to his wife's family (*Survey of London*, 18 (1937), 12). The Jacobean house, which comprised four wings around a central courtyard, clearly was regarded as being old fashioned, and Northumberland immediately employed Edward Carter, who succeeded Inigo Jones in 1643 as Surveyor of the King's Works, to oversee extensive alterations. Work continued under Carter until 1649 and recommenced in *c.*1655. There is a submitted account

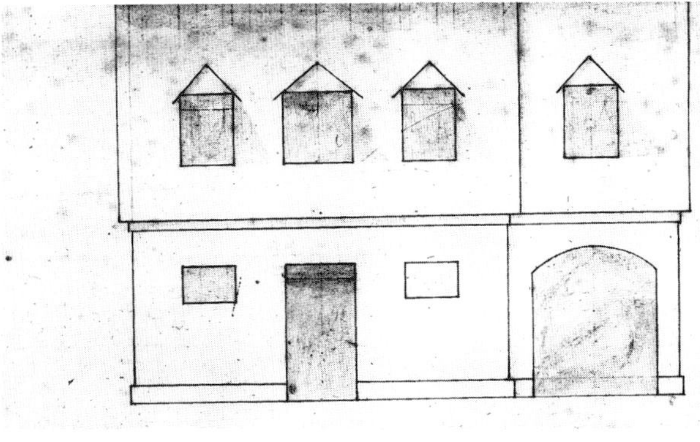

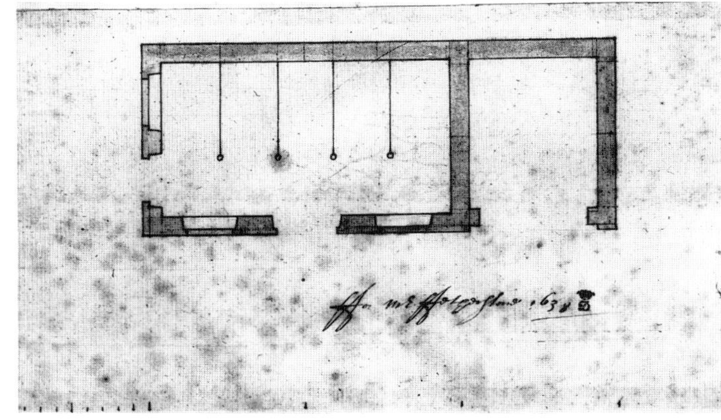

105 (*above*). Hassenbrook Hall: sketch elevation and plan for the stables designed for Henry Fetherstone

106 (*right*). Northumberland House: design by Webb for a chimneypiece and overmantel, engraved by John Vardy

107 (*above*). Nun Appleton House: views of the north and south fronts, executed *c.*1655–60 by Daniel King

108 (*right*). Nun Appleton House: design for a composite capital for 'Lo ffay' which incorporates the Fairfax lion

for the period 1655–7 from Edward Marshall, the mason, and, in a letter of 17 Oct. 1658, Webb wrote to him: 'I must desire you to make a modle in Clay of this pedestall for the Earle of Northumberland about ye bignesse of this draught.' It might be presumed that Webb was in charge of the work from the beginning of the period worked by Marshall. (Webb's letter: RIBA, Boy. Coll. 17; published by W. Grant Keith, 'Six Houses in Search of an Architect', *Journal of the RIBA*, 3rd ser. 40 (1933), 732–3.) Both men were engaged also in 1656 in making estimates for work at the 10th Earl's Syon House, Middlesex (see below), in one of which reference is made to a further estimate by Webb for a brick wall for the garden of Northumberland House (Percy Archives, Alnwick, U III 5).

Office of Works craftsmen were employed in both building campaigns at Northumberland House: Thomas Stevens (mason), Zachary Taylor (carpenter), and John Embree (Sergeant Plumber) worked on the house during the period 1642–9 (Percy Archives, Alnwick, U III 2; British Library Film no. 394); Maurice Emmett (bricklayer) and Richard Ryder (carpenter, who had worked with Webb at Wilton) worked on the house with Edward Marshall during the period 1655–7 (Percy Archives, Alnwick, U III 2; BL Film no. 394).

Marshall built the great stone stairs which John Evelyn was swift to criticize as 'too massie, ... without any neeate Invention' (*The Diary of John Evelyn*, ed. E. S. de Beer (1959), 391, 7 June 1658). The stairs, according to the engraving published by R. Dodsley (*London and its Environs Described*, v (1761)), ran along the entire 82′ of the central river frontage of the house, with two ascending flights to each side of the first-floor dining-room door. These survived until their rebuilding by Thomas Cundy in 1821. (The elevation of the river front as it appeared in 1819, and plans of *c.*1750 and 1821, were published by D. Owsley and W. Rieder, *The Glass Drawing Room from Northumberland House* (1974), 26.)

Webb's surviving interior designs are for an overmantel, for 'ye dining roome ... 1657' and for a chimneypiece and overmantel for 'the withdrawing roome ... 1660'. The latter incorporates Webb's favoured palm-frond motif. It was published as a design of Inigo Jones by J. Vardy (*Some Designs of Mr Inigo Jones and Mr Wm Kent* (1744), pl. 9) (pl. 106).

NUN APPLETON HOUSE, YORKSHIRE

(pls. 107–8)

Lord Fairfax

*c.*1650

Decorative work. Designs for composite capitals (Bk. of Caps., fos. 7–14).

The attribution of work by Webb for Lord Fairfax is based on the faint inscription, 'Lo ffay', on the design for a capital; on the inclusion of the Fairfax lion in some of the designs, and on the incorporation of military trophies in another (pl. 108). The dating of *c.*1650 is suggested by the positioning of the designs in the 'Book of Capitols' between Wilton (1649) and the Physicians' College (1651).

The engraved views of Nun Appleton House by Daniel King (pl. 107), executed in *c.*1655–60, depict a two-storey house with hipped roof, cupola, and cross wings (BL Harley MS 2073, f. 126: see H. Kelliher, *Andrew Marvell: Poet and Politician* (BL exhibition catalogue, 1978), 46–7). The house celebrated in Marvell's poem, 'Upon Appleton House', was built in part upon the site of a Cistercian nunnery:

> A nunnery first gave it birth
> (For virgin buildings oft brought forth);
> And all that neighbour-ruin shows
> The quarries whence this dwelling rose.
>
> (ll. 85–8)

The estate had come to the Fairfax family after the Dissolution and William Fairfax appears to have built the first secular house on the site in the 1550s or 1560s. The building of the new mansion on the site was begun, probably, in the 1630s or 1640s (cf. E. S. Donno (ed.) *Andrew Marvell: The Complete Poems* (1976), 248). Thomas, 3rd Baron Fairfax, Commander-in-Chief of the Parliamentary army *c.*1645–50, succeeded to this property in March 1648. He resigned from his military duties in 1650, and we might presume that it was upon his retirement that he employed Webb on the completion of the house.

Although Nun Appleton was altered in the eighteenth and nineteenth centuries, a substantial amount of the seventeenth-century fabric survives. It is a red-brick, double-pile house with an entrance on the north side into a cross passage, divided by an arcade from the off-centre hall. Beyond the hall, to the west, a staircase with seventeenth- and eighteenth-century balusters is thought to be situated in roughly the same position as the original stair. The secondary stair in the seventeenth-century house was placed symmetrically at the opposite end of the house, beyond the withdrawing-room.

King's views of Nun Appleton depict the cupola on the north side of the house, placed over a prospect room of three bays' width which projected above the cornice. This is alluded to in Marvell's lines on 'the swelling hall [which] | Stirs, and the square grows spherical' (ll. 51–2).

In the early eighteenth century Nun Appleton was bought by William Milner of Leeds, who made significant alterations. He removed the wings, roof, and cupola, added a third storey, and probably refenestrated both of the main fronts. The appearance of the house after these alterations is shown in Samuel Buck's drawing of *c.*1720 (BL Lansdowne MS 914; published in *Samuel Buck's Yorkshire Sketchbook*, introduced by I. Hall (1979), 324). Substantial additions were made by E. B. Lamb in 1863 and by B. Chippindale in 1920. Lamb's wing has been demolished, but Chippindale's west tower survives.

Recent investigation of the house has provided further evidence for dating. The presence of medieval or sixteenth-century masonry in the cellars, providing the foundations for the north wall, indicates that the present house was built in part upon an earlier structure. The uncovering of a seventeenth-century mullioned window in this north wall indicates that the building of this side of the house, hitherto presumed to have been datable to the eighteenth century, was coeval with the south side.

The only details to survive in the house which can be attributed with confidence to Webb are the capitals of the pilasters which frame the north-side entrance door (within the modern porch), and the adjacent lion's head keystone. The capitals are of the rudimentary acanthus type which appear in the 'Book of Capitols' as designs for the hall. Four more of Webb's capitals survive, resited in the garden. Two of them, of magnesian limestone, greatly eroded, are mounted on columns; two more are placed next to the fishpond. The south side centrepiece is framed by giant brick half columns, which might date also from the Webb period.

PHYSICIANS' COLLEGE, LONDON

(pls. 109–11)

The Royal College of Physicians

1651–3

Designs for Library, Repository, and Consulting Room, 1651 (*Worcs. Coll. Cat.* 75–80); designs for composite capitals (Bk. of Caps., fos. 18–20). Building destroyed in Great Fire, 1666.

In 1651 Dr William Harvey set in train the building of 'a Library and a Repository for Simples and Rarities' (C. E. Newman, 'The First Library of the Royal College of Physicians', *Journal of the Royal College of Physicians, London*, 3/3 (1969), 299–307). Harvey, a friend of Inigo Jones, probably had been responsible for commissioning a design for an anatomy theatre from the aged architect in *c.*1649 (*RIBA Cat.* 13). Two years later the design for a new building on a site at Amen Corner, near St Paul's Cathedral, was entrusted to Webb. Building began in 1652 and was completed the following year. John Aubrey described it as 'a noble building of Roman architecture (of Rustique work with Corinthian pillasters) . . . a great parlour (a kind of Convocation House) of the Fellows to meet in belowe; and a Library above. . . .' (Newman, 'First Library').

Webb's plan, elevation, and sections depict a two-storey building, arcaded at ground-floor level, with the library and repository above, a restatement in classical terms of the traditional monastic arrangement of first-floor library over cloister (pls. 109 and 110). The design is Roman in manner, being reminiscent of the early cinquecento Villa Farnesina by Peruzzi. The drawings do not accord with Aubrey's description; evidently it was decided that an arcaded ground floor was a luxury and this space became a consultation-room with an adjoining parlour.

The library was designed on the stall system, having a central aisle with cubicles to each side. Composite half columns decorated the ends of the bookcases, which were set at right angles to the walls, giving the impression of a colonnaded nave with side chapels. In the adjoining repository, the order was raised on a stylobate of the same height as the desks in the library. The exhibits were arranged in free-standing cases or on tables, not attached to the walls. In 1660, according to the catalogue compiled by the Harveian Librarian, Christopher Merrett, there were seventy-four exhibits, several surgical instruments, and 1,278 books; most of these were lost in the Great Fire (Newman, 'First Library').

Webb's designs for capitals are for 'The Library', 'The Repository' and 'ye Front' (pl. 111). The latter is comparable with his design for The Vyne, a pared-down acanthus, but the other two include more specifically medical references. The Library design depicts the Torch of Life and the Aesculapian serpent. The serpent, a symbol of renovation, was sacred to the god of the medical art since it was believed to have the power of discovering healing herbs. The design for the Repository includes the inscription ΡΑΡΜΑΚΑ ΘΕΟΥ ΧΕΙΡΕΣ* (Drugs are the Hands of God), a phrase which is ascribed variously to the celebrated physicians Herophilus and Erasistratus. 'Hands' in Greek is an idiomatic expression for 'agents'; a rather more literal interpretation of the phrase appears on the title-page of *Pharmacopoeia Londinensis* (1618): there, above the motto, a divine hand issues from a cloud to grasp an arm by the wrist.

It is particularly unfortunate that Webb's building should have survived for so brief a span, since it provides us with a rare example of his abilities as an institutional rather than a country-house designer. It is deserving of our attention, furthermore, as a precursor of Wren's Trinity Library, Cambridge.

* It should read: ΦΑΡΜΑΚΑ . . .

SOMERSET HOUSE, LONDON

(see also pp. 103–7; pls. 69–71)

Royal Works

*c.*1628–65

*c.*1628/9–1633/4: work with Inigo Jones on designs for water stairs (*RIBA Cat.* 46–9).

1638: work with Inigo Jones on unexecuted designs for palatial rebuilding (*RIBA Cat.* 50; *Worcs. Coll. Cat.* 17–19).

1661–4: new range towards the river (Campbell, i, pl. 16).

1664–5: apartments facing north towards the backs of houses on the Strand, for Queen Henrietta Maria; attributed to Webb (*King's Works*, v. 255–6).

The drawings for the water stairs, with gates framed by obelisks, represent Webb's earliest surviving works for Inigo Jones (*King's Works*, iv. 263). This design was superseded by the executed design which consisted of a projecting platform with a straight flight of steps down to the water. The gates were framed by piers with

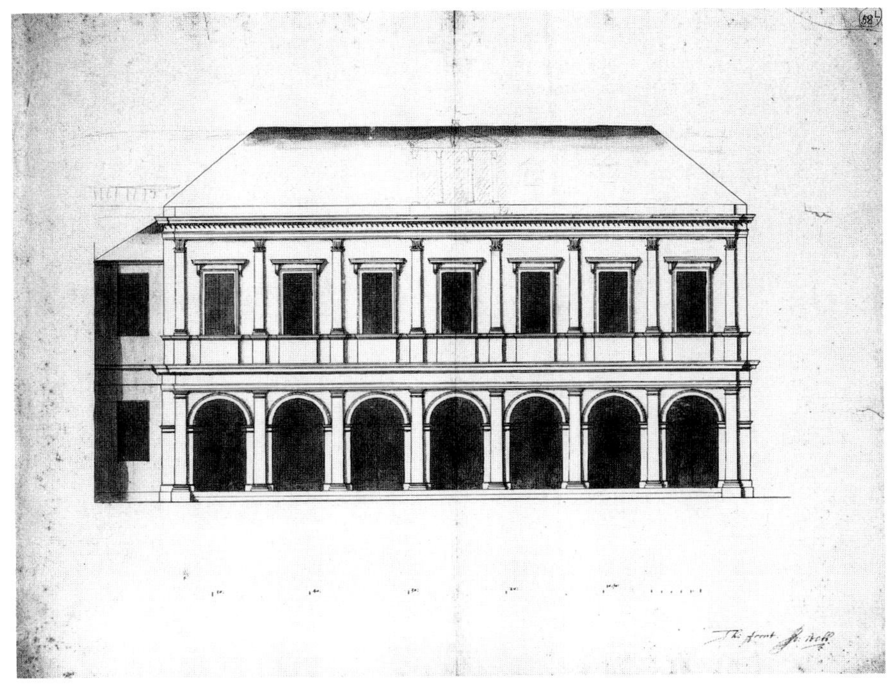

109. Physicians' College: design for the front elevation

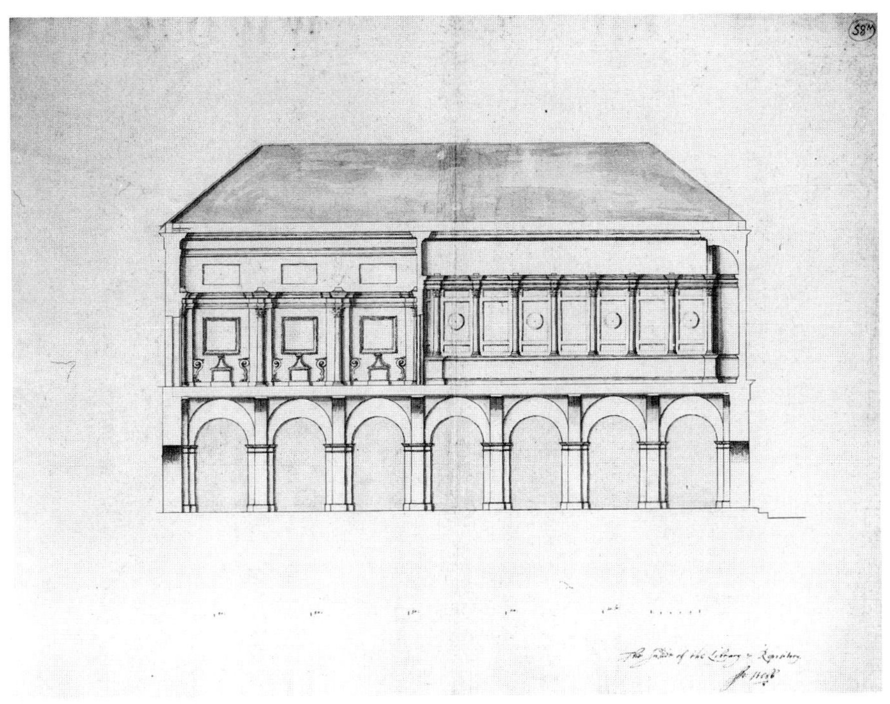

110. Physicians' College: longitudinal section showing the internal wall elevations of the first-floor Library and Repository

111. Physicians' College: design for a composite capital for the Library, incorporating the Torch of Life and the serpent, emblematic of Aesculapius, the god of the medical art

side pieces bearing relief carvings of river gods (*King's Works*, v, pl. 33).

ST PAUL'S CATHEDRAL, LONDON

(pls. 13, 112)

Royal Works

1633–63

1633–41: employed as 'Clerk engrosser'. Drawing of a pulley for raising stones (Strafford Letters, vol 24–5 (133), 14 July 1637; Wentworth Woodhouse Muniments, Central Library, Sheffield).

1663: prosecution of minor repairs.

The restoration of old St Paul's Cathedral was only marginally an Office of Works' concern. Although Inigo Jones was architect to the commission for rebuilding, he was acting in an honorary capacity. However, the initiative behind the rebuilding was the King's; further, he paid for the west front and portico (*King's Works*, iii. 147) (see pl. 13).

As clerk engrosser, Webb received no official payment but was paid directly by Inigo Jones for 'double engrossing' the account books, 'one for the paymaster, and one to remaine in the office, and for his Attendance'; also 'for drawing, entering into a ledger book the bargains made from time to time with the workmen, coppying several designs and mouldings and making the tracing according to Mr Surveyor's direction for the workmen to follow' (Works Accounts 1–15, Apr. 1633–Sept. 1641, St Paul's Cathedral Library; another volume for 1639–40 at Lambeth Palace Library: FP 321). A document relating to the *modus operandi* of the restoration describes the respective contributions of Jones, his 'substitute' Edward Carter, and Webb himself, who noted: 'Mr. Webbe copied all ye designs from ye Surveyors Invention, made all ye traceryes in great for ye worke, & all ye mouldings by ye Surveyors direction so yt what the Surveyor invented & Mr. Webbe made, ye substitute saw putt in worke & nothing else' ('Inigo Jones and St. Paul's Cathedral', *London Topographical Record*, 18 (1942), 41–3).

A letter and drawing in the Strafford papers provide further evidence of the nature of Webb's involvement in the works. The 1st Earl of Strafford was Lord Deputy of Ireland. Secretary of State Sir Francis Windebank wrote to inform him that 'His Maty hath been pleased to imploy the Earl Marshall (Lord Arundel) & Mr Jones Surveyor of his Works in the procuring of Marble for his use out of Ireland', requesting that they should be given 'all furtherance & assistance in the Service' (Strafford Letters, Vol. 17 (121), 15 July 1637; Central Library, Sheffield). The memorandum of instructions for the stones which were required for St Paul's, and the drawing of a pulley for raising them, are in Webb's hand. These are entitled 'Mr. Surveyors direction for Marbles to be sent out of Ireland: And for a Capstone to rayse great stones with ease', and are countersigned in Jones's hand: 'pp Inigo Jones' (see D. Howarth, 'Lord Arundel as an entrepreneur of the arts', *Burlington Magazine*, 122 (1980), 690–2, where the drawing is published as being by Inigo Jones).

The design for the single masted pulley and capstan was taken by Webb from Cosimo Bartoli's illustrated edition of Alberti's *L'architettura*, a copy of which was owned by Jones (pl. 112). Such machines had been used by the Romans (see C.J. Singer and E.J. Holmyard, *A History of Technology*, ii (1956), 659–60), but it must be presumed that the raising of stones of the size required for St Paul's was an unusual requirement in Britain; hence the need for Webb to provide an illustration of the method.

The work achieved at St Paul's was the remodelling of the whole of the exterior, apart from the central tower, and the addition of the great west portico, for which, according to Webb, Jones 'contracted the envy of all Christendom upon our Nation, for a Piece of Architecture, not to be parallell'd in these last Ages of the World' (Webb, *A Vindication of*

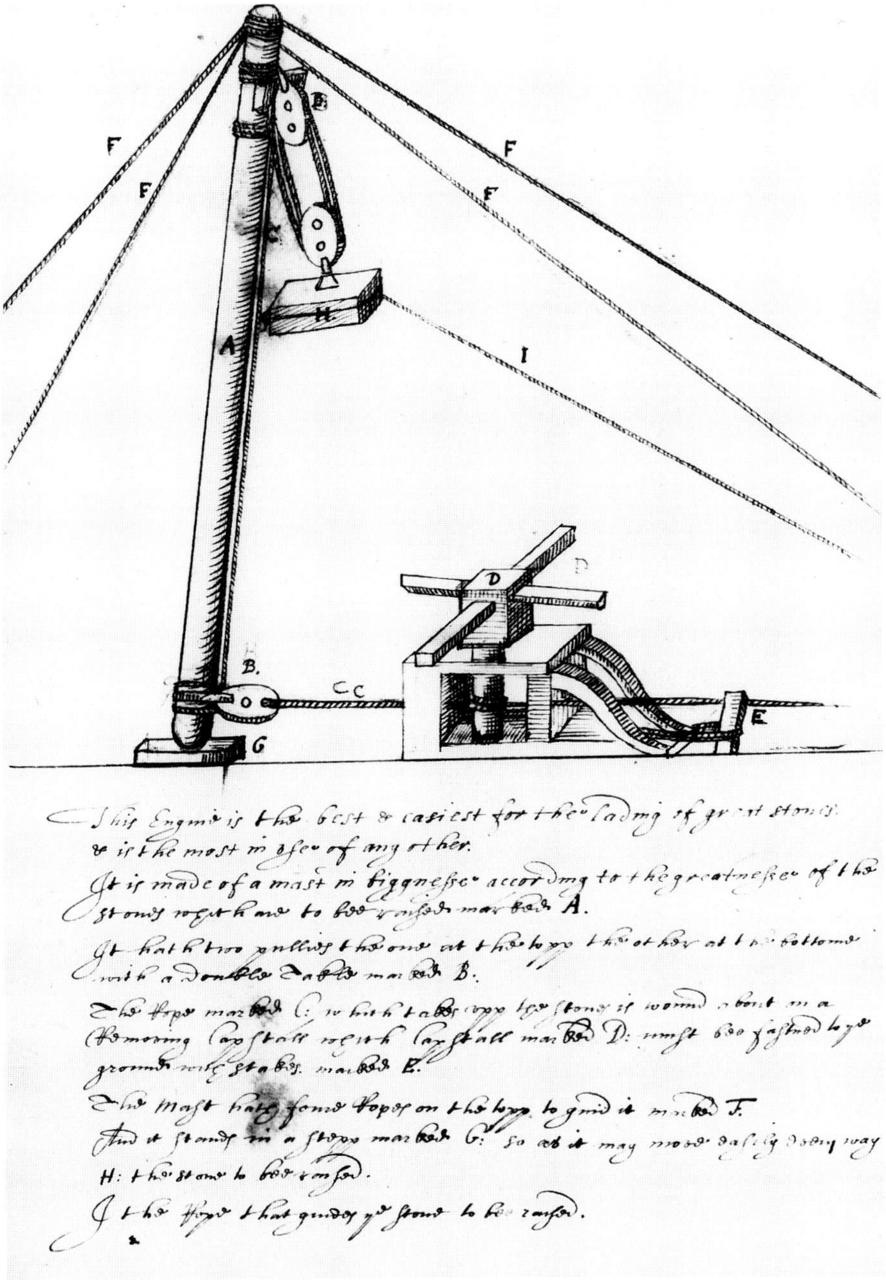

This Engine is the best & easiest for the lading of great stones & is the most in use of any other.

It is made of a mast in bignesse according to the greatnesse of the stones which are to bee raised marked A.

It hath two pullies the one at the topp the other at the bottome with a double cable marked B.

The Rope marked C: which takes upp the stone is wound about in a Removing Capstall which Capstall marked D: must bee fastned to ye ground with stakes marked E.

The Mast hath some Ropes on the topp to guid it marked F.

And it stands in a stepp marked G: so as it may move easily every way

H: the stone to bee raised.

I the Rope that guides ye stone to bee raised.

112. Old St Paul's Cathedral: Webb's design for a pulley for raising stones, made in 1637 in his capacity as Inigo Jones's clerk engrosser on the Cathedral works

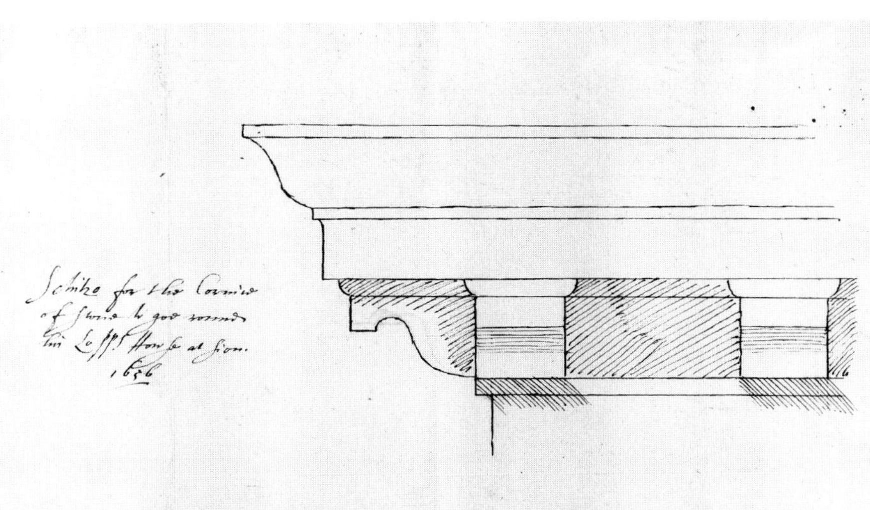

113. Syon House: design for a new stone cornice to go around the house, 1656

Stone-Heng Restored (1665), 48). The portico, the largest in northern Europe, was short lived: 'It was barely finished before civil war clashed over the cathedral, disrupting the corporate body which governed it, dispersing its property, and raping its fabric' (J. Summerson, 'Inigo Jones', *Proceedings of the British Academy*, 50 (1964), 191). The portico survived the Great Fire but was demolished in 1687.

In 1663 a Commission was constituted to investigate the repairs which were needed after the depredations of the Interregnum, and a report was submitted by the Surveyor, Sir John Denham, Webb, and Edward Marshall. They noted the ruinous vaulting, the perilous state of the roof, the defaced and decayed interior and the 'barbarously spoiled' columns of the portico (*Wren Society*, 18 (1941), 13–14). It is customary to blame the barbarous population for the ravages suffered by the Cathedral during the Interregnum, but the extent of the restoration required lends force to the remarks which Dean Sancroft expressed in a letter to Wren in 1668 in which he referred to:

> two great defects in Inigo Jones' work; one that his new case of stone in the upper Walls (massy as it is) was not set upon the upright of the Pillars but upon the Core of the Groins of the vaulting: the other, that there were no keystones at all to tie it to the old work; and all this being very heavy with the Roman Ornaments on the Top of it, and being already so far gone outward, cannot possibly stand long (C. Wren, *Parentalia* (1750), 132).

After their report, Webb and Denham were able to prosecute some minor repairs, refusing payment for 'new making the hip of the south end of the roofe, where it was cut away and spoiled' and removing houses which had been built against the sides of the Cathedral (Malcolm, *Londinium Redivum*, iii (1803), 83). The Great Fire, which ruined the body of the church, rendered redundant any plans for further repairs to Jones's building.

SYON HOUSE, MIDDLESEX

(pl. 113)

The 10th Earl of Northumberland

1656

Sketch of cornice and estimates for various works, apparently unexecuted (Percy Archives, Alnwick, U III 5).

During the period in which they were working on Northumberland House in the Strand, Webb and Edward Marshall were involved in making estimates for various works at the 10th Earl's country house, Syon, just outside London. Estimates were made for vaulting a cellar, adding chimneys, renovating the roof, and adding a new stone cornice to go all round the house (pl. 113). Webb recommended the building of a portico and 'other worke done with severall considerable Accommodations', but work does not appear to have been carried out.

Marshall made a structural survey of the house in which he noted that the ashlar facing of the walls was leaning towards the internal courtyard, having been separated by damp penetration from the brick, supporting walls. He suggested that, although the danger was not imminent, repairs should not be long delayed.

THE VYNE, HAMPSHIRE

(pls. 114–16)

Chaloner Chute, MP; Speaker of the House of Commons (1659)

1654–7

Alterations to existing house, including new chimneypieces and portico (extant). Designs for composite capitals (Bk. of Caps., fos. 27, 36a). Measured drawings of north (portico) front, internal door, and aedicule by Flitcroft, who attributes the design to Inigo Jones (*RIBA Cat.* 171). Agreement between Chute and Edward Marshall, mason, 4 Mar. 1654 (Hampshire CRO, Chute papers 31M57/627); payments, 1655–7 (31M57/627–9). Attribution of the portico to Webb (H. Walpole, *Anecdotes of*

114. The Vyne: the projecting portico on the north side of the house. It is of brick, stucco rendered, with stone capitals and bases and a wooden pediment which carries the arms of the Chute family

Painting, ed. R. N. Wornum, iii (1862), 93). See also C. W. Chute, *A History of The Vyne in Hampshire* (1888).

Chute bought The Vyne in 1653 from William, 6th Lord Sandys, descendant of William, 1st Lord, Lord Chamberlain to Henry VIII, who had built the house in the early sixteenth century. A family connection links this commission with Chevening (see above): Chaloner the younger, Chute's son by his first wife, married Dorothy, the daughter of Richard, Lord Dacre of Chevening. Richard died in 1630 and his widow, also Dorothy, in 1650 became the second wife of the elder Chaloner Chute. Her stepson Francis was responsible for commissioning Webb's work at Chevening (T. Barrett-Lennard, *An Account of the Families of Lennard and Barrett* (1908)).

Marshall was responsible for all the alterations at The Vyne, following 'such directions as shall be from time to time given him by the surveyor' (i.e. Webb; not named in the agreement). This work involved the regularization and renewal of the battlements on the chapel and of the windows on both fronts of the house, the removal of various buildings which ran down to the river, and the addition of a portico to the north, garden side. Inside, alterations were made in the hall, below the chapel, and in the cellar, and payment was made for nine new chimneypieces. The programme subsequently was extended to include work on the staircase, the chapel, and the bridge over the river.

Webb's portico is of considerable importance, in being the first projecting temple front to be applied to an English house (pl. 114). It is of brick, stucco rendered, with stone capitals and bases to the composite columns and piers. The capitals are austerely pared down, showing the acanthus before its central leaves had come to fruition (pl. 116). The pediment is of wood, with a shield carved by Marshall which bears the Chute coat of arms.

Of the chimneypieces recorded in Marshall's accounts, two were of white marble, six of Portland stone, and one of 'Italian raunce'. In the house now there are two on the first floor which are certainly by Webb: in the Gallery (pl. 115), a white marble chimneypiece with garlands cascading down from a cartouche, set over a broken pediment; and in the Library, a stone chimneypiece with columns clothed in tiers of upright leaves and its lintel carrying the Chute arms flanked by palm fronds (this room became a library in the early nineteenth century; the chimneypiece formerly was in the corner Tapestry Room). Two others, situated in the Drawing Room and the Dining Room on the ground floor, may be attributed to Webb. The Drawing Room chimneypiece is wooden, painted to resemble stone, with caryatids at each end and swags and scrolls which curl botanically along the jambs and lintel. The stone chimneypiece in the Dining Room appears to incorporate earlier jambs, over which a classical frieze of female heads and garlands is placed.

In the grounds of the house three further structures from the Webb period are worthy of note. The rusticated gatepiers, reset at the entrance to the short south drive, might be attributed to him, but the summerhouses, both red brick, centrally planned, domed pavilions, are unlikely to be his. One of them, described as being 'in the uncourtly style of Mills' (N. Pevsner and D. Lloyd, *Hampshire* (1967), 638), was used for a long time as a pigeon-house and might have been intended always for this or a similar use. The other has been extended and is now in use as a cottage.

The Vyne itself was altered in the eighteenth century by John Chute, who was responsible for building the monumental staircase which provides a suitably classical, although rather theatrical complement to Webb's portico. In the nineteenth century the house devolved upon William Lyde Wiggett, who assumed the name of Chute. His alterations included the addition of battlements to the north front to match those on the chapel, and the addition of blind gothic windows to the chapel itself (M. McCarthy, 'John Chute's Drawings for The Vyne', in

115 (*left*). The Vyne: white marble chimneypiece in the Gallery

116 (*below left*). The Vyne: design for a composite capital

117 (*below*). Wrexham: design for a composite capital for the Hall of Sir John Trevor's house, incorporating the Trevor wyvern

G. Jackson-Stops (ed.), *The National Trust Year Book 1975–76*, 70–80).

WHITEHALL PALACE, LONDON

(see also pp. 107–125; pls. 73–86)

Royal Works

*c.*1637–*c.*1664

Unexecuted proposals for a new royal palace, catalogued by M. Whinney, 'John Webb's Drawings for Whitehall Palace', *Walpole Society*, 31 (1946), 45–107; with additions in *Worcs. Coll. Cat.* The schemes follow Whinney's classification.

P. (21 sheets) Designs by Inigo Jones, *c.* 1637–9, drawn by Webb (Chatsworth 68–81, 84; *Worcs. Coll. Cat.* 28–9).

K. (9 sheets) Designs by Jones and Webb, *c.* 1637–9, drawn by Webb (Chatsworth 86–7; *Worcs. Coll. Cat.* 30–40; Kent, i, pls. 1–50).

C. (5 sheets) Obtained by Colen Campbell from William Emmett. It is here suggested that these are from the Wren office rather than by Webb. A further drawing by Emmett is a redrawing made in 1717 from a lost original (British Museum Print Room: British Museum, *Catalogue of British Drawings*, i (1960), 305, 377–9, pl. 119b; Campbell, ii, pls. 2–19).

E. (16 sheets) Designs by Webb, *c.* 1645 (Chatsworth 82–3; *Worcs. Coll. Cat.* 41–54).

T. (3 sheets) Designs by Webb, *c.* 1647–8 (Chatsworth 66, 85; *Worcs. Coll. Cat.* 55).

D. (1 sheet) Design by Webb, 1661 (Chatsworth 48).

Z. (2 sheets) Not by Webb; possibly attributable to Willem de Keyser (Chatsworth 67; *Worcs. Coll. Cat.* 56).

S. (11 sheets) Designs by Webb, *c.*1663–4 (Chatsworth 49, 56–65).

WILTON HOUSE, WILTSHIRE

(see also pp. 57–69; pls. 30–44)

The 4th and 5th Earls of Pembroke (the 4th Earl died in 1650)

*c.*1638/9(?)–*c.* 1651

Late 1630s: designing ceilings and doors for the new south range of a quadrangular house which had been substantially rebuilt by William Herbert, 1st Earl of Pembroke, in the mid-sixteenth century; the 1630s work was overseen by Isaac de Caus.

1648–*c.* 1651: rebuilding the upper stages of the towers of the south range and refitting the state rooms after the fire of 1647. Much of this work survives, although there have been alterations by the 9th, 'Architect', Earl, with decorative work by Andien de Clermont (1730s), and by James Wyatt (1801–12). For a full discussion see RCHME, *Wilton House and English Palladianism* (1988).

Ceilings: 1630s (*Worcs. Coll. Cat.* 58–9, 61–5); 1649 (*Worcs. Coll. Cat.* 60; *RIBA Cat.* 172; Ashmolean Museum, Cotelle Album 89A). Doors: 1630s (Wiltshire CRO 2057 H1/1a). Composite capitals and a cartouche: 1649 (Bk. of Caps., fos. 1–6, 39). Account Books: 1650–1 (Salisbury papers, Hatfield: Private & Estate MSS, Accounts 168/2; published by H. M. Colvin, 'The South Front of Wilton House', *Archaeological Journal*, 111 (1954), 187–8). Campbell, ii, pls. 61–7; iii, 57–60: plans of ground and first floors, elevation of south front, sections of Double Cube and Single Cube rooms; loggia, grotto, and stables (de Caus); gatepiers (Webb); perspective.

Two drawings by Webb have been published as being perhaps for the Cube rooms (Victoria & Albert Museum 3436—66–7; O. Hill and J. Cornforth, *English Country Houses Caroline* (1966), 86), but the presence of emblematic eagles, rather than the Herbert wyverns, argues against this suggestion.

WOOLWICH DOCKYARD, LONDON

Royal Works

After 1663, possibly 1667

Fortifications. In 1636, the responsibility for the design and maintenance of military works passed to the Board of Ordnance, but the changeover of responsibility from the Royal Works was gradual. According to his petition of 1669, Webb was recalled to the King's service in 1663 to work on the new palace at Greenwich, to initiate others into the art of the Court masques, and to superintend the fortification of Woolwich Dockyard: 'At Wolwich day and night hee discharged his duty about ye fortifications there to your Majesties good content' (PRO, SP 29/251 120; *Wren Society*, 18 (1941), 156). The design of fortifications was at this time regarded as being a proper concern of the architect: Inigo Jones owned and annotated copies of Gabriello Busca's *L'architettura militare* (1619) and Buonaiuto Lorini's *Le fortificationi* (1609) and Webb himself owned books on the subject. After the architect's death Robert Hooke 'saw books at Faithornes of Webb about fortifications and Engines' (H. Robinson and W. Adams (eds.), *The Diary of Robert Hooke 1672–1680* (1935)).

Webb had demonstrated his abilities in this field during the Civil War when he 'sent to the King at Oxford the designes of all the fortifications about London, their proportions, the number of Gunns mounted on them, how many Souldyers would man them, how they might bee attempted & carried and all particulars relating thereto in writing' (PRO SP 29/5 74.1). The precise nature of Webb's work at Woolwich is not known. After the Dutch attack on Chatham in June 1667, ships, many of them good ones, were sunk deliberately at Woolwich to prevent the Dutch from coming up the river. Guns were then placed there and at Deptford, and on 23 June Pepys went to Woolwich 'to see the batteries newly raised; which, indeed, are good works to command the River below the ships that are sunk, but not above them' (*The Diary of Samuel Pepys*, ed. J. Warrington, ii (1953), 494). The hurried nature of the operation accords with Webb's working 'day and night' and this might well be the work to which he was referring in his petition.

WREXHAM, FLINTSHIRE

(pl. 117)

Sir John Trevor

*c.*1650

Designs for composite capitals: (Bk. of Caps., fos. 15–17; Chatsworth Album 26, no. 125).

Sir John Trevor II (1596–1673) owned two houses in Wales: Trevalyn Hall in Denbighshire, built in 1576, and Plas Teg in neighbouring Flintshire, built *c.*1610 (Trevalyn Hall: *Country Life*, 132 (1962), 78–81; Plas Teg: *Country Life*, 132 (1962), 134–7; for the Trevors, see Lady Enid Sophia Jones, *The Trevors of Trevalyn* (1955)). Trevor was a convinced Puritan and Parliamentarian who was pardoned in 1660 when he retired from public life. Webb's drawings probably were produced as part of a remodelling or renovation of Plas Teg. They represent designs for 'The Front', 'The Hall' (pl. 117), and 'The Great Chamber', for 'Sr:Jo:Trevor at Wrexham in Flintshire'. The drawing in the 'Book of Capitols' for the Great Chamber capital duplicates the one in the Chatsworth Album, on the verso of which is the fragmentary inscription: 'Pirro 41/not taken'. The designs appear to have been unexecuted. Their positioning in the 'Book of Capitols' between Wilton and the Physicians' College suggests a dating of *c.*1650.

APPENDIX I. THEATRE DESIGNS

WEBB, by his own account, studied under Inigo Jones not only architecture but also masques and triumphs.[1] Furthermore, 'at Whitehall hee made yor [Majesty's] Theater, and thereby discovered much of the Scenicall Art, wch to others than himselfe was before much unknowne'.[2] During the 1630s he worked as Jones's assistant on the Court masques, designing the auditoria of the Paved Court Theatre at Somerset House for *The Shepherd's Paradise* (1632–3) and of the Great Hall at Whitehall for *Florimène* (1635).[3] He also made drawings for scenes for *Britannia triumphans, Luminalia, Salmacida spolia,* and the *Queen of Aragon.*[4] In addition to this collaborative work, he produced drawings after Jones[5] and annotated others by the master,[6] which indicates perhaps that a theoretical text on the theatre was at some time in his mind. In 1656 he stage-designed for the first time alone, but neither at this time nor later did he take further Jones's own revolutionary staging procedures, so his 'discovery' was in fact a revealing, for the benefit of a new audience, of those ideas of Jones which had remained unexploited during the Interregnum.

In 1647 an ordinance for the suppression of 'Stage-playes and Interludes' was issued, empowering the 'Lord Mayor, Justices of the Peace and Sheriffs of the City of London and Westminster and the Counties of Middlesex and Surrey' to enter into all houses where plays were being performed and arrest the offenders, who would be 'punished as Rogues, according to Law'.[7] It was by an act of some ingenuity, therefore, that Sir William Davenant modestly staged a production of the *Siege of Rhodes* in Rutland House in 1656. This was an epoch-making event, being the first opera to be produced in England, employing recitative to tell the story, the first public play to have women on the stage, and the first to use movable scenery.[8] Webb produced five scene designs and a proscenium, applying the techniques of Jones's masques to the drama, but because of limitations of space the side scenes were fixed and only the back shutters were changeable. These were illustrations, of some topographical accuracy, rather than settings for action (pl. 118). A shortened version of the complete play was enacted—a full production with three extra scenes being put on in the Duke's Theatre, Lincoln's Inn, at the Restoration.

The Rutland House proscenium was the same size as that of the Cockpit Theatre, Drury Lane. This was not accidental. Anthony Wood, in his memoir of Davenant, relates that the author

> contrived to set up an Italian Opera to be performed by declamations and music: . . . This Italian opera began in Rutland house in Charterhouse yard . . . and was afterwards translated to the Cockpit in Drury Lane, and delighting the eye and ear extreamly well, was much frequented for several years. So that he having laid the foundation of the English stage by this his musical drama, when plays were, as damnable

[1] SP 29/5 74.1 (see App. II).

[2] PRO SP 29/251, 120, pub. in *Wren Society*, 18 (1941), 156 (see App. II).

[3] BL Lansdowne MS 1171; J. Orrell, *The Theatres of Inigo Jones and John Webb* (1985), 113–48.

[4] Devonshire Collection, Chatsworth; S. Orgel and R. Strong, *Inigo Jones, The Theatre of the Stuart Court* (1973), nos. 335, 386, 399–400, 405, 409, 413, 445–6.

[5] *The Triumph of Peace;* Orgel and Strong, *Inigo Jones*, nos. 268–9.

[6] *The College of Augurs;* Orgel and Strong, *Inigo Jones*, no. 115. *The Shepherd's Paradise;* Orgel and Strong, *Inigo Jones*, nos. 247, 249, 254.

[7] C. Firth and R. Rait, *Acts and Ordinances of the Interregnum*, i, (1911), 1027.

[8] W. Grant Keith, 'The Designs for the First Movable Scenery on the English Public Stage', *Burlington Magazine*, 25 (1914), 29–33, 85–98; R. Strong, *Festival Designs by Inigo Jones* (1967), nos. 107–12.

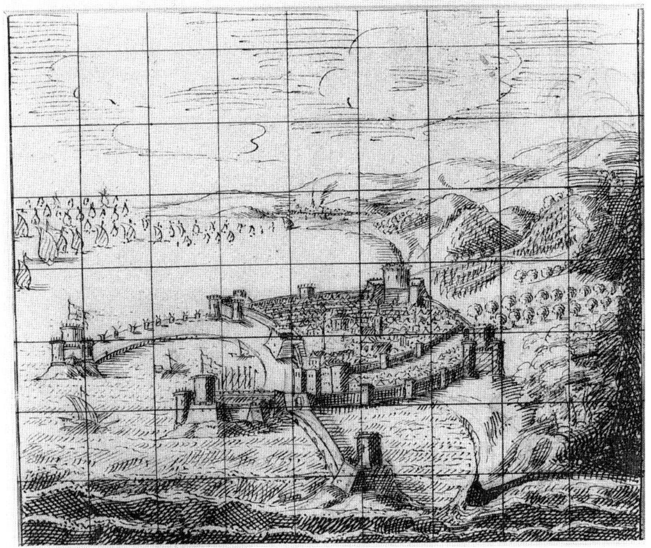

118. *The Siege of Rhodes:* scene design for Act I of Davenant's opera, showing 'the true prospect of the City of Rhodes', beneath 'a lightsome sky', with the Turkish fleet making towards a promontory

120. *The Tragedy of Mustapha:* design for 'The Queen of Hungaria's Tent', scene 6 of the play by the Earl of Orrery, performed in 1666 by Davenant's company at the Hall Theatre, Whitehall

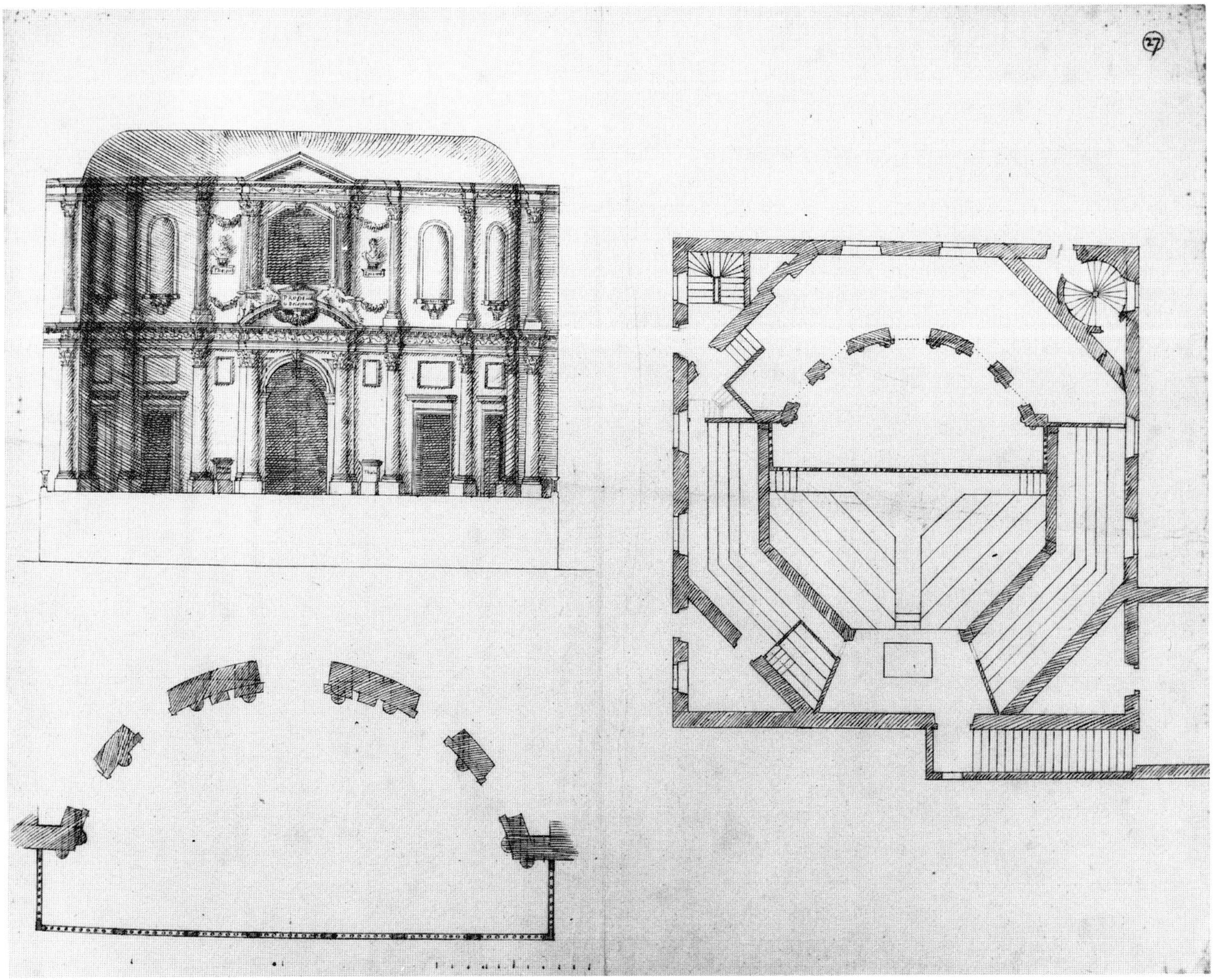

119. Cockpit Theatre, Whitehall: plan and elevation of the stage and plan of the theatre; drawing of the building reconstructed in 1629–31 by Inigo Jones, which also shows the improvements which Webb himself made in 1660–2

things, forbidden, did after his majesty's restoration, revive and improve it by painted scenes, at which time he erected a new company of actors under the patronage of James duke of York, who acted several years in a tennis court in Little Lincoln's-inn-Fields.[9]

Webb next was involved in work for the theatre in 1660 when he was preparing Whitehall for the Restoration of Charles II. The Cockpit Theatre, on the opposite side of Whitehall from the Banqueting House, had been reconstructed in 1629–31 to the designs of Inigo Jones. This is illustrated in a drawing by Webb (pl. 119) which also shows the improvements which he made in 1660 and in 1662: a new stage floor, extra gallery accommodation, a rail and balusters upon the stage, and the addition of fireplaces.[10]

The Cockpit stage, following Palladio's Teatro Olimpico, had a permanent scene forming an architectural background.[11] Such a fixed scene did not allow for the elaboration of scenic arrangement developed by Jones in the masques. Although Webb appears to have provided drawings for back scenes at the Cockpit, the space, and therefore the possibilities for spectacle, were limited.[12] Hence his making of 'yor Theater' in 1665, at which time the Cockpit fell into disuse and was demolished about ten years later.

The Great Hall of Whitehall Palace was built by Wolsey in 1528. Measuring 70 feet by 40 feet, it had a stage with enough space for movable scenery and had been used for masques (including *Florimène*), although, lacking galleries, accommodation had been limited. In August 1660 it was again in use when the King watched 'dancing on the ropes', and in 1665 steps were taken to make it more suitable for use as a permanent theatre. Between February and April work took place to make it ready for 'masking, plays and dancing'.[13] The stage was altered and boxes were set up around it, a gallery was erected at the southern end, a new platform was created over the stage 'for ye hanging up of the workes & frames of ye sceenes', four heated tiring-rooms were made at the northern end, new doors, stairs and passage were provided and provision was made for 'ye musick', at a total cost of £737 6*s*. 2¼*d*. On 20 April Pepys recorded: 'This night I am told the first play is played in White Hall noon-hall, which is now turned to a house of playing.' He visited the theatre for the first time in October of the following year, when he found it 'very fine, yet bad for the voice, for hearing'.[14] This defect was corrected in 1675 when a new ceiling was installed to improve the acoustics. At the same time, accommodation was increased by the addition of two side galleries. By 1675 at least, the theatre was in use as a public theatre, and might well have been so from the beginning.[15]

The Hall Theatre stage was of the Jonesian type, with a proscenium arch, wings, and sliding shutters. Webb's plan and section of the all-purpose staging arrangements was inscribed: 'for the Queens Ballett in the Hall at Whitehall 1665—To bee used also for Masques & Playes. 1. The Tragedy of Mustapha'. Seven drawings by Webb of scenes for *Mustapha* survive at Chatsworth (pl. 120).[16] The play was performed in 1666 and, so far as we know, marked the end of Webb's continuation of the theatrical tradition inaugurated by Inigo Jones. His contribution to that tradition has been summarized by John Orrell: 'Webb systematised what Jones invented or

[9] A. Wood, *Athenae oxonienses*, iii (1813–20), 802.

[10] *Worcs. Coll. Cat.* 4.

[11] Webb produced a design, apparently unrealized, for a scenic theatre based on the Teatro Olimpico: *Worcs. Coll. Cat.* 15–16, 249. The occasion for this design remains unknown. It is discussed by Orrell, *Theatres*, pp. 160–7.

[12] W. Grant Keith, 'John Webb and the Court Theatre of Charles II', *Architectural Review*, 57 (1925), 49–55.

[13] PRO Works 5/8; see also *King's Works*, v., 271–2, and Orrell, *Theatres*, pp. 168–85.

[14] S. Pepys, *The Diary of Samuel Pepys*, ed. J. Warrington, ii (1953), 109, 353.

[15] *Survey of London*, xiii, pt. ii (1930), 51–2.

[16] Grant Keith, 'John Webb and the Court Theatre', pp. 50–1.

adopted, and in the course of his quite deliberate studies became technically more adept perhaps than even Jones had been, especially in the design of auditoria. Yet he never passed beyond the circumference of Jones's talented invention in matters relating to the stage.'[17]

[17] Orrell, *Theatres*, pp. 189–90.

APPENDIX II. PETITIONS

1. Webb's Petition of 1660[1]

To the Kings most excellent Majesty
The humble petition of John Webb Architect
Humbly Sheweth

That yor petitioner was by the especiall comand of yor Maties Royall father of ever blessed memory, brought up by Inigo Jones esq. yor Maties late Surveyor of the Works in ye study of Architecture for enabling him to do yor Royall father and yor Maties service in ye said Office. In order whereunto he was by Mr Jones upon leaving his house at the beginning of the late unhappy warre appointed his deputy to overrule the said place in his absence wch yor petitioner did, until by a Comtee of parliamt in ye yeare 1643 he was thrust out, as being entrusted for his Maty since wch time yor petr hath patiently acquiesced in confidence of yor Maties glorious returne wch now after so many calamitous years happily succeeding the Lords & Comons in parliamt & Councell of State have confess'd none more able than yor petr (as he hopes yor Royall Maty shall find) to discharge ye trust of being Surveyor of yor Maties works, and accordingly he hath & is preparing ye Royall houses for yor Maties reception the charge whereof upon their severall Surveys amounting to 8140li 5s 2d yor petrs credit stands solely engaged for, he having as yet received 500li only of ye said summe.

Yor petrs humble prayer therefore is that yor Maty would be pleased gratiously to cast yor eye upon yor petitioner as yor loyall subject and by yor Maties gratious grant settle upon him the Surveyors office of yor Majesties works whereunto yor Royall father designed him & to that end only ordered his education. Otherwise after his many sufferings and imprisonments during the late warrs for his loyalty to the Crowne yor petitioner standing engaged as above said instead of reaping the fruits of his fidelity and long studyes may together with his whole family be ruined at last for ever without your Majestyes Royall favour.

And yor petr as in duty bound shall continually pray for yor Maties most prosperous & happy raigne.

2. 'A Breife of Mr Webbs case'—supporting his Petition of 1660[2]

That hee was brought up by his unckle Mr Inigo Jones upon his late Majestyes comand in the study of Architecture, as well that wch relates to building as for Masques, Tryumphs and the like. That he was Mr Jones Deputy and in actual possession of the Office upon his leaving London and attended his Matie in that capacity at Hampton Courte and at ye Isle of Wight where he received his Maties comand to designe a Pallace for Whitehall which he did untill his Maties unfortunate calamity caus'd him to desist.

That he was Mr Jones Executor & there is 1500li due to him in that regard upon Arrears of Mr Jones's wages. Besides 500li Mr Webb carryed his Matie sewed up in his waistcoate through

[1] PRO SP 29/5 74. [2] PRO SP 29/5 74.1.

all ye enemys quarters unto Beverley in Yorkshire wch being afterwards discovered Mr Webb was plundered to the purpose and a long time kept in prison being close prisoner for a month.

That Mr Webb sent to the King at Oxford the designes of all the fortifications about London, their proportions, the number of Gunns mounted on them, how many Souldyers would man them, how they might bee attempted & carried and all particulars relating thereto in writing. That Mr Webb hath made ready Whitehall as his Matie sees in ye space of a fortknight upon his own credit having yet received 500li only of 8000 and odd pounds.

That Mr Denham may possibly as most gentry in England at this day have some knowledge in the Theory of Architecture but nothing of ye practique soe that he must of necessity have another at his Maties charge to doe his businesse whereas Mr Webb himselfe designes, orders and directs, whatever given in comand without any other mans assistance. His Matie may please to grant some other place more proper for Mr Denhams abilitye and confirme unto Mr Webb the Surveyors place wherein he hath consumed 30 yeares study there being scarce any of the greate Nobility or eminent gentry of England but he hath done service for in matter of building, ordering of meddalls, statues and the like.

JOHN WEBB

3. Webb's Petition of 1669[3]

To the Kings most Excellent Majestie.
The humble Petition of John Webb Esq. Surveyor assistant for yor Majestys works at Greenwich.
Most humby sheweth

That in 1660 yor Majestie was gratiously pleased, to conferr yor Petitioner a grant for ye reversion of Sr. John Denham's place, wch past yor Royall Signet and privy seale, and ye Lord Chancelor's recept also, whereupon ye patent was ingrossed, and was never yet recalled by yor Majestie, but stopped at the greate Seale by Sr. John Denham, under pretence only yt yor Petitioner was elder than himself adding withall that if I had his reversion hee could not sell it, yet since he hath given his consent under his hand likewise. After having prepared Whitehall for yr Majesties happy restauration, yor Petitioner withdrew into the country, from whence afterwards in 1663 by yor Royall appointment being sent for, to react for yor Majestie at Greenwich, hee readily obeyed. At Wolwich day and night hee discharged his duty about ye fortifications there to yor Majesties good content. At Whitehall hee made yor Theater, and thereby discovered much of the Scenicall Art, wch to others than himselfe was before much unknowne; yet for all these services, both for yor Majesties honor and pleasure hee never received any reward. It is true, yor Majestie was gratiously pleased to grant yor Petitioner a Salary of £200 p Ann for Greenwich; but Dread Sir it hath been so slowly paid that yor Petitioner hath spent out of his own estate little lesse than £1000 in ordering that worke, besides the neglect of his owne houshold affaires.

The humble desire of yor Petitioner is, to know yor Royall pleasure, how in this conjuncture hee shall dispose of himselfe, for although hee acted under Sr. John Denham, a person of honour, hee conceives it much beneath him, to doe ye like under one, who in whatever respects is his inferiour by farr. May yor Majestie please if not to confirm yor Petitioner's Grant as in the honor of a King you appear to bee obliged, then to Joyne him in Patent with Mr. Wren and hee shalbee ready to instruct him in the course of the office of yor works, whereof hee professeth to bee wholy

[3] PRO SP 29/251 120; first published in *Wren Society*, 18 (1941), 156, where it was dated 1668; the document itself is undated; Wren succeeded Denham as Surveyor in 1669.

ignorant, and yor Petitioner, if you vouchsafe, may take care of yor Majesties works at Greenwich, or elsewhere as hitherto hee hath done.

And yor Petitioner shall ever pray for yor Majesties long and happy raigne.

John Webb

APPENDIX III. FAMILY MATTERS

JOHN WEBB's early life is shrouded in mystery. Little Britain, where he was born in 1611, is in the parish of St Botolph: unfortunately, there are no surviving church records dating from before 1637, and there are no rate books earlier than the 1680s. The records kept by the nearby St Bartholomew's Hospital of properties which it owned in the area, refer to a John Webb who paid rent for a house 'within the close' from 1601 until 1617.[1] The tenants of these houses would be expected to have worshipped at St Bartholomew the Less—a church for which records survive, but with no mention of Webbs during the period in question.

It might be presumed that John Webb remained in the area of Little Britain until he joined Inigo Jones, who from 1630 had a house in Scotland Yard, near to the Office of Works. Webb is recorded as living in Theeving Lane, Westminster, in January 1644,[2] then in Green's Lane, Charing Cross. He was in Scotland Yard again from 1650.[3]

During the 1650s Webb continued to run his architectural practice from Scotland Yard,[4] but after the death of Inigo Jones he was able, also, to set himself up as a country gentleman in Butleigh, Somerset. It was to Butleigh that he retired, briefly, after the disappointments of the Restoration, taking all his papers with him. These were transported back from Somerset to his house in Greenwich in 1665, to help him with his designs for the interior of the Palace. In both the second Stonehenge book and in his *Essay* on China, Webb signed himself 'of Butleigh': he clearly was keen to be seen as a member of the squirearchy.

Webb's purchase of Butleigh Court followed his wife's inheritance in 1652 of £2,000 from Inigo Jones. Anne Webb was the daughter of a first cousin of Jones[5] and the architect made her his principal beneficiary. His will stipulated that the money was 'to be laid out for a Jointure for her by my executor [i.e. Webb] within one yeare after the proving of this my will'.[6] A further £1,000 was bequeathed by Jones for division amongst the five children which the Webbs had at that time. This was held and used by the parents until Webb's death, when his settlements upon the children included their outstanding legacies.

Webb's financial affairs were complex. He agreed in 1653 to pay Thomas Symcocks £8,420 for the Butleigh property, much of which was already mortgaged.[7] Payment in instalments followed and Symcocks agreed to vacate the premises by March 1654.[8] A major incumbrance upon the property, £1,500, was for the 'servinge of Mr. Symcocks children'.[9] Symcocks had in 1641 set aside parts of the estate to provide for his younger children after his death (which took place in 1676), and Webb took over the obligation with the property.

Symcocks's financial problems were considerable and in 1671 he sold to Webb, for £2,000 (of which Webb paid, initially, £950), the impropriate parsonage of Butleigh, which had been

[1] St Bartholomew's Hospital Archives; the rents are recorded in Ledgers no. 3 (1589–1614) and no. 4 (1615–28).

[2] Noted at the beginning of Book VII of his copy of Serlio (RIBA).

[3] *King's Works*, iii. 157–8.

[4] The letters to Sir Justinian Isham at Lamport were all written from Scotland Yard.

[5] A. Pritchard, 'A Source for the Lives of Inigo Jones and John Webb', *Architectural History*, 23 (1980) 138–40.

[6] Webb's copy of the will is at Somerset CRO DD/S/BTO.

[7] PRO C8/115/183.

[8] Somerset CRO DD/SE/48; Deed of Defeazance.

[9] PRO C8/237/65.

excepted, specifically, from the first sale of property.[10] The parsonage was inherited by Webb's second son William, and he was obliged by his father's will[11] to pay Symcocks and his children the remaining monies owing to them.[12] The financial transactions of both Webb and Symcocks were complicated by their predilection for entering into mortgage agreements. Webb's children spent a great deal of time, money, and effort in litigation after their father's death, endeavouring to reach agreement about the ramifications of his dealings.

Despite the complexity of his arrangements, or perhaps because of them, 'att the tyme of his death he was allwayes esteemed to be a very rich and wealthy man as well in real and personal estate'.[13] Of the eight children who survived him, Webb mentioned seven in his will. His eldest son, James, apart from a bequest of furniture and household goods, had been catered for already in a separate settlement drawn up in 1670 between Webb and Ralph Farmer of Bristol, whereby £2,000 was to be paid as the dowry of Farmer's daughter Katherine, who was to marry James. In return for this, the 'mansion house, gardens and orchards of Butleigh, 30 acres of meadow and pasture, 220 acres of comon and the perpetual advowson of the vicarage' were to be settled on James and Katherine and their children. By virtue of this marriage settlement, Katherine Webb, following the death of James (intestate) in about 1690, 'did hold and enjoy the whole of Butleigh'.[14]

John Webb's eldest daughter, also called Katherine, was bequeathed pictures and furniture, having received her portion already upon her marriage to Dr John Westley, at least ten years before.[15] William, the second son, inherited the parsonage, as well as 'my Librarie of Books and alsoe all my prints and Cutts and drawings of Architecture of what nature or kinde soever and my will charge and desire is that he shall keepe them intire together without selling or imbezzling any of them'. As we have seen (p. 8), dispersal of the collections was under way within three years of Webb's death.

Webb's third son, Henry, later described as a merchant in the City of London,[16] inherited £800 and all his father's household goods at Greenwich. Also at Greenwich was Webb's silver case of mathematical instruments which he bequeathed to his six-month-old grandson, John, the son of James and Katherine.

Webb's other daughters, Elizabeth, Martha, and Rebecca, each received £600 from their father, Elizabeth getting an additional £200 which she was owed from the will of Jones: the other two must have been born after 1652. Elizabeth married 'John Radford of Butleigh, clark'; Martha married 'Francis Drew of Lyme Regis in Dorset, gent' and Rebecca married 'Robert Hole of Prestley in Somerset, gent'.[17] Another daughter, Anne, appears to have incurred her father's displeasure, for, although he bequeathed to her daughter Frances 20 shillings to buy a ring, the same bequest as he made to Katherine's and Dr Westley's daughter Elizabeth, he fails to mention her at all in his will. She might have received her portion already, following her marriage to Philip Jegowe, a merchant, but it was claimed in 1692 that she was still owed £600.[18] By this time, Jegowe had died and she had married Gregory Alford. The last member of Webb's family to benefit from his will was his sister, Bridgett Moore, to whom he left an annuity of £5.

Webb made his will on 24 October 1672, 'being sicke of Bodie but of perfect mind and memorie'. He appointed his 'dear and beloved wife Anne' his executor. He died on 30 October and was

[10] Ibid.
[11] PRO PCC 145 (EURE); PROB 11/340.
[12] PRO C8/208/91.
[13] PRO C7/386/66.
[14] PRO C7/365/6.
[15] Westley referred to Webb as his father-in-law in 1662: Bod. Carte MS 31, fos. 440–1.
[16] PRO C8/349/181.
[17] Ibid.
[18] Ibid.

buried, as he had wished, in the aisle of Butleigh Parish Church, on 4 November. The will was proved two days later.

Webb's grandson John died in 1712, leaving a two-year-old daughter, Catherine.[19] The estates devolved upon her after the death of her mother Elizabeth in 1734. Catherine died in 1738, the same year as her husband, Thomas Riggs, and the property and lands, valued at just over £16,000, passed from the Webb family to her executor and heir, James Grenville.[20]

[19] Parish registers, Butleigh.

[20] Revd. E. F. Synge, *Butleigh—A Thousand Years of a Somerset Parish* (1973), 32–3.

SELECT BIBLIOGRAPHY

FULL references to sources are given in the footnotes. The following list is confined to those books which have proved to be indispensable for the study of the architecture of John Webb.

COLVIN, H. M., *A Biographical Dictionary of British Architects 1600–1840* (1978).
—— (gen. ed.), *The History of the King's Works*, iii–v. *1485–1782* (1975–82).
DOWNES, K., *English Baroque Architecture* (1966).
HARRIS, J., *Catalogue of the Drawings Collection of the RIBA: Inigo Jones and John Webb* (1972).
—— *The Palladians* (1981).
——ORGEL, S., and STRONG, R., *The King's Arcadia: Inigo Jones and the Stuart Court* (1973).
—— and TAIT, A. A., *Catalogue of the Drawings by Inigo Jones, John Webb and Isaac de Caus at Worcester College, Oxford* (1979).
HILL, O., and CORNFORTH, J., *English Country Houses Caroline 1625–1685* (1966).
RYKWERT, J., *The First Moderns* (1980).
SUMMERSON, J. *Architecture in Britain 1530–1830* (1970).
—— *Inigo Jones* (1966).
WHINNEY, M., and MILLAR, O., *English Art 1625–1714* (1957).
WITTKOWER, R., *Palladio and English Palladianism* (1974).

INDEX

(Bold figures represent plates)